WAR IN THE PEACEABLE KINGDOM

ALSO BY THE AUTHOR

Fort Pitt: A Frontier History

Guyasuta and the Fall of Indian America

Hessians: Mercenaries, Rebels, and the War for British North America

Major Washington's Pittsburgh and the Mission to Fort LeBoeuf

WAR
IN THE
PEACEABLE KINGDOM

The Kittanning Raid of 1756

BRADY J. CRYTZER

WESTHOLME
Yardley

Westholme Publishing, LLC
904 Edgewood Road
Yardley, Pennsylvania 19067
Visit our Web site at www.westholmepublishing.com

ISBN: 978-1-59416-345-6
Also available as an eBook.

Printed in the United States of America

"War is the continuation of politics by other means."

—Carl von Clausewitz, *Vom Kriege* (*On War*)

CONTENTS

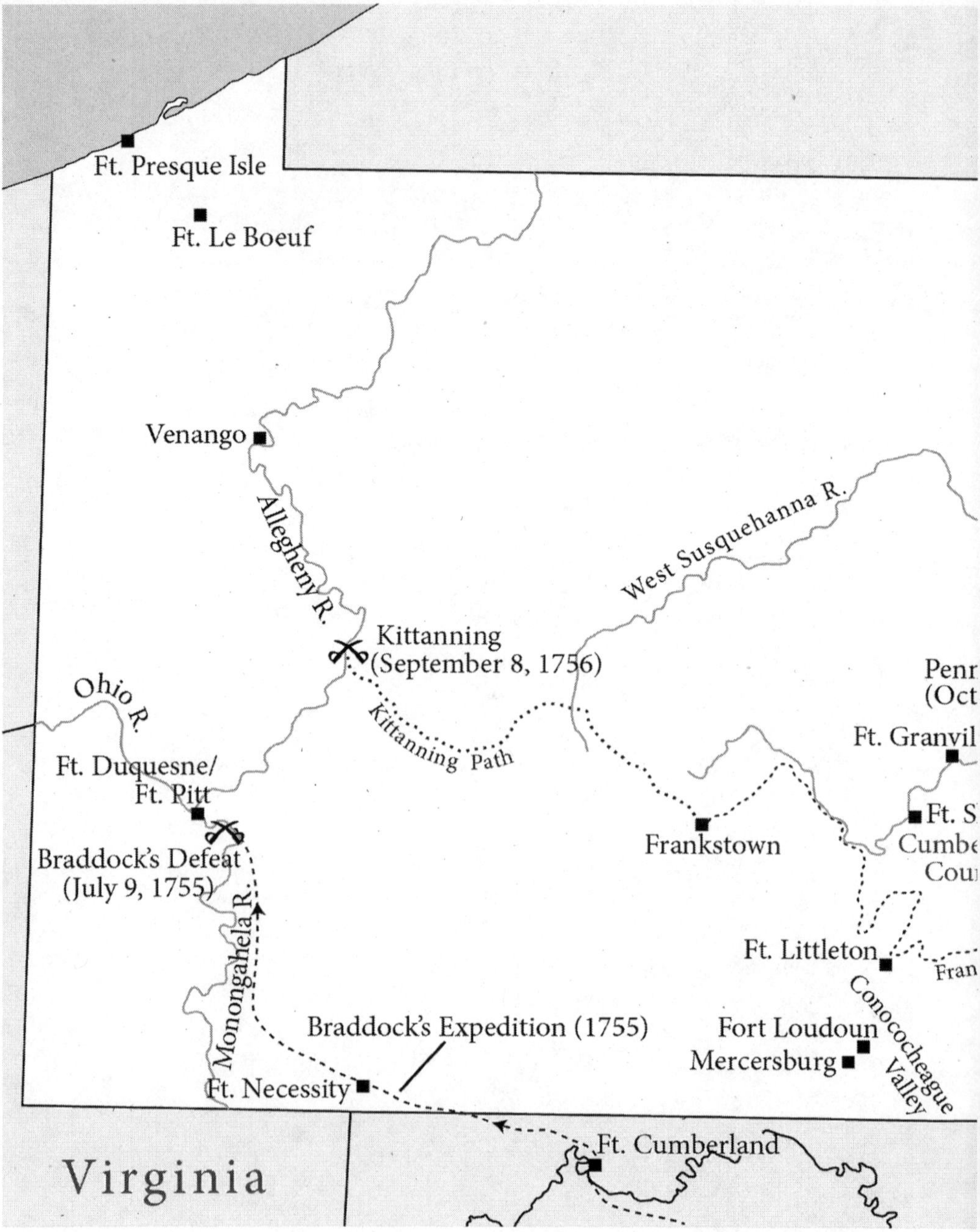
Ft. Presque Isle
Ft. Le Boeuf
Venango
Allegheny R.
West Susquehanna R.
Kittanning
(September 8, 1756)
Ohio R.
Kittanning Path
Ft. Duquesne/
Ft. Pitt
Braddock's Defeat
(July 9, 1755)
Monongahela R.
Frankstown
Ft. Granvil
Ft. S
Cumbe
Cou
Penr
(Oct
Ft. Littleton
Fran
Conococheague
Valley
Braddock's Expedition (1755)
Fort Loudoun
Mercersburg
Ft. Necessity
Ft. Cumberland
Virginia

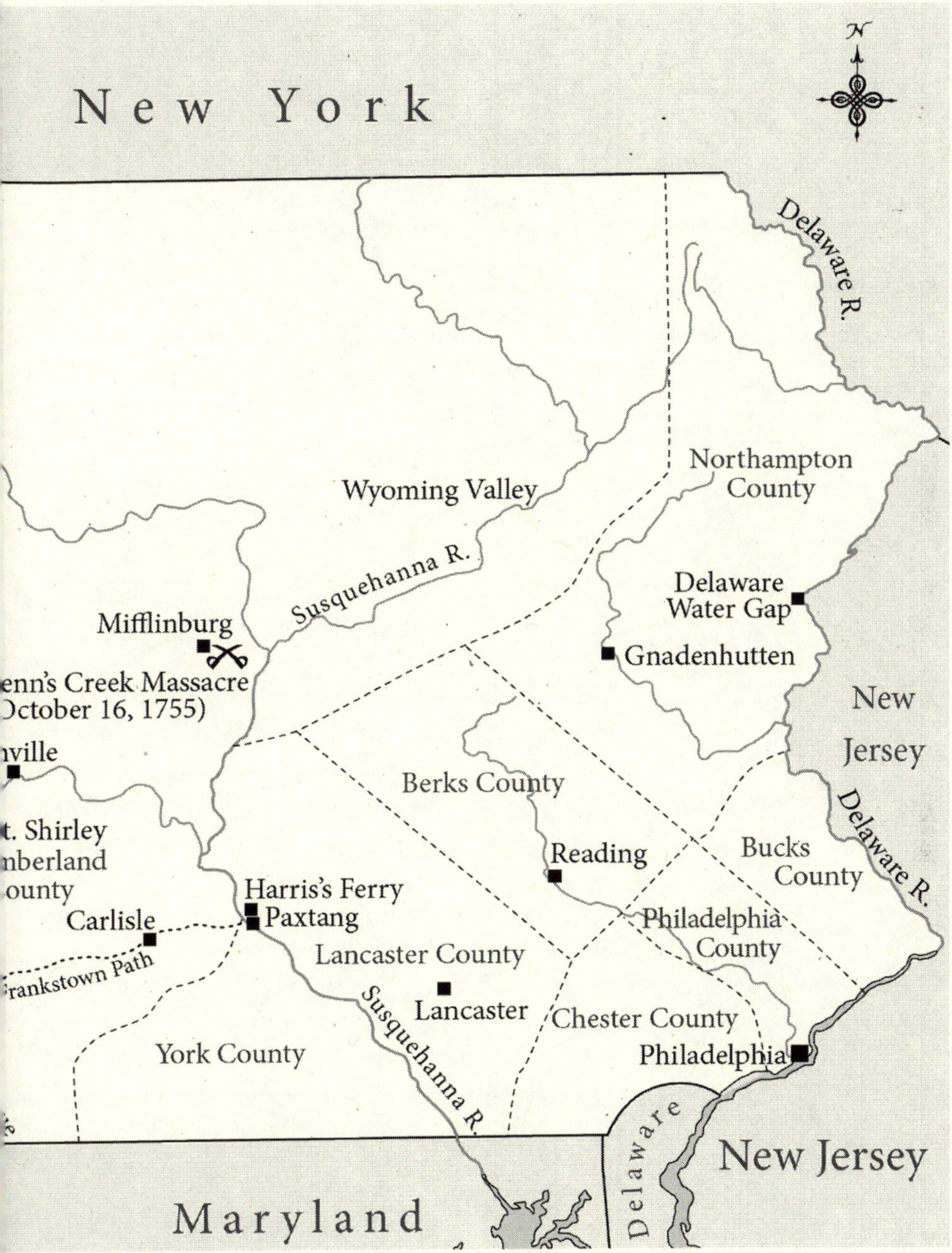
New York
Delaware R.
Northampton County
Wyoming Valley
Susquehanna R.
Delaware Water Gap
Mifflinburg
Gnadenhutten
enn's Creek Massacre
)ctober 16, 1755)
New Jersey
ıville
Berks County
t. Shirley
nberland
ounty
Reading
Bucks County
Delaware R.
Harris's Ferry
Paxtang
Carlisle
Philadelphia County
Lancaster County
Frankstown Path
Lancaster
Susquehanna R.
Chester County
York County
Philadelphia
Delaware
New Jersey
Maryland

List of Illustrations

PROLOGUE:
A Political War

By the summer of 1756 the Pennsylvania Frontier was devastated by war. In the previous eight months, thousands had fled the backcountry for the safety of Philadelphia and Virginia, leaving smoking homesteads in their wake. The enemy that they faced was unlike any other and often attacked sight unseen with no warning, and even less mercy. These raiders pillaged, plundered, and kidnapped their way into the public consciousness of British North America, and no colony had suffered their wrath as much as William Penn's "Peaceable Kingdom." Raids occurred suddenly, without notice, and communities were virtually erased from the map; homes were burned, farms were razed, and families were forever separated. The men were murdered, the women and children abducted, and all the while colonial authorities remained deaf to these victims' cries. Penn had founded the colony nearly seventy years earlier as a "holy experiment" of peace, fraternity, and equality under the law. Now, though, it seemed that the province had never been more divided, and its very soul was being lost in the process.

But what could have brought the New World's most liberal and free colony to this wretched condition? And more importantly, who was to blame? These were all questions that plagued the colony of Pennsylvania, and there seemed to be plenty of blame to go around. For some the guilt fell squarely on the native Ohioan raiders that waged war on the people of the west, yet for others the problem was believed to have stemmed from the colony's own internal failures. In Philadelphia, the finger pointing was done on a partisan basis, and in the backcountry blame often had more to do with one's ethnic heritage. Whatever the case, this was the dark secret of the widely romanticized memory of William Penn's Peaceable Kingdom. His colony was by design a melting pot, and the inherent prejudices that came with a blended society were bubbling to the surface. They had been there for some time, but were only now revealed by the terrible arrival of a world war.[1]

The story of the Kittanning Raid is one of politics. Although the event itself was a mere flashpoint in the history of the North American Frontier, the debates, brawls, and murders that led to it are of the utmost importance. These quarrels would involve some of the greatest minds of their day and reveal the worst of humanity. Men like Benjamin Franklin, Robert Hunter Morris, Thomas Penn, and John Armstrong were just a few of the figures that have made this event so vital to understanding its role in the greater spectrum of an imperial world. But these familiar names are not the only people who made their mark on the period, and all too often leaders like Shingas, Tewea, Scarouady, and Teedyuscung are simply left out of the story. This story take place in the midst of a global conflict that meant many different things to *many* different peoples. It is only in the light of that complicated revelation that the Kittanning Raid can be fully understood.

FOR THE PEOPLE OF THE DELAWARE NATION, theirs was a legacy lost. Long before the arrival of Europeans the Lenni Lenape (or "Original People") ruled the Delaware River Valley that conjoined modern Pennsylvania and New Jersey. They had developed a society based on family, kinship, and trade that allowed them to live in harmony with the many other native peoples around them. When the first European ships arrived to the region, they were welcomed into this system. Although many today have adopted the view that the immediate arrival of Europeans was "the beginning of the end" for the American Indian, this was not the case in the Lenape world. The first foreign settlers came in small groups with little support, and they soon learned that unless they sought out the support of an established local power they would be sure to die. Truth be told, many Europeans *did* die early on, but they soon found that by inserting themselves into the existing Indian system, they could prosper as well. Like all of the peoples of the Delaware River Valley these earliest white settlers traded, hunted, and farmed; they created a world that was very different from the Old World, but it was all their own.[2]

In time, however, the balances of power shifted. As more and more white-sailed ships arrived on the shores of the New World, the old regimes fell by the wayside. Collapsing under the weight of new settlement, the Lenape saw their ancient system failing as well. It was then that the Original People resorted to violence as a means of retaining power, and the violence that they inflicted shook the newly arrived Europeans to their very core. The settler families had never seen the level of violence that could be inflicted by an Indian raiding party, and the Lenape delivered a clear message to their new neighbors: this land was still theirs. In the years that followed peace was again the norm, but the realities of an imperial world soon brought turmoil. New Europeans arrived, bringing with them old rivalries from across the sea, and these foreign powers inevitably clashed. Suddenly the Atlantic Seaboard of North America found itself in a race for conquest, and the Lenape struggled to maintain a neutral peace. It was under these circumstances that the English king won control of the Lenape homeland and changed their destiny forever. By the middle of the seventeenth century, officials claiming to represent New York arrived to meet with the natives, and the two worlds clashed in violent struggles yet again.

Finally, in the 1680s, a new order arrived on the continent—this one not under the banner of war but the open hand of friendship. William Penn had been granted a charter to preside over a proprietary colony, and he made a concerted effort to work *with* the Lenape rather than wage war against them. He came to the Western Hemisphere with a vision of creating a "Peaceable Kingdom," and for the next two decades the Pennsylvanians and Lenape (now called Delawares by the English) lived in peace. Upon Penn's eventual demise, though, the relationship soured. The old issues emerged, and land became the ultimate currency. In 1737 the descendants of Penn executed their boldest plan yet to dismember the Lenape world, and succeeded in a scheme to confiscate nearly all of their traditional homeland.[3]

It was then that the Delawares, now a mere shadow of their former selves, elected to pursue their own freedoms. Most migrated west, and many who believed that peaceful diplomacy might still win the day remained close by in the Susquehanna River Valley. Still others, though, sought total disconnection from the new colonial powers of North America, and settled far over the Appalachian Mountains in the depths of the untamed Ohio Country. It was among this group, known as the Western Delawares, that the most disaffected and zealous Lenape found a fresh start at a village they called Kittanning. In time, even these distant lands would be threatened by new European settlement, and under the leadership of a warrior chief named Shingas they would wage a war to defend it.[4]

When the decision finally came to "take up the hatchet," Shingas and his warriors were not fighting a war of *revolution* but of *reclamation*. Their story was of a legacy lost, and the eventual war to regain it. The first part of this book will detail their struggle.

IN WHAT FELT LIKE A WORLD AWAY, the city of Philadelphia was hotly divided. As the capital of Pennsylvania, the city's denizens met for regular battles in the building that would one day be known as Independence Hall. In 1756 it was merely called the "State House," and there was nothing liberating about it. From its inception Pennsylvania was founded as a proprietary colony, meaning that sovereignty in strictly provincial affairs lay in the hands of the ruling Penn family alone. There was an assembly elected by the residents of the colony, but no laws would be passed without first being approved by the governing executive. While it appeared to be a democratic system by design, that was only partially true. The governor was the proprietor himself, and as was customary, he was mostly absent from the colony. In the wake of William Penn's death in 1718, rule fell to his sons. In 1756, it was Thomas Penn who inherited the lion's share of his father's proprietary power. Rather than living in the colony on one his family's many vast estates, Penn instead made his home in England, quite literally a world away.

To protect his interests in the colony Thomas Penn handpicked a series of subordinate "lieutenant governors" to command in his place. They were often Penn loyalists by necessity and given very strict instructions on how they should govern. For the absent Penn, the most vital obligation that he commanded of his lieutenants was that they must protect his inherited interests at all costs. As part of his proprietary prerogative, Penn was able to impose a virtual tax-exempt status on all of his estates within the boundaries of Pennsylvania. Therefore, any time that a bill should come across his lieutenant governor's desk that included revenue drawn from Penn family lands, the subordinate was given strict orders to veto it at all costs. To show his seriousness, Penn even threatened his would-be executives with legal penalties should they ever sign such a bill. While the proprietor saw no issue with this stance, as the colony bore his family name, the assembly of the people balked at the notion. Thus developed the greatest political tug-of-war in the history of colonial America.[5]

The colony of Pennsylvania was divided into two political camps, and the differences between them were stark. Representing the Penn family and their wealthy associates was the Proprietary Party, and although they represented only a small portion of the assembly, they very definitively controlled Pennsylvania's executive wing. Opposing them was the Quaker Party, and due to the Friends' deep roots in the province's origins, they had controlled the assembly since the earliest days of its existence. As the Quaker faith demanded complete nonviolence from its adherents, one of the central tenants of the party was that Pennsylvania would have no army. As North America developed into a continent of *many* imperial powers in the eighteenth century, this rigid position became increasingly unpopular. In what would be only one of many small conflicts with the empire of New France, a rising political star named Benjamin Franklin took it upon himself in 1747 to raise an "association" to defend the capital in the event of French invasion. The ideologically rigid Quakers cringed at the notion, but it made the Bostonian Franklin wildly popular. In 1751 he was elected to the Pennsylvania Assembly and became a driving force in the colony's contentious politics.

Franklin's ambition was great, but to climb the ladder of success he would need to battle two enemies. On one hand, he would quarrel with the Proprietary Party over the issue of taxes, particularly on the Penn family estates. On the other, though, and perhaps more importantly, was the opposition that he faced from within his own Quaker Party. As a non-believer, Franklin only joined the Quaker Party out of political expediency, and he was not alone. He quickly became the dominate voice of a faction that attempted to rebrand the party from one of nonviolence to anti-proprietary populism. He and his followers had no issue with the creation of an army, but they did take issue with the descendants of William Penn refusing to aid in its funding by adhering to their tax-free policy. By the mid-1750s, it became apparent that the forces of the British and French empires were marching toward war, and the defense of the colony took precedence over every other issue in Pennsylvania. In 1754 the partisan division in Philadelphia threatened to undermine the safety of the entire colony. Recently appointed Lieutenant Governor Robert Hunter Morris lobbied the oppositional legislature to fund the creation of a military force, but the Quaker-dominated assembly would not budge. The pacifist faction objected based on religious grounds; and Franklin's anti-proprietary wing, due to Penn's built-in tax immunities.[6]

Under these circumstances, Robert Hunter Morris and Benjamin Franklin would engage in one of the greatest feuds in American political history. Although they were both in agreement that a military force should be established, they were miles apart on how to achieve it. The ensuing grudge match between these two men would grow to take on almost legendary status, and it would skyrocket Franklin to the forefront of American politics. The second portion of this book will detail their many political quarrels, and the deep partisan divisions that defined them.

In the wake of one of the worst disasters in the history of the British Empire, the Western Delawares and their Ohioan allies declared war on the Pennsylvania backcountry. From October 1755 to August 1756, the Frontiers of the province became what one commentator called "a theatre of bloodshed and rapine." As hundreds were killed, maimed, and taken prisoner, the Scots-Irish settlers of the Frontier demanded a harsh response from their capital; what they received was inaction. While the western edge of the colony burned, the factionalized government in Philadelphia sparred and quibbled over legislative details and seemed more interested in winning partisan battles than defending the lives of their citizens. Finally, in July 1756, Pennsylvania suffered a devastating blow when Fort Granville, one of its primary posts west of the Susquehanna, was raided and burned. Its garrison was taken hostage, its commander was killed, and the settlers of the Frontiers prepared to rise in rebellion against Philadelphia.[7]

With the Peaceable Kingdom more divided than ever before, Lieutenant Governor Robert Hunter Morris and Lieutenant Colonel John Armstrong devised a raid on the village of Kittanning, the apparent source of their colony's tormentors. On September 8, 1756, Armstrong led three hundred Scots-Irish volunteers from their homes in Cumberland County to march on the settlement, and they attacked without warning at dawn. It was the first time in the history of William Penn's "holy experiment" that an army ever marched under its flag. In what can best be described as a sudden outburst of revenge-fueled chaos, Kittanning was stormed and burned by the rangers of the Pennsylvania backcountry. By the end of the raid and the six-hour engagement that followed, the entire village was left in smoking ruins, leaving one of its primary war sachems dead. By all accounts it was a tremendous victory for Governor Morris and his hawkish Proprietary Party, and would prove to be a death knell to the pacifist wing of the Quaker Party in the October 1756 elections. Armstrong and his army returned to the battle-scarred east as heroes, and they were welcomed with great fanfare. The first military medal ever cast in North America was designed in their honor, and even the England-based Thomas Penn returned to join in the celebrations. But still, despite his newfound glory, Lieutenant Colonel John Armstrong expressed lingering doubts about the entire campaign, and many viewed the entire raid and destruction of Kittanning as nothing more than bloody political theater. The Kittanning Raid, along with its controversial aftermath, will be examined in the third part of this book.[8]

More than any other campaign in the whole of the Seven Years' War, the Kittanning Raid allows for an examination of the murky intersection of war and politics. The legislative machinations that brought about its formation were complex, and the people involved were deeply invested in its ultimate outcome. This is a story of empire, rebellion, freedom, and revenge; most importantly, though, it is one of conflict. Whether pitting the Western Delaware against the Wyoming, the Scots-Irish against the English, or the Proprietary Party versus the Quaker, by 1756 the politics of the Peaceable Kingdom were nothing short of tribal.

When understood through that lens, perhaps the burned-out ruins of Kittanning express that sentiment most eloquently of all.

ONE

The Original People

On October 1, 1753, a council of alternative worldviews began. Situated approximately 125 miles west of Philadelphia, Carlisle was a far cry from the colonial capitol. While Pennsylvania's first city grew in an organized and thoughtful fashion from the banks of the Delaware River, Carlisle was a rough sketch of the new America. Stone houses were few and far between in the 1750s, and the majority of the town was a motley assortment of log-hewn dwellings made by hand. Even the courthouse, which the forty-seven-year-old Benjamin Franklin now approached, was nothing more than a hasty construction of local timbers pieced together by local craftsmen.

Franklin was well aware of the stakes presented by the meeting that awaited him. He had been handpicked by the governor to personally meet in council with the many Indian nations that resided in and around the colony of Pennsylvania. Diplomacy was a vital part of Franklin's unique skill set, but over the next three days he was more likely to hear grievances and absorb criticism than to negotiate any meaningful solution. This was not uncommon for councils such as this, but the location of the meeting was what proved to be a nuisance for the entire Philadelphia delegation that accompanied Franklin. In the past such events would undoubtedly be hosted in the capitol itself, but recent developments had made such a venture impossible. In the years leading up to the day's council, policymakers in Philadelphia were repeatedly troubled by scenes of wild drunkenness courtesy of their native guests. As these meetings would often last for days or weeks, the intoxicated spectacles would be a cause of great distress for the city as a whole. Time and again the polite diplomats would attempt to dissuade this behavior by prohibiting the sale of liquor to the visiting sachems, until finally deciding that no more council fires would be burning in Philadelphia for the foreseeable future.

It was because of this decision that Franklin and his delegates slogged westward from the creature comforts of their home city to the emerging city of Carlisle, a Wild West in its own time. Carlisle was made up of hundreds of recent immigrants to the New World seeking a fresh start in what remained of William Penn's Peaceable Kingdom. They were new arrivals of Irish, Scottish, Welsh, and English descent, but most notable among them were the Scots-Irish. Often marginalized and hearty, the Scots-Irish had planned on taking full advantage of Pennsylvania's lenient policies of religious freedom to promote their Presbyterian social order. They soon found, though, that they were almost as unwanted in Philadelphia as the native peoples that had formerly resided there.

Unwelcomed but not undeterred, the Scots-Irish continued their travels westward until they had made a home for themselves on the fringes of Pennsylvania society. Their settlements soon became unofficial boundaries between the colonial borders and the dark Frontier that lay west of the Appalachian Mountains. First among their settlements was the city of Carlisle, and in less than five years it had become recognized as the Quaker colony's gateway to the West. For all of those reasons Benjamin Franklin now found himself in the midst of this newly fashioned Frontier metropolis, and while its residents were a far cry from his usual company, they represented the expanding future of Pennsylvania.

The scene inside the log-hewn courthouse was highly representative of the New World in the 1750s, and especially so of the emerging colony. Joining Franklin were other colonial representatives, including Richard Peters and Isaac Norris, as well as a who's who of Carlisle's emerging social elite. Among them was John Armstrong, an Irish immigrant who had been instrumental in the design, conception, and construction of the city just two years earlier. Not only was he responsible for the bustling town, but he was also a driving force behind the creation of the new Cumberland County. Now, only two weeks shy of his thirty-sixth birthday, the future certainly seemed bright for the young entrepreneur. If there was ever an individual who embodied the spirit and practicality of the colony's westward push, it was Armstrong.

Across from them sat a delegation of a very different sort, but with equal designs for the future of the Western lands beyond the Appalachians. Seated crosslegged on the floor and puffing casually on tobacco pipes were the over one hundred representatives of the many tribal nations that compromised the eighteenth-century population of the region called "the Ohio Country." A vast expanse of wilderness that stretched eastward from the Allegheny Mountains to modern Indiana, the Ohio Country and its namesake river were of great importance to many interested nations, both Indian and European alike. Franklin was struck by the scene before him, and took great care to account for all parties present, claiming them as "the most considerable Persons of the Six Nations, Delawares, Shawonese . . . Twightwees, and Owendaets." They had little in common before the emergence of the English on the Eastern Seaboard, and were only brought together in the decades since by a series of broken treaties and lawless circumstances that were spinning out of their control.

When the council fire finally ignited, two figures sat across from one another in silence. On the side of the colonial delegation was John Armstrong, a man whose prowess and standing among his own people had made him a pillar of the Scots-Irish community. Unlike the policymakers in Philadelphia who discussed new counties and city planning in an abstract way, it was Armstrong who was overseeing these plans of expansion personally. From Carlisle to the creation of Cumberland County, he was quite literally supervising the growth of the colony through his own actions. On the other side of the darkened room was a man of equal ambition, though of far different means. Shingas sat defiantly as a man who had positioned himself as a leader of the Delaware people of the Ohio Country. Like Armstrong, Shingas traced his lineage back to a family name of good standing, and planned on using the shifting tectonic plates of colonial politics to his own advantage. Although neither would play a major role in the deliberations at Carlisle, history would inexorably link them together in the years to come.

The meetings would last for three days, each seemingly more confusing and futile than the one before it. Early in the proceedings the many sachems hesitated to engage Franklin and his delegates until the proper exchanges of goods and gifts had occurred. While this delay was quite frustrating for the Philadelphia delegation, the offerings were essential for the tribal delegates and of great importance in Indian diplomacy. By the second day of the conference such goods had arrived and were distributed, but for all of the postponement there was little of actionable substance proposed by the sachems. Speaking throughout the conference on behalf of his subject peoples was the Iroquois Scarouady. For almost a century, the Iroquois had been de facto rulers of the Ohio Country and the imperial masters of their subject peoples in attendance. Although the Shawnee and Delaware had great men of their own present, the supremacy of the Iroquois Confederacy and their strong alliance with the British conditioned that only an Iroquois leader would address them in council.

As Franklin had conjectured, the council was primarily centered on a series of complaints and grievances, but none of which the governor of Pennsylvania had much control over or time to consider; chief among them was the English rum that had become such a great scourge of native life. With great passion, Scarouady declared: "These wicked whiskey sellers, when they have once got the Indians in liquor, make them sell the very clothes from their backs. In short, if this practice be continued, we must inevitably be ruined. We most earnestly, therefore, beseech you to remedy it."[1]

The council fire burned until October 3, when the parties expressed their mutual concerns and began to go their separate ways. But for the laundry list of concerns that Scaroudy had expressed, there was one common theme at the core: land. For as varied as the complaints may have been, they all centered on the inherent struggles of two populations struggling for control over the same piece of territory. From the Indian viewpoint, the Scots-Irish were moving westward and claiming land as their own—vacant land, in the eyes of the settlers. As the settlers were technically living in Pennsylvania, it was beholden to Franklin, his colleagues, and the colonial government to solve these problems. The urgency and concern, whether fair or not, was not shared by the colonial government. What the natives viewed as unfair treatment and abusive practices, the Pennsylvanians saw as nothing more than progress and profit. In short, it was a natural consequence of success in the New World.

For all of the cumbersome discussions over that three-day meeting, however, it was not sufficient to claim that all parties were fairly represented. The Iroquois leadership and the colonial government were certainly given an adequate voice, but the subject classes were far from heard. For all of the pleasantries and formalities that Scarouady and Franklin's delegation shared, equally silent were the men who actually resided in the areas presently in dispute. From their vantage point in upstate New York, the Iroquois were quite distant from the realities on the ground in the Ohio Country; equally so was the colonial government in Philadelphia regarding the needs of the Scots-Irish in and around Cumberland County.

Unknown to the powerful parties at the time, this disconnect had lit a slow-burning fuse on the fringes of their societies. While the Scots-Irish harbored an intense animosity toward the Quaker elites of the capitol, the subjected peoples of the Iroquois did the same. For a leader like Shingas, the past loomed large. Despite the long history of freedom and dominance once shared by his own Delaware people, in 1753 he served as a mere adjunct to Scarouady and the Iroquoian power that he represented. The collective chiefs of the disaffected subject nations never spoke to any of the Pennsylvania delegates out of respect to tradition and custom, and they would have undoubtedly been unsatisfied by the Iroquois expression of their own complaints.

They would have felt equally so of the treaty that followed. The Pennsylvania delegates offered the tribal leaders £1,400 of goods in the form of ceremonial gifts, as well as horses to aid in carrying them westward. As a closing, they also promised the collective sachems a quantity of rum, "on Condition it be not delivered . . . until you shall have passed the Mountains."[2]

While at face value the Treaty of Carlisle was of little consequence to the parties involved, it was indicative of the troubling rifts that were forming across Pennsylvania and its Frontiers. An often forgotten council, it would soon serve as a disastrous harbinger for the calamitous years to come. While neither Franklin nor his Iroquois counterpart knew it at the time, a war was set to begin that would tear at the political fabric of the Peaceable Kingdom like never before.

THE ANIMOSITY FELT BY SHINGAS throughout the council at Carlisle was one of deep historical roots, and stretched far beyond any of his own personal experience. The Delaware, or Lenni Lenape in their native Algonquian tongue, had a long-standing agreement with the new colony of Pennsylvania since its inception in 1682, based on mutual respect and a sense of shared prosperity. However, in the many years since William Penn's demise, the multi-layered relationship that they shared with the colonial government was stripped away with little regard for past promises or treaties. The Lenape paid little mind to the changes in ideology that came with each new governor after Penn, and expected that the contracts signed by the two groups should be binding regardless of who currently held the executive title. Those promises, however, were broken, and the Delaware that were willingly removed from their ancestral homeland soon left their heirs in a downward spiral of forced relocation that seemed impossible to stop. In short, Shingas was swept up in a stirring political movement that hoped to restore the proud nature of Lenape life while carving a new, autonomous place for the tribe in the newly emerging America.

Tracing the history of the Lenape people is a challenging and frustrating affair. While historians often take comfort in the certainty that European-style documents and ledgers can provide, all too often a similar study of the Indian world can be daunting. For most of modern history, the scholarship of the eighteenth century offered little on the roles of native peoples in larger North American affairs simply because the traditional methods of research rarely bore enough fruit to justify its continuation. As North American history was so often driven by European accounts, a distinctly European narrative soon developed to explain how an untamed wilderness became the modern United States of America. It was only beginning in the 1980s that new waves of historians cast aside these thoughts and boldly stepped away from their comfort zones. Only then did they discover that Indian America was a vibrant place, and its inhabitants were far more than mere pawns in a larger game of Old World chess.

The history of the Lenape people has been painstakingly extracted from oral tradition as well as the reinterpretation of previously studied European accounts. Almost immediately however historians realized that the standard song of "Indian history" was far more complicated than previously understood. The Eurocentric view of the native world has been one of "tribes," "chiefs," and "braves" that was more likely handed down by Hollywood Westerns than actual facts.

Perhaps no single Indian peoples illustrate this point better than the Delaware.

While many Indian nations and confederations did possess the traditionally recognized social structures passed down through modern popular culture, those seeking it from the Delaware would come up decidedly empty. The name Lenni Lenape literally translates into "original people"—or, perhaps, "real people"; it was understood by its owners as an insistent and forceful declaration that they were the *first*. What they were claiming to be the "first" of remains a point of debate among anthropologists and historians, but other native groups such as the Iroquois often referred to them as a "grandfather" people. This insinuation brings forward the notion that the Lenape, or "Delaware" as the English would later call them, were in some ways understood to be the ideological ancestors of many of the customs often considered to be "Indian."

The territorial homeland of the Lenape was vast, and for many seeking to preserve their roles as Originals, this comes as an affirmation of their true power. Some have claimed that their possessions stretched as far north as Connecticut, the lower Hudson River Valley, and parts of Manhattan Island. Others, however, cite more conservative estimates, placing them in the states of New Jersey, Delaware, and eastern Pennsylvania. None, though, dispute that the true heartland of the Lenape was the Delaware River Valley. It was in this place that the Lenape's distinct culture and unique social patterns set them apart as the dominant Indian force of the region, and cemented their way of life as an old order in the soon-to-be Middle Colonies.[3]

Perhaps the greatest single hindrance to accurately tracing the history of the Lenape as a people is the distinct lack of cohesion that so defined their existence. Unlike other tribal affiliations on the American East Coast, the Lenape did not view themselves as a combined people or nation. They understood in a broad sense that there was a historical and ancestral link with the peoples that also lived in their region, but there was never a collective sense of national destiny to be found. Instead of viewing the Lenni Lenape as a monolithic nation moving in one shared direction, historians should attempt to study them as they understood themselves. Compared to neighboring tribes like the impressively organized Iroquois Confederacy, the Lenape were a loose smattering of peoples with no sense of centralized power. Unlike the Iroquois, who had a clearly defined political center in upstate New York from which major policies were debated, the Lenape instead found sovereignty on a local level. By the dawn of the eighteenth century, the Iroquois had brought together five member nations and developed a uniquely federal system in which member nations were provided clear and systematic representation; for the Lenape, such decisions centered around powerful men who only affected control over relatively tiny villages. The Lenape saw each family as its own state, and each village its own nation.[4]

This was not to claim, however, that the Lenape were completely unaware of their shared heritage with their kin of the Delaware River Valley. The Lenape were quick to recognize language as a unifying factor among their brethren. From only minor dialectical differences ranging from village to village, the Lenape could discern with whom they might find a common strand of mutual cultural understanding. In the most basic sense, the greatest contributor to the confusion and debate surrounding Lenape territory comes from a simple question: *who is a*

Lenape? While many will claim a wide swath of territory encompassing much of the Northeast, others take a more narrow view. This is based on the fact that the Lenape were only one part of a larger classification known as the Algonquian-language family. Made up of many different nations, the Algonquians all spoke a similar tongue, but with enough distinctions that they must be recognized as separate languages. Three of these groups would have each claimed to be their own unique polity: *Unami*, *Munsee*, and *Unalachtigo*. Despite their own perceived differences, to the outsider they were so similar in language and culture that they were all considered to be *Lenape*.[5]

For the newcomers to make such a simplistic generalization was no fault of their own. The group categorized as the Lenape did in fact live in very similar ways. Whether Unami, Unalachtigo, or Munsee, the basics of village life were largely the same. A village was typically made up of a handful of familial bands living in single-family units. Rather than living in the Iroquois-style longhouse as extended families, the Lenape preferred smaller domed structures made of bark and timber, housing only a nuclear family. Their relatives were not far away, as they comprised the remainder of the village, but they did not all live under the same roof as was so common in the Iroquois fashion. Land was cultivated primarily for growing the now-famous "three sisters": corn, beans, and squash. Men would supplement the village by hunting, and because the Lenape preferred to locate themselves near water, fishing was also central to their regular diet. Although they were proficient farmers, the Lenape did not practice the European method of crop rotation to conserve the vitality of their land. Instead, they simply planted the same parcel of ground until the fields went fallow and then relocated the village. Later, Europeans would stumble across vacant settlements that were the colonial equivalent of ghost towns and refer to them as "Old Towns." In this communal system, though, a unique political and social order would emerge, centered entirely around the village collective.

At the center of the Lenape worldview was the family. In Europe, families were most often delineated through the father's line. In this way, long-standing and reliable lines of descent could be established in support of its most vital institution: inheritance. By tracing heritage using a patrilineal standard, the survival of the twin pillars of land and personal fortune could be guaranteed from one generation to the next. It was a system that stood at the very core of European governance, and was accepted as nothing less than an economic system of divine inspiration. While this system had lasted for over a millennia in the Old World, the view from Indian Country was quite different. In the Lenape world, land as an asset of personal ownership was a foreign idea, and therefore to pass it down from one generation to the next was rarely considered.

Instead of regarding family lineage as a simple means of guaranteeing the transfer of assets over time, the Lenape worldview placed much more importance on the value of kinship. By the dawn of the seventeenth century, European diseases had diminished Native America down to only a fraction of its pre-Columbian level; some estimates claim as high as 90 percent casualties in less than a hundred years. Because of this terrible scourge, much more value was placed on the actual family members than any personal assets. In short, the Lenape kinship system was not designed to preserve the wealth of a family, but rather the family itself. Unlike the patrilineal society that ruled over Europe, Lenape society based its lineage through the mother. With this system in place grandmothers, mothers, and sisters held a special significance unseen in the European world.[6]

Disease, warfare, and famine were viewed as existential threats in the New World after European arrival; although these challenges would prove to be disastrous, major societal shifts developed as a result. It was in the preservation of family *members* rather than family *wealth* that Lenape society persisted into the seventeenth century, and women were the distinctive beneficiaries. In the Lenape world women were viewed as integral to any household, and the fringe benefits would have seemed incredible to a European outsider. A Lenape woman was free to marry a man of her choosing, and equally free to pursue divorce. Unlike her European counterparts, whose marriages were arranged for political expediency, the Lenape woman possessed the final approval on any such venture. While her husband would have certainly completed the tasks that were too dangerous or physically taxing, the Lenape woman was responsible not only for child-rearing but the planting and harvesting of crops as well. Unlike European households, where fathers played a significant role in their children's lives, a child's maternal uncle was more likely to be his guide and mentor. Perhaps most galling to the European sensibility was the notion that when personal ownership of land, equipment, or the home itself came into dispute, it was always the woman who was the perceived owner of the property.

From this highly localized system developed a strong sense of freedom and autonomy among the many Lenape peoples; the immediate family superseded any concession to a larger political body. In place of preordained hereditary chieftains, the Lenape instead relied on popularly approved spokesmen, or *sachems*, to express their grievances when dealing with foreign powers. When it came time to sit in treaty with other Indian peoples or wayward European travelers, the Lenape sachems truly spoke for their own constituents, because they often knew them personally. Other tribes such as the Iroquois, as time would prove, relied much more on making broad statements that benefited the national collective first, rather than the individual. Among many other reasons, this would make the Iroquois a much more attractive negotiating partner for the great empires of Europe in the decades to come.

Despite the woman's immense role in Lenape life, she would never serve as a true sachem of her people. The role of the male within the community was never inferior, but it came with gender specific expectations. Males gained prestige and status based on their mother's clan affiliation, and women were regular deciders on matters of which of their sons, grandsons, or nephews would represent their people in council. In an especially apt description of an interaction with the Lenape, William Penn wrote: "Their government is by Kings which they call *sachema*, and those by Succession, but always of the mother's side; for Instance, the Children of him that is now King, will not succeed, but his Brother by the Mother, or the Children of his Sister, whose sons (and after them Children of her Daughters) will reign . . ."[7]

For William Penn, a man who owed his place in Europe's grand socioeconomic hierarchy completely to the practice of primogeniture, this statement speaks volumes. Somewhat meandering and quizzical, Penn unknowingly identified the very essence of the Lenapes' political design. Like many other colonists of his day, this female-oriented classification system was entirely foreign to him, yet in their trivializing accounts historians have found a veritable wealth of information.

As time would pass in Lenapehoking ("land of the Lenape"), dwindling numbers and scarcity of resources would cause great shifts in organization and political control. From this somewhat chaotic world, new divisions of Delaware culture would emerge— most notably the aforementioned clan system. By the middle of the eighteenth century, the notion of the "clan" would come to dominate Lenape life, and give order to a way of life that was steadily disappearing. While historians debate the origins of the clan system, by the year 1700 there were three distinct kinship groups: the Turkey, Turtle, and Wolf. Oral traditions speak of a bygone era in which as many as thirty such designations existed, yet by the age of colonization these three would come to dominate the Lenape political scene. As the society was wholly matrilineal, the clan affiliation of a child would be descended through the mother. Because of falling population, a village of fifty or sixty people would unquestionably consist of members of every clan. If a woman of Wolf heritage birthed a child whose genetic father was Turtle, the child would always be considered Wolf. In this way the Lenape adjusted to the changing circumstances around them, and in the future the clan structure would be one of the last visible vestiges of the perceived "golden age" of Lenape society.[8]

By the arrival of Europeans to the Atlantic Seaboard, Lenape society was at a cultural zenith that would soon begin a stark decline. The arrival of European diseases, wars over access to trade, and loss of a territorial homeland would ravage the Original Peoples' way of life. Despite these encroaching factors, the most vital essence of Lenape life would never falter: their sacred love of freedom and autonomy. The notion that no outsider, whether European or Indian, would ever reign over a Lenape man, woman, or child was held in the highest regard. While these sentiments were ever-present, by the dawn of the eighteenth century they would be tested as never before.

Perhaps the single greatest lingering myth of Pennsylvania's earliest colonial experience was that of the great benevolence of its founder William Penn. Known as the Peaceable Kingdom, the notion has persisted for centuries that Penn arrived in the Delaware River Valley with thoughts of freedom and equality, and that his most gracious beneficiaries were the Lenape themselves. This idea has persisted since the 1680s and has since become a point of pride for many Pennsylvanians seeking a tangible connection to the colonial era. With its perpetuation, however, another more injurious belief has also persisted: that the Lenape were merely reactionaries in the exchange.

While the idea of Penn's peace and pacifism taking hold in the New World may sound comforting to moderns, it also carries with it the distinct prerequisite that the Lenape were likewise transformed by his goodly Quakerism. In truth, this generality obscures the clear reality that the Lenape of the Delaware River Valley had already been dictating their own policies to other Europeans for decades. By Penn's arrival in 1682 they had developed a clear strategy for how to maintain their own culture in the face of new colonial encroachments.

In the eyes of many, the history of colonial America begins with the arrival of the English on the Eastern Seaboard, but quick examination soon reveals a very different story. Keeping in mind the Lenape that had resided in the Delaware River Valley for centuries, the Dutch were the first Europeans to truly explore and claim the region known as the Middle Colonies. Beginning with the arrival of Henry Hudson in 1609, the years that followed saw the United Netherlands continuously imprint themselves in the wild New World. By 1614 they had explored the Hudson, and a year later they began building forts. Finally, in 1623, New Netherland was officially declared, and Fort Nassau was built at modern Gloucester City, New Jersey. With its construction, the Dutch had staked their claim to *Lenapehoking*.

Or had they?

One of the most enduring misconceptions surrounding the Lenape system was the idea that no person controlled land in any way. While European-style ownership of land in the hereditary sense did not exist, the Lenape believed very strongly in communal rights to land use.

When the first Dutch arrived they were few in number, and in the strange New World they were in no position to force themselves on anyone. From their earliest interactions, the Lenape had made it known that their new neighbors could certainly use their land, but were clear that the use would only be temporary. Already by the 1620s, in other parts of North America, new colonists were settling on what they viewed as vacant land. They were establishing homesteads and plantations at a rapid rate in Virginia and New England, and each time they chipped away at the ancestral homelands of the Indian peoples that they encountered. The Lenape were the undoubted masters of the Delaware River Valley, and for them this permanent encroachment was indefensible.[9]

This driving fear of losing land to a smattering of newcomers created a world in which the Lenape dictated the terms of European settlement; rather than being mere bystanders, the Original People did everything possible to retain that title. As their sphere of influence began to shelter Finns, Swedes, and Dutch migrants, it was understood that the Lenape were the true power of the region. For the Dutch, whose primary interest resided in trade, the need for a plantation-style settlement offered very little. In its place came temporary wooden stockades and forts, and so long as they played by the Lenape's rules the region flourished in trade of all manner of goods. Anything else would be rebuked with harsh retaliation. The most striking example of this preemptive chastisement came in 1631. That year, Dutch entrepreneurs purchased a plot of land near modern Cape Henlopen, Delaware, from a community of southern Lenape called the Sickoneysincks. After a few short weeks the settlers began to lay the foundation for what appeared to be a traditional whaling station and plantation. In swift fashion, the Lenape razed the settlement and killed its residents. While it appeared that the "Swanendael Massacre" had been an unprovoked act of war, for the Lenape it was a clear message that their existing arrangement had no room for such permanent settlement. To avoid the loss of territory experienced by the Indian nations to their north and south, the economy had to remain trade-based; to allow an agricultural market to develop would be disastrous, and it was to be stifled at all costs.[10]

The message sent at Swanendael was unmistakable: the Lenape were willing to kill to retain control. Over the next thirty years, the Delaware River Valley became a contested region of Europeans and Indians jockeying for control over the lucrative trade network that had developed there. The Lenape found competition and ultimately defeat at the hands of the neighboring Susquehannocks, but the trade goods enriched the region in spite of the violence.

That status quo changed drastically, however, in August 1664, when a contingent of four English frigates boldly sailed into the harbor of New Amsterdam (Manhattan Island). With no aid coming and very little chance of reasonable success, Director General Peter Stuyvesant signed over control of the city to the English. It was at this moment that the fragility of empire was revealed: although the Dutch flag flew throughout the colony, the Netherlands was overextended and in no position to defend its namesake. Although the Second Anglo-Dutch War (1665–1667) would start only months later, a final peace agreement in 1667 officially handed New Netherlands and its capital city to the English, and forever altered the fate of North America.[11]

As king of England, Charles II would name the colony after his brother, the Duke of York. In the time-honored tradition of hereditary nepotism, the capital would gain his title as well. For the Lenape this represented a radical shift in the future of their lands. They were not aware at the time, but somewhere on Manhattan Island a cartographer was drawing a sketch of the king's New York, and their coveted domain was squarely in the middle of it. For the Lenape this new claim was deeply troubling; in colonies from New England to Virginia to the Carolinas the English had a well-known *modus operandi*—land.

With the acquisition of New York, the English now possessed an empire in North America that stretched from Massachusetts to South Carolina and offered them almost complete control of the Atlantic Seaboard. As their settlers poured into the colonies, they broke ground with an enthusiastic fervor and only as much regard for their Indian neighbors as necessary to carve up the landscape. The Lenape were aware of the immediate threat, but because of the important matters in and around Manhattan the English were able to spare few soldiers to tramp through the Delaware River Valley. Some settlers moved into the region, but because their numbers were so sparse they tended to disappear into the blended society already present. By 1668, though, the king's new grip began to tighten. That year Francis Lovelace was appointed governor of New York, and began to fashion the colony in an image more suitable to his own tastes. Formerly of Virginia, Lovelace believed very little in negotiating with Indians at all and dismissed many of their sacred customs out of hand. With valuable land at stake, the Lenape took up the hatchet against the new settlements that sprang up across their homeland.[12]

In this violent period the English governor and Lenape sachems clashed on many different levels; one noted example was the Indian compensation for the dead. Because of dwindling numbers, it was a typical custom in the Indian world for one band to repay another following the death of a kinsman with trade goods. There was no expectation of surrendering the murderer, as to do so could have been catastrophic to the demographic integrity of the village. For Governor Lovelace, this notion was not only foreign but absurd. When a Lenape warrior would raid a settlement and kill a settler, Lovelace demanded that the guilty culprit be handed over to colonial authorities. As a show of their ever-present dominance over the Delaware River Valley, the Lenape openly defied Lovelace and revealed his impotence. Throughout his tenure, Lovelace even attempted to goad the allied Swedes, Finns, and Dutch into siding with the Crown, but was often dismissed with equal temerity. Lovelace would never remain in power long enough to achieve his great showdown with the obstinate Lenape, as he would be removed from office. In 1673 the Dutch briefly recaptured the colony, and Lovelace was sent back to England in disgrace.

After the interregnum of Dutch occupation in 1673, the Duke of York reclaimed the land a year later and installed Edmund Andros as its new executive. Andros was a cunning figure, brilliantly well-connected in the English world, and following almost a decade at the helm of New York would also go on to govern New England, Virginia, and Maryland. For all of his pedigree, however, Andros would prove to be an extremely valuable figure in the lives of the Lenape, and certainly in the future of the Middle Colonies. When Andros assumed power, he found himself backed into a proverbial corner; Indian rebellions were ravaging New England (King Phillip's War) as well as Virginia (Bacon's Rebellion). The Lenape had already threatened to incite a similar war in the Delaware River Valley, and Andros's predecessor had delighted in the prospects.

To spare New York the devastation of its neighboring colonies, Andros reached out a hand of respect to the Lenape with hopes of repairing the relationship. Like all colonial governors, he had plans of gobbling up large tracts of land, but unlike others he was facing an opponent that still retained practical control of a huge piece of his colony.

Andros undid many of the reforms championed by Lovelace regarding compensation for Lenape casualties and new trade, and for nearly a decade peace prevailed. This was not a testament to his generosity, but it did speak to his practicality. Andros recognized that he may have walked tall in Manhattan, but the *Lenapehoking* remained out of his reach; in order to make New York profitable and prosperous, he would need to bend to the Lenapes' wishes. In this regard, the Lenape forcefully manipulated the colonial politics of the New World to uphold their long-held standard of freedom and fairness.[13]

The fortunes of the Lenape changed in October 1682, when a ship called the *Welcome* landed on the shores of the Delaware River. Onboard was William Penn, and what he brought with him was a royal charter granting him a new colony and a fresh vision for the New World. For most of his youth, Penn was part of a marginalized religious sect known as the Society of Friends, or Quakers. Although he was born into one of England's elite families, Penn saw nothing but anguish for his fellow sectarians, and utilized his substantial pedigree to alter their fortunes. After the death of his father, Admiral William Penn, the younger man was able to leverage a £15,000 royal debt into a substantial landholding in North America. This would famously become the origin story of the colony of Pennsylvania, although "New Wales" was the modest Penn's preferred title.[14]

For Penn, this new colony would provide a safe haven for not only his Quaker brethren but for religious minorities of all backgrounds. While it sounded quaint, there had never been anything like it tried in the New World before. The New England colonies were founded on the principles of religious isolation rather than true freedom, and the ill treatment of Quakers in those Puritan settlements was evidence enough to stir Penn into action. But like other governors of New York before him, Penn understood that he had been granted a land already claimed by many peoples. His policy toward those established residents would play a major role in determining whether or not his "holy experiment" would prove a success or failure. While Penn's generosity of true religious freedom was a welcome declaration for the many different protestant families living in his new colony, there would be little to celebrate if he could not maintain good relations with the native peoples who resided there. In a letter written prior to his arrival, Penn wrote to the Lenape:

> Now this Great God hath been pleased to make me concerned in your part of the world, and the king of the country where I live hath given me a great province therein; but I desire to enjoy it with your love and consent, that we may always live together as neighbors and friends . . . I have great love and regard towards you, and I desire to win and gain your love and friendship by a kind, just, and peaceable life . . . and if in any thing any shall offend you or your people, you shall have a full and speedy satisfaction . . . .[15]

And so, with only the most benevolent of intentions, William Penn set about continuing the conciliatory terms of Edmund Andros and fostering good relations with the Lenape. With the looming shadow of Swanendael still hanging over the recent history of the Delaware River Valley, Penn understood that there was no greater threat to his Peaceable Kingdom than to incite the powerful Lenape who controlled it. As a Quaker who believed that the divine light of God resided in all people, no militia would protect and serve his colony. To guarantee safety, proactive maneuvers to curry favor with the Lenape were essential. From the Indian perspective, this was welcome news, as they had a new English partner who appeared to desire the same standards they had set forth decades earlier. Penn wanted land and colonial expansion, and the Lenape were comfortable with that so long as he was willing to do so in the spirit of honesty and clarity. Armed with treaties and anxious to purchase from the Lenape under fair and equitable terms, Penn set about building his colony.

In these circumstances historians begin to toe a fine line between history and legend. As the story has been told, Penn met with the Lenape sachems, including the notable Tamanend, to enshrine these virtues in treaty. It was there in the shade of the fabled Shackamaxon Elm that the Peaceable Kingdom was born, and the divine light of God shone forth on this new colony of Pennsylvania. While it makes for a powerful scene, historians have found little evidence that this now-critical meeting ever took place, and no document matching its description; it seems that this immensely important treaty may be nothing more than a creation myth. While no document survives that can rightfully lay claim to being the Shackamaxon Treaty, Penn does write that in his first year he sat in council with many Lenape sachems; these events though lack important details that would tie them to the glory of this extraordinary meeting. Why, then, would the colony of Pennsylvania benefit from perpetuating this tale as its genesis? Knowing the recent history of conciliation toward the Lenape customs by New York governor Andros, it may have been far easier for colonial administrators to accept this notion than to question it.

For Penn, it seemed that having the natives as his ally rather than his enemy was the safest way to ensure his colony's safety. He would go on to offer his Indian neighbors the most fair and equitable terms seen anywhere in English North America, even at the expense of his own European sensibilities. The young colony of Pennsylvania respected and followed the traditions that had ruled the Delaware River Valley for centuries, and stories of Penn's benevolence traveled far and wide. As much as later Quakers enjoyed ascribing these policies to divine inspiration, the Lenape had already been living under them for generations.[16]

It was a peaceable kingdom of their own making.

FOR THE AVERAGE EUROPEAN SETTLER in the seventeenth century, North America was a continent of unknowns. The most pressing threat was always the one most visible, and the prospect of some greater challenge was always just beyond the next mountain ridge. When attempting to understand life in the colonial Delaware River Valley, the Lenape appeared as the most evident Indian power in the region—however, the New World was a vast place with a political hierarchy all its own. If the early settlers of the Atlantic Seaboard could have had a bird's-eye, macro view of North America when they first landed, they would have seen a far more complicated picture than they first assumed. While the Lenape enforced their practical control over the Lenapehoking, they were but one small group in a much greater world. Only two hundred miles north, the greatest council fire on the North American continent burned, and it was starting to swell.

The most dominant Indian force of the American Northeast during the sixteenth and seventeenth centuries was the vast and powerful Iroquois Confederacy. Made up of five different nations this native empire brought together the Seneca, Cayuga, Onondoga, Oneida, and Mohawk tribes into a semifederal system located in upstate New York. The Haudenosaunee, or "People of the Longhouse," granted each member nation its own freedoms to control their territory as they pleased, but met in regular council near modern Syracuse to craft policy thought best for the confederation as a whole. It was an entirely innovative system, which, when mobilized, allowed the Five Nations to pool their resources and manpower to become the most impressive power on the continent. For smaller groups on the periphery, the Iroquois were a constant and looming threat. From their position in upstate New York they could effectively raid and attack tribes from the Saint Lawrence River Valley to the Great Lakes, the Ohio Country, Maryland, and New England. By the year 1600, there was little doubt as to where the true power of the Indian Northeast lay, and the much smaller Lenape constantly lived in the shadow of the Iroquois.[17]

While much of the history of Native America before the Europeans remains a mystery, the titanic shift that came as a result of their arrival is undeniable. Using European sources, historians are able to trace the major changes ushered forth by the Dutch fur trade. As most European settlements began as trading posts on the Atlantic Coast, marginal groups like the Lenape were the first to benefit; before long, however, the wealth of new commerce drew the attention of their imperial neighbors. First, with the French along the Saint Lawrence River, the Iroquois hoped to insert themselves into these pockets of trade and eventually monopolize them completely. Their policy toward the smaller nations in their way was nothing short of total conquest. In one of the most brutal and bloody eras in the history of North America, the Iroquois took up the hatchet against all neighboring tribes that traded with European merchants. This terrible period of decades-long conflict became known as the "Beaver Wars."

The Beaver Wars were numerous and complex. They often forced European colonies into alliance with local tribes to stop the imperial Iroquois, and, although rarely, they were sometimes successful. For the purposes of this work, though, the focus will be placed on how these events affected the Lenape specifically and served to redirect their fortunes in a terrible new direction.

When the fur trade reached its full vigor in the early seventeenth century, the Lenape would have believed that the greatest threat to their control of the Delaware River Valley lay in the form of the neighboring Susquehannock. An Iroquoian-speaking people with a deep hatred for the Iroquois Confederacy, the Susquehannock had a traditionally hostile relationship with the Lenape for generations. When Europeans entered the fray, the two nations regularly battled each other for access to Dutch traders. By the 1640s a combination of warfare and smallpox had given the Susquehannock a distinct advantage over the Lenape. For most of the middle of the century the Lenape were effectively paying tribute to the Susquehannock, and in many ways subsisting at their whims. It came at terrible cost, but as contentious as this conflict seemed neither tribe understood how localized it truly was. In the 1660s the greatest Indian superpower on the continent would set its sights on the river valleys they called home, and the Beaver Wars would engulf Lenapehoking.

For, as formidable as the Lenape appeared to the English settlers whom they encountered, the greater political crisis of the larger Indian world was certainly taking its toll. The decade of the 1660s saw bands of Iroquois warriors channel down the Susquehanna River Valley into the heartland of the Susquehannock world. Using calculated raids, and with the help of another smallpox epidemic, the expanding empire added yet another nation to their great banner of conquest; by the year 1677, the Iroquois had driven the Susquehannock to extinction.

Through assimilation and warfare the Susquehannock were removed from the history of North America, and their tributary subjects were spoils to the victorious Five Nations. With the signing of a treaty in 1677, the Lenape officially became subjects of the vast Iroquois Empire. They were soon given the ceremonial label of "woman," signifying that they had lost their ability to make war without the consent of their new rulers. It was an unexpected twist for the Lenape, but subsisting in a weakened state remained superior to suffering the fate of the Susquehannock.[18]

The Lenape themselves had been badly diminished by the arrival of William Penn. While they numbered approximately eight thousand in 1600, they were barely four thousand by 1682. In the grander scope of Indian North America they were marginal, but in the Delaware River Valley they still loomed large as the most visible native polity. For all of their dominance, the Iroquois were largely absent rulers; they spoke in council on behalf of the Lenape, and demanded regular tribute in the form of European trade goods. Although far from ideal, the Lenape took advantage of the space given and reasserted some control over their traditional homeland. When William Penn first arrived to his colony boasting of overtures of peace and equality, he was unknowingly dealing with a Lenape people that were in severe decline. Whether known at the time or not, the initial period of treaties and equanimity shared by the Lenape and Penn was one of the last times that the Original People would ever experience the freedoms and self-determinism that had defined their culture for so long.

The graceful partnership between William Penn and the Lenape was short-lived. Only two years after his arrival in the New World, Penn returned to England. Although the Lenape hoped that they would retain a controlling share in this new colonial vision, they were soon disappointed. By 1687, the population of the colony of Pennsylvania had exploded to over eight thousand, and for the first time in their history the Lenape were the minority in the Delaware River Valley. With this dramatic shift, they lost much of the power that they had retained after falling to the Iroquois, and few believed that Lenapehoking would survive as a viable homeland. By the turn of the eighteenth century many Lenape had begun migrating westward away from the Delaware River to the Susquehanna; the former home of the now-extinct Susquehannock had proven itself to be a viable place of settlement.[19]

But already by 1710 it seemed that the Susquehanna, too, was slipping from their grasp. Pennsylvania's population reached over twenty thousand, and many resettled Lenape still felt as though their sacred freedoms were being infringed upon. For these disaffected few, the only place to experience true independence in their daily affairs was to relocate ever farther west beyond the ominous Appalachian Mountains. To consider such a move was a dangerous proposition; settling in the Ohio Country would mean blazing new trails and trekking over three hundred miles from their ancestral roots. It was a stark notion that interested only a minority of Lenape, but it was an attractive option for the most bitter and disaffected among them. By the year 1720, some Lenape began to settle in this distant region, and by 1730 tiny villages became staples of the Allegheny River Valley. It is important to stress that a full-scale exodus westward was considered an extreme position for the Lenape. Even by 1730 the majority of their population still lived east of the Appalachian Mountains, and some even stayed in the traditional realm of Lenapehoking; only a choice idealistic few, however, considered retaining the Delaware River Valley as their permanent home. For those who could see themselves living peacefully alongside the Pennsylvania colonists but still valued the essential autonomy that their ancestors had procured, the reasonable middle ground was to claim and settle the Susquehanna River Valley. In time these political divisions would bisect the Lenape into distinct camps, and the events of 1737 would further drive a wedge into the Original People.

William Penn died in 1718, and in many ways his "holy experiment" died with him. Because of the hereditary nature of colonial control, Penn's sons inherited their father's namesake of Pennsylvania. Like the late William, his heirs—John, Richard, and Thomas Penn—were Quakers, but unlike their father they were far more concerned about worldly affairs of colonial governance than any divine quest. Despite their practicality, by 1737 the Penn sons found themselves in dire financial straits; they hoped that land acquisition would be a means of righting their colonial ship. For the Penn family, expanding Pennsylvania's landholdings was their right, and the precedent cemented by their father was to fairly and equitably negotiate with the Lenape. There was no such practice in any of the other English colonies on the Eastern Seaboard by that time, and the tradition was largely a personal devotion of the late William. By the time John, Richard, and Thomas took the reins of the colony, it appeared that standards were an antiquated note of the past.[20]

By 1737 the family debt that the Penns had accrued was directly tied to the solvency of the colony; even more than that, it was tied to the untold fortunes Pennsylvania stood to produce in the future. Despite William Penn's great legacy, settlers had abandoned the Peaceable Kingdom mentality long before his earthly demise. Following the first decade of the eighteenth century, settlers began to move into clearly defined Lenape territory of their own volition, without deed or title. Although it troubled the Lenape who remained in the Delaware River Valley, there was a sense that the colonial government would still live up to its word.

It did not.

By the time Penn's heirs took control of the colony, there were hundreds of illegal settlers living and farming on Lenape land. Even more, there were German immigrants relocating into the colony because of their unhappiness with New York's policies. From the Lenape viewpoint, these plantations were an affront to their stake in the region and nothing short of the work of squatters. Although they were displeased, the reality set in that the Lenape remnant were in no position to fight this encroachment. Sensing weakness, the Penn heirs and the infamous Provincial Secretary James Logan set out to capitalize on the disrepair of the broken Lenape people. In 1737 James Logan and Thomas Penn called the Lenape sachems into council, and claimed that they had uncovered an unsigned (yet still legally binding) draft of a treaty created in 1686. This mysterious document was said to have granted the late William Penn land north of his initial purchase as far as a man could walk in a day and a half.[21]

The Lenape leadership was not convinced. Although Logan and Penn tried their best to hurry their counterparts into signing this nefarious treaty, negotiations soon broke down. Only later that year, when the opposition parties met again—this time at Logan's plantation—was a deal struck. Using cartographers, surveyors, and judicial specialists to their advantage, the Pennsylvania delegation overwhelmed the Lenape and convinced them to strike a land deal. In accordance with the terms of this uncertain treaty, the Penns were entitled to as much land as a man could walk in a day and a half. This standard measurement in the Lenape world would give the Quakers a limited amount of land and, though not ideal, would allow the natives to retain some of their ancestral home. What came next was as unexpected as it was devious. Using long-distance runners and a map that badly skewed their route, the Penns' "walkers" were able to carve out a piece of land that stretched from modern Wrightstown, Pennsylvania, deep into the Lehigh River Valley. From there the cartographers employed a deceptive (yet agreed upon) line running 90 degrees east toward the Delaware River. The Lenape who accompanied the walkers left in disgust soon after the treachery was revealed, and by the end of the time allotted the colony of Pennsylvania had acquired over 750,000 acres of land—roughly the size of Rhode Island.[22]

Leaving no doubt as to its finality, the 1737 treaty read:

> The Delaware Indians fully clearly and absolutely remove, release, and forever quit the claim unto the said John Penn, Thomas Penn and Richard Penn all our Right, Title, Interest, and Pretensions whatsoever of in or to the said Tract or Tracts of Land and every Part and Parcell thereof so that neither we nor any of us or our children shall or may at any Time hereafter have challenge, claim or demand any Right Title Interest or Pretensions whatsoever of in or to the said Tract or Tracts of Land or any part thereof, but of and from the same shall be excluded and forever debarred.[23]

The "uncovered" treaty from 1686 was almost certainly fraudulent, and the Lenape who fell victim to its subversion were left with little recourse. When the treaty was ratified in 1737, most Lenape had moved west into the Susquehanna River Valley and the Ohio Country. Those who remained along the Delaware were a distinct minority of ideologues that maintained an unrealistic hope of staying in their ancestral homeland. They had very little real power to challenge the Pennsylvanians on their dealings, and required an outside moderator to express their concerns. As they were a subjected people, such a task would fall on their imperial masters; the Iroquois Confederacy was the Lenapes' last hope of settling this disagreement in a fair manner.[24]

Five years after the ratification of the "Walking Purchase," Thomas Penn and Secretary James Logan called upon the Iroquois to meet in council at Philadelphia. In the decades since the British had emerged as the dominant European superpower in North America, the Iroquois Confederacy had joined in a chain of mutual friendship and alliance known as the Covenant Chain. Since its inception, the Anglo-Iroquois coalition had greatly benefited the Crown, and served to retain the Five Nations as the dominate Indian superpower on the continent. Representing the discredited Lenape was the Onondaga headsman Canasetego, and while the Lenape were hopeful, there was little doubt among the Quakers about whom he would side with. In an impassioned and emasculating speech, the Iroquois admonished the Lenape for their discontent: "We Conquer'd You, we made Women of you, you know you are Women, and can no more sell Land than Women . . . for all these reasons we charge You to remove instantly. We don't give you the liberty to think about it. You are Women; take the Advice of a Wise Man and remove immediately."[25]

With this single pronouncement, the Lenape were left with no recourse. The conspiracy of interests that had first united the Iroquois Confederacy with Britain's North American colonies remained firm. Even in the face of a treaty that was produced in bad faith, with the express purpose of denying a native community ownership of their land, the Haudenosaunee were unflinching. The Lenape commitment to autonomy and freedom was gone; it seemed that the destiny of the Original People would no longer lie in the valley that they called home.

In the 1740s the Lenape were at a crossroads. The position of strength and control that they exercised in the seventeenth century was a thing of the past; they were now a marginalized and disenfranchised people. For those Lenape who sought to retain their lost legacy, the prospects were grim. The Iroquois Confederacy controlled their political fortunes and it was unlikely to release its grasp. If the Lenape were to become a free people again, they would need to recalibrate their collective understanding of what true independence actually was. The ways of their ancestors were not going to return as they knew them, but they could be replicated in a place far on the periphery of the New World by a younger generation. The discussion would soon ignite as to how far they should travel, and that largely depended on the level of fervor, anger, and disenchantment that one felt. In this there were many arguments, but on one point there was no debate; the future of the Lenape pointed in only one direction.

West.

ON OCTOBER 4, 1753, THE COUNCIL HELD at Carlisle officially broke. Satisfied by the results, Benjamin Franklin and the Pennsylvania delegation hurried back to Philadelphia. In a rush to return to the cosmopolitan capital, the colonial representatives left the nasty, brutish, and short realities of the Frontier behind them. Carlisle was a rough place, and although the Scots-Irish families that lived there were undisputedly Pennsylvanians, they had little in common with the Philadelphians. For most in the east, the settlers of the Frontier were a convenient buffer from the terrible truth that was the Frontier. They came to the New World with little to offer in the way of education or wealth, and to the Quaker elites they were much better served while out of sight and out of mind. While Franklin was an open-minded champion of the average Pennsylvanian, he fled hoping that their fears had been put to rest. Likewise, the Iroquois delegation who spoke so openly on behalf of their subject peoples returned to their homeland in the Mohawk River Valley.

With the old Indian order now decades old, the Five Nations rested on the hopes that their imperial underlings would be likewise satiated. The Lenape, Shawnee, and Wyandot were thinly spread across the Ohio Country, and their masters hoped that they were too few in number to mount any substantial challenge to their supremacy.

Both the Philadelphians and Iroquois were pleased with their efforts at Carlisle, but neither could truly comprehend the dangerous rumblings that were occurring amid their underclasses. John Armstrong was a bystander in the council that had just ended, but he was no background character in the emerging Frontier city. He laid the plans for Carlisle and oversaw its construction; no matter how his wealth and favor grew, his thick Irish brogue always gave him away. He may have been a welcomed guest in the east, but in Carlisle he was truly among his kin. Their problems were his own, and although Franklin's delegation could simply leave it behind, it was Armstrong who would be called upon to implement true change.

At the same time, the Delaware sachem Shingas wrestled with his own political duties. He was a headsman of the Lenape who relocated to the far west, and as his party crossed the towering Allegheny Mountains he, too, was reaching a crossroads. He was gifted a title of "king" by the Iroquois and British, and he was a valued leader of the Lenape of the Ohio Country. His obligation was to his people, but he began witnessing a dangerous political shift. In the Ohio Country the Lenape were growing restless, and their anger was directed at the Iroquois who had effectively silenced them for a generation. Shingas also felt this strain, and his continued inaction would be viewed as a tacit endorsement of Iroquois domination. If the Lenape warriors of the region were to revolt, he would need to choose a side; the Original People could be free again, but not without the terrible scourge of war.

The council at Carlisle left both Armstrong and Shingas at a loss. As much as the Iroquois had let down the Lenape, the Pennsylvanians had disappointed the Scots-Irish. Each demanded a solution to the growing conflict between Settler and Indian, and both were given little more than shallow promises. The conspiratorial Anglo-Iroquois status quo known as the Covenant Chain had effectively silenced both peoples, but change was brewing on the Frontier. Two rival empires from an ocean away were preparing for war, and the Peaceable Kingdom would be divided like never before.

TWO

Invasion

To those in the east, the world beyond the mountains was dark and ominous. They envisioned it as a backcountry that was as mysterious as it was endless. For the average Philadelphian in the 1750s, the Ohio Country was one of the great paradoxes of living in an imperial age; for, as formidable as the Frontier seemed, they knew that one day it would likely be theirs. Exploring these vast, unknown reaches of the New World was not for the faint of heart—it was a difficult task. Had the residents of the capital any means to actually take on the trial of exploration, they would have found the Ohio Country to be a very different place than their imaginations had suggested. In the region that encompassed modern western Pennsylvania, a fertile and unique community was developing in a land blessed by geography. Home to three major waterways with countless tributaries, the Ohio Country was a nearly vacant land only decades earlier. Since the expansion of the English on the Atlantic Coast had boomed, refugee peoples from many Indian nations had resettled along the banks of these rivers and creeks with hopes of starting anew, and distinct communities were developing each year. The regenerative power of this place was no more evident than in the Delaware village of Kittanning.

As early as the 1720s, the Delaware—seeking greater independence and isolation—had made the Ohio Country their chosen destination. Since their sojourn began, they had developed a political bent that valued localized autonomy, and the remoteness of the Allegheny River Valley had proven to be well suited to their needs. Meandering some 150 miles through dense wilderness and mountainous terrain, the Allegheny River steadily flowed south, providing a natural corridor for trade and travel. By comparison, it was not the Delaware or even the Susquehanna, but its reliable temperament allowed for a transplanted community to settle with some degree of familiar comfort. Along the banks of the Allegheny just forty miles north of its meeting place with the Ohio River sat the village of Kittanning, a place that was well established by 1753 as the social and political heart of the newly aligned Western Delaware peoples.

If Philadelphians could have seen this place before the opening shots of the war that would ultimately destroy it, they would have been pleasantly taken by its serenity. Kittanning, pronounced "*Kit-han-nee*" by the Lenape and interpreted roughly as "at the great stream," was much more a collection of settlements as opposed to a singular village. Situated on both the east and west banks of the Allegheny River, Kittanning (also known as Attiqué in Iroquoian) was home to nearly four hundred people. If viewed from above, the settlement would not have appeared as one large, circular Delaware-styled village, but it would have contained seven individual bundles of homes. They would have sat nestled within the safe confines of a valley carved out by the river itself, and the many burning fires would have dotted the valley throughout the day and night. Along the banks of the Allegheny grew a field of corn, beans, and squash that would have sustained the families nearby. In time, this quiet crossroads of the native world would develop a vile and odious reputation, but in 1753 it was where men hunted, women farmed, and children played.[1]

It was also the place that Shingas called home.

All throughout the immediate region communities like Kittanning had sprung up, some of more note than others. Some fifty miles west was Kuskuskies on the Shenango River, and twenty miles south of there was the village of Saucunk on the Beaver River. While both of these paled in comparison to Kittanning, the closest Delaware settlement that came close to being its rival was located approximately sixty miles to the north—a community called Venango. Also situated on the Allegheny River, Venango was on the rise, and would continue to grow in importance as the larger geopolitical circumstances of the region changed. By the time Shingas and the other Delaware delegates that had met previously in Carlisle returned, though, changes were already evident.

Almost immediately following their arrival in the region, the Delawares that had fled seeking greater control over their own affairs soon found that they would not be alone for long. In the 1740s many European sutlers and traders followed them to their new settlements with hopes of profiting in trade goods. Although it was unexpected, these enterprising newcomers were typically welcomed by the Delawares; as they were in such a distant place, their mundane commodities became especially valuable. Their presence was an undeniable agent of change, and one of the great sources of material for modern historians wishing to study the blending effect of Frontier life. Kittanning was a Delaware village in every sense of the word; community and kinship remained the foundational bedrock of the community. The physical appearance of the place, though, would have been far more familiar to the Pennsylvanians than expected. The most common form of domestic dwelling in any Delaware village was the domed structure sometimes called the wigwam. Built first from a frame of bent saplings, the structure was next covered in bark and usually designed to house a single nuclear family. The first Europeans to arrive in *Lenapehoking* would have seen this design throughout the landscape, but this was not the case for fur traders and trappers at Kittanning. The wigwam would most definitely have been present on the banks of the Allegheny, but more startling would have been the number of European-style log cabins peppered among them.

The single greatest myth of the North American Frontier always centered around the notion that two cultures met and inevitably clashed. With acknowledgment that times of peace and trade did occur, the sense that the Frontier was a place of constant push-pull politics was generally accepted among the administrators of the colonial East. In many ways, this sentiment still exists today; however, even cursory glances at accounts from those on the Frontier soon reveal a startling truth: the Frontier produced far more *fusion* than *friction*. For the Delawares, these European newcomers represented a vital part of their regional economy, but the lessons of the past still loomed large. Regardless of how many rich and valuable goods these white traders brought into the Ohio Country, the Delawares refused to allow permanent settlement. Throughout their earlier history, the Delawares had maintained the reputation of being a fair and accommodating people, but the sting of the past still resonated. They were now determined to maintain control of their new home, and they would not sign it away as they had the Delaware River Valley.

The vast majority of Western Delawares agreed on this point, and none of them more so than the sachem Shingas. While the largest of Kittanning's settlements was located on the eastern bank of the Allegheny, the site of the modern city bearing the same name, Shingas and his family kept their home on the opposite shore. Like so many other figures in Native American history, Shingas's early life will never likely be uncovered. What we know of him comes from the European historical record, but his impact on the eighteenth-century Frontier is not in doubt. Shingas was a respected leader in the unfolding political climate of the Ohio Country, and his allegiance was first and foremost to the Delawares. He was viewed as a great champion of the self-reliant ideology that fueled the Westerners, but he was also viewed as a man with two masters. To many he was called "king," but to the Delawares that word did not exist in any meaningful form. He was bestowed his title by the Iroquois; they saw him as a trusted collaborator ideally suited for maintaining control.

His relevance to the larger history of the Delawares, though, was not limited to a mere appointment by a distant power. A member of the Turkey clan, Shingas was the nephew of the powerful sachem Allumapees (also known as Sassoonan), who was present at the fateful council that legitimized the Walking Purchase of 1737. In the wake of his passing, Shingas lobbied greatly to see his brother Pisquetomen placed as the successor to Allumapees, but the Pennsylvanians would not support the decision. Angry and disenchanted, it was this slight that drove Shingas to the cause of the West, and his intense distrust of colonial authority only strengthened in the years that followed. Despite the fact that the Delawares did not practice the hereditary kingship of the European model, Shingas was viewed as a natural leader due to his close relation to his highly regarded uncle. While his exact role in Western Delawares' life will never fully be known, the fact that he carried a high degree of regard among his people was evidenced by his selection as their "king."

At the village of Logstown along the banks of the Ohio River, a council was held in June 1752 by the Iroquois Confederacy and the colony of Virginia. Although the area is within the boundaries of Pennsylvania today, the Ohio Country was a disputed land for most of the eighteenth century, and Virginia regularly attempted to assert its control over the region. The purpose of this council was to reaffirm Iroquois control by electing a leader to represent the growing Delaware community of the West; for reasons only assumed to be his already high stature, Shingas was the selection. The man responsible for this "coronation" was the Seneca Tanacharison, known among the English as Half-King. As a local viceroy, Tanacharison was a unique figure who would prove vital to maintaining Iroquois control over the Ohio Country. For the Half-King, it was his duty to be the eyes and ears of the Iroquois in the region; and just as the Delawares were still subjects of the Five Nations, it would be he who represented them in council. Just as was the case a generation earlier in the East, the Delawares were represented regularly in council with the British, but had no right to voice an opinion of their own.

Perhaps another indication of his role was the fact that Shingas was not present at his own selection as king. In his place, his brother Tamaqua was honored in ceremony. According to the Virginians present at Logstown, the Iroquois Tanacharison delivered the following speech to seal Shingas's selection:

> Nephews, you receiv'd a Speech last Year from your Brother, the Governor of Pennsylvania, and from us, desiring you to choose one of your wisest Counsellors & present him to us, for a King, as you have done it, we let you know that it is our Right to give you a King, and we think proper to give you Shingas for your King, whom you must look upon as your Chief, & with whom all publick Business must be transacted between you & your Brethren, the English. On which the half King put a laced Hat on the Head of the Beaver, who stood Proxy for his Brother Shingas, & presented him also with a rich Jacket & a suit of English Colours, which had been delivered to the Half King, by the Commissioners for that Purpose.[2]

With Shingas now labeled as the leader of the new Western Delawares, an aura of legitimacy soon followed. He had won over his own people long before the Iroquois appointed him king, but surprisingly the Pennsylvanians soon followed suit. Despite the fact that they had disregarded the recognition of his brother as the rightful heir to Allumapees's title a decade earlier, Shingas was now viewed as the leading sachem of the West. That is not to say, however, that he was the lone king of the Original People.

Some 250 miles east of Kittanning in the Wyoming Valley lived another sachem of the Delawares, a man who would be exonerated by history for a commitment to peaceful resolutions and thoughtful concessions. Born in the area of Trenton, New Jersey, Teedyuscung's path to kingship was very different than that of his Western counterpart. Much like Shingas, Teedyuscung had been displaced by the nefarious Walking Purchase, but unlike his fellow chieftain did not immediately assume a hardline stance. He sensed that the Delawares' way of life was facing an existential threat, and in the years immediately following his removal from the Delaware River Valley, Teedyuscung assimilated into the greater European world. He settled into a Moravian mission and became Christian. He wore European clothes and learned to speak English. He even adopted the name Gideon to make his transition more complete. By the Indian standard, he had done everything possible to integrate himself into the tribe of the English—yet these steps would prove to be only temporary.

For reasons that will likely remain unclear, Teedyuscung began to waiver on his commitment to the Moravian mission at Gnadenhutten.

He began to involve himself more in the politics of the Frontier, paying close attention to the struggles of the Delawares. He was deeply offended by the designation of "women" that the Iroquois had thrust upon his people, and regaining their lost freedoms became central to his beliefs. Where he differed from Shingas and the Western Delawares was not so much in their distaste for the Five Nations but in his sense of loyalty to his former English comrades. Shingas had made it clear that land speculators and settlers were entirely unwelcome in the West, yet Teedyuscung had lived among the Pennsylvanians and believed that the two communities could live together in relative peace under the right circumstances. He soon used his position in the mission to begin preaching a political message of self-reliance to his fellow Delaware converts, and by the 1750s had convinced dozens to take up his cause. His partisans would next follow him to the Wyoming Valley, and he would ultimately take on the title of king. With this declaration the Pennsylvanians were forced to come to terms with the notion that the Delawares were truly divided; Teedyuscung and Shingas would fly the banners of the Eastern and Western Delawares with great fervor. While it makes for a poetic dynamic, Teedyuscung and Shingas would have little in common, and no natural relationship would develop. In the ancient tradition of the Delawares, their two communities would rarely meet, and they exercised great control over their own pockets of territory. In the years to come, historians would compare these two men in ways that made little sense in their own time. Both men would stake their claim to history as passionate visionaries seeking renewal of a long-broken Delawares society, but they would be remembered very differently.

For as much as Teedyuscung would be praised in the years to come for his inclination toward peaceful resolution, Shingas would become the uncontested face of terror for thousands on the Frontier.

THE YEARS LEADING UP TO SHINGAS'S ASCENSION to king of the Western Delawares were of great consequence to Native America as a whole. Like many his age, presumably in his mid- to late-forties by the year 1753, Shingas had personally witnessed major shifts in imperial policy from three major empires competing for dominion in North America. Since their agreement to the English king, known as the "Covenant Chain," the Iroquois had found that their position on the continent was dropping considerably. Originally a mutually beneficial arrangement modeled after one shared with the Dutch of New Amsterdam, the English version was far less satisfying. Unlike the Dutch, who traded quality goods regularly with the Iroquois, the English economy produced far less exchange. The materials that the English traded were satisfactory, yet their ties to the Old World power made them necessary allies in a war they had not expected, and produced results they had not desired.

For nearly six centuries the relationship between the empires of Britain and France had been one of almost constant war. Certainly battles and gunfire were not constant, but the two superpowers regularly competed economically, culturally, and of course militarily. Since the fourteenth century, most of the combat experienced had been on the continent of Europe itself, and—due to the sparse amount of land that was unclaimed—was typically over a small river valley or critical mountain pass. But despite the geographic limits of the petty prizes for which they quarreled, the war was always representative of a national pride and competing vision for Western society. In the sixteenth century this tradition of competition took both kingdoms away from the continent in a race of a different sort: empire. For the next 150 years, Britain and France jockeyed for position around the globe, taking with them armies, fortune, religion, and culture. As the French began to explore the Indian subcontinent, so did the English. As the English ventured to the New World, so did the French. They carried with them countless elements of their own worldviews, and their now-cherished institution of warfare came along for the journey.

By the eighteenth century the French and the British grappled with a startling new truth. The causes of conflict may have been familiar, but the warfare would never be the same again. Unlike previous outbursts of violence that saw small battles flare up only to be hastily settled by laborious peace treaties, the new warfare was a global enterprise. As the superpowers agreed to blows in London and Versailles, it was the forests of North America and the blue waters of the Caribbean that experienced the bloodshed. With this new high-stakes development came the unmistakable desire for victory, and a global war would require distant allies. World war was a new concept for both peoples; empire was the art of conquest but the science of collaboration. In foreign theaters across the globe, the British and French raced to gain favor with local populations that would allow them to assert their own control over new territories as well as defend them in battle. It was in this mold that the Covenant Chain rose to international prominence, and that would ultimately force the Iroquois Confederacy into a position they had not anticipated.

What began as a mutual agreement based on trade became a terrible drain on the power of the Haudenosaunee. The trade goods that they received from the British were plenty, but the effect of war with the French and their allies was a burden they could not endure. Their population suffered, their numbers dwindled, and their economy became unsettled. At a time when the Iroquois seemed perched to become the unquestioned Indian superpower of the American Northeast, countless raids, ambushes, and the ever-present threat of disease threatened to topple all of their previous gains. Facing an internal political turmoil brought on by the strains of their contractual obligations, the Iroquois Confederacy had decided to pursue a radical change in their own imperial policy.

In what became known as the Great Settlement of 1701, the Iroquois sent diplomatic parties to both Montreal and Albany with hopes of stopping their troublesome decline. With the British, the Iroquois sought merely to extend the terms of the Covenant Chain; the British believed that their Iroquois allies were pleased with the arrangement and satisfied to see it continue. What the New Yorkers did not know, however, was that the Iroquois were also brokering a deal in the heart of New France's Saint Lawrence River Valley. The ultimate result of their French dealings was not an agreement of alliance but a simple declaration that in the event of another (almost inevitable) war with the British, the Iroquois would remain neutral and their warriors would stay home. To sweeten the deal, the French at Montreal offered the Iroquois access to their extensive trading network in the Great Lakes at Detroit, and the deal was done. While the French knew full well that the Iroquois were staunch British allies, the English-speaking colonists at Albany were unaware that the duplicitous meeting had ever taken place.

The maneuver was cunning and downright *imperial*, but its completion had successfully repositioned the Iroquois as extraordinary power brokers on the American Frontier. On the surface, the Great Treaty of 1701 was satisfactory to all parties involved. The French had no pretenses to acquiring and holding land in the Iroquois domain and sought only to expand their incredible network of trade. The British on the Atlantic Coast held land acquisition as their most pressing priority, and as such viewed the Five Nations as willing partners in this venture. In the middle of it all were the Iroquois, becoming richer and more influential than they had been in decades, and they emerged as the premiere native empire of the new eighteenth century. Like children of divorce, the Iroquois played the two superpowers against one another throughout the period. They parlayed the modest trade goods of the British to extract more lucrative exchange from the French, and in times of war they passed important British military and economic intelligence to the gracious French.[3]

This game of conspiracy served the Iroquois well for the first decades of the eighteenth century. In the War of the Spanish Succession (1701–1714) they positioned themselves astutely between the two powers. Although the war was primarily a European conflict, the small portions fought in North America revealed the stylistic imperial differences between Britain and France. Britain's was a system based on land acquisition; what new soil they tilled they considered their own to keep. Using this method, the Crown's holdings grew slowly but substantially, and were thereby neatly displayed on cartographic charts across the empire. The French, however, sought to build an economic empire based on trade rather than landholdings. Using the rivers and lakes of North America like a circulatory system, French traders and trappers were able to navigate incredible distances into the continent. Their dual command centers were Quebec in the north and Louisiana in the south, and the land in between was the key to their riches. The great artery that connected the Saint Lawrence River and the Mississippi was the Ohio, and the people that lived nearby would be key to their continued success. For this reason, the Ohio Country became central to the French vision for the New World, and winning the favor of its inhabitants would be a tremendous lift for King Louis's dominion.

The utter importance of the Ohio Country was revealed after nearly thirty years of peace in which the Iroquois proved to be the primary beneficiary. In 1744, hostilities flared again in an event known globally as the War of the Austrian Succession, but in the British colonies as "King George's War." Unlike the prior conflict, this event drew North Americans into extensive combat operations, and a new precedent for global warfare was set. The critical flashpoint of combat in this vast new theater came when the fortress of Louisbourg was captured after an extended siege. Situated at the mouth of the Saint Lawrence River, this British conquest wreaked immeasurable havoc on the very lifeblood of New France. With the Saint Lawrence being the primary point of entry into the aforementioned circulatory system of New France, the capture of the fortification at its mouth served to effectively close its economy. No new trade goods could get into the rivers and streams to which it flowed, and the trade network that had flourished for so long quickly began to wither. With their entire economy at risk of collapse, Indian nations across the continent grew anxious at the resulting trickle of French goods; it was then that the British appeared as willing partners to fill the worrisome vacuum.

It was in this development that the Delawares whom Shingas represented received their first taste of reclaimed freedom. With the British now committed to replacing the French as the primary suppliers of trade goods to the famished Indians of the West, new opportunities for trade soon came available in villages like Kittanning. Across the Ohio Country, strange new faces emerged seeking to engage in trade or exchange, and most importantly they were willing to do so without the approval of the Iroquois Confederacy. For the first time in half a century the Delawares could once again broker their own deals on their own terms, and because of greater developments abroad they could do so without their imperial masters looking over their shoulders. For a people desperate to regain the freedoms lost in generations prior, the War of the Austrian Succession manifested itself as the tremendous opportunity that the Western Delawares had been waiting for.

From the perspective of Quebec, the advancement of British traders into the Ohio Country was wholly unacceptable. While they themselves had no proper designs for the region itself, the Ohio River was a vital connection between their northern and southern spheres of influence; to lose that middle ground was to have their trading network severed in half. This new development stirred officials of New France into action, and in the summer of 1749 an exploratory expedition was launched under the command of Pierre-Joseph Celeron de Blainville. An officer of France's colonial military wing, Celeron de Blainville floated his men through the Ohio Country placing lead plates at river junctions deemed to be of high importance. These plates, which explicitly claimed the land for King Louis XV, were only the opening shots in a cold war that would lead to hostilities greater than most involved could have ever imagined.

For the Indian nations of the Ohio Country this was a troubling affair. Though the new influx of trade goods was a proverbial rising tide that benefited nearly all of them, the fact that France was now "claiming" land was a worrisome twist. The position of strength that both the Iroquois Confederacy and their subjected peoples had fostered was based on neither European empire being able to truly plant roots in the region. If one was beginning to do that, however, the other was likely to respond in kind. Their positions as mediators had given them great power, and if they had any hope of remaining as the "middle men" they would need to act quickly. Astute observers of shifting political winds, the natives began to craft a policy that was nothing short of an imperial balancing act: if the French presence was going to increase, they would need to do everything possible to ensure that the British kept pace. All of this, however, had to be done on their terms—a task that would prove to be entirely unmanageable.

Following Celeron de Blainville's bold actions to claim the region for France, the situation for the Ohioans only worsened. More British settlement trickled into the Allegheny, Monongahela, and Ohio river valleys from across the mountains, which served only to embolden the French. In the spring of 1753 New France began an incredibly expensive and ambitious effort to permanently stamp their label onto the region: they would build forts. At about the same time as the treaty council in Carlisle, agents of New France were completing construction on two forts, Presque Isle on Lake Erie and Le Boeuf just fifteen miles to its south. Even more pressing, they had very open designs at building two additional posts southward along the Allegheny River, the greatest being a bold statement of ownership at the Forks of the Ohio to be called Duquesne. At this critical juncture, two rivers—the Allegheny and the Monongahela—converge to form a third. This third river was the Ohio, the coveted westward passage leading directly to the Mississippi River. When completed, this chain of forts would effectively command all of the major arteries of the Ohio Country, and when taken into consideration with the rest of New France and Louisiana would unify an empire spanning a distance equivalent of Paris to Moscow.

The emergence of New France as the most present, if not most powerful, European empire in the Ohio Country put both the British and the natives on high alert. The Indian policy of strategic neutrality became paramount, and Ohioan sachems of the Delawares, Shawnees, and Mingos all attempted to maintain the status quo. For their part, the British colonial governors struggled to agree on how precisely to confront this new threat. It was not until Virginia seized the initiative that any action was taken, and the results would be historic but far from effective. As the wealthiest colony in North America, brandishing an official charter claiming its borders "from sea to sea," Virginia had great designs on the Ohio Country. One of its most powerful influences came in the form of a land speculation conglomerate known as the Ohio Company of Virginia. Made up of a veritable who's who of Virginia elites (including the lieutenant governor), this cabal of investors stood to lose an untold fortune if France actually took possession of the Ohio Country. Although it was publicized as a retaliatory action in defense of the Crown, the Old Dominion only took action when it seemed that the pocketbooks of its highest officials were in jeopardy. For this reason a young, well-connected planter named George Washington was selected to lead the colony's great foray into the wilderness. At only twenty-one years old, no one could have predicted how special the young Washington would become; there was no mistaking, however, that this mission would be only the first step on a much greater journey.

Washington kept a detailed account of his three-month expedition, and the urgency of the Delawares in the region can be easily identified. The young Washington arrived near the Forks of the Ohio on Saturday, November 24, and noted that "at the place where the Ohio company intended to erect a fort, lives Shingiss, king of the Delawares. We Called upon him, to invite him to council at the Loggstown . . . Shingiss attended us to the Loggstown . . ." At the meeting described, Washington met with the Iroquois Half-King Tanacharison to reaffirm their Covenant Chain obligations to one another in the face of the new French incursion. By all accounts, Shingas was present at this council along the Ohio River and also pledged his continued support to the Crown.[4]

For all practical purposes, Washington's mission produced little in the way of results. He traveled to Fort LeBoeuf and delivered an official letter demanding that the French vacate the Ohio Country; they did not. Aside from nearly dying twice of his own inexperience (once from falling into the icy Allegheny), Washington was unknowingly caught up in a desperate torrent of shifting native politics. The Iroquois and their subjects, including the Western Delawares represented by Shingas, had no real attachment to the British worldview, but they did desire an increased British presence in the Ohio Country to counter that of New France. They did not seek British migration into the West, as that virtually guaranteed a loss of territory. However, they were anxious to see a British military post placed somewhere in the vicinity of the Forks of the Ohio. Fort Duquesne, a French post that was not yet built by 1753, would have been stifled by the preemptive construction of a British fort at its intended location. This would increase the overall European presence in their lands, but it would also allow them to maintain their powerful position as mediators. The key was balance, and without it the scales might tip irrevocably against them.

At the end of January, George Croghan, a man considered by many to be the face of British trading in the Ohio Country, held council at Logstown. During these meetings the various sachems of the region reaffirmed their position and expressed their desires. The Half-King Tanacharison plainly made his case, and did not mince words:

> We now request that our Brother the Governor of Virginia may build a Strong House at the Forks of the Mohongialo, and send some of our young Brethren, their Warriors, to live on it; and we expect our Brother of Pennsylvania will build another House somewhere on the River where he shall think proper, where whatever assistance he will think proper to send us may be kept safe for us, as our Enemies are just at hand, and we do not know what Day they will come upon Us. We now acquaint our Brethren that we have our Hatchet in our Hands to strike the Enemy as soon as our Brethren come to our assistance.[5]

On February 2, at that same council, the Delaware Shingas, too, expressed his position: "I am glad to hear all our People are of one mind. It is true I live on the River Side, which is the French road, and I assure you . . . that I will neither go down or up, but will remove nearer to my Brethren the English, where I can keep our Women and Children safe from the Enemy."[6]

It seemed that in the face of a growing French presence, the British had a mutual ally in the peoples of the Ohio Country. That fact alone, however, would not be enough to stave off the French advance, and by early 1754 the Virginians doubled down on their efforts. Within weeks of the council at Logstown, Virginia had begun construction on a new post at the Forks of the Ohio to be named Fort Prince George. Tanacharison ceremonially laid the first log, but the pomp and circumstance was not to last. Shortly after its construction began, a French force floated down the Allegheny River and recaptured the site. They greatly outnumbered the paltry skeleton crew that Virginia had mustered, and began construction of Fort Duquesne. Upon its completion it would serve as the critical link in the chain of forts that completed their vast North American empire.

Unaware that their efforts to build a fort of their own at the Forks of the Ohio had failed, Lieutenant Governor Dinwiddie once again called upon the young George Washington to venture back into the Ohio Country. Given orders to act in a defensive manner against any French attempt to impede the construction of their fort, Washington (now twenty-two years old) led over 1,800 men back into the wilderness. While it seemed like a much greater imperial affair, Dinwiddie commissioned Washington without any authorization from London, and this oversight would soon have drastic consequences.

On May 23, Claude-Pierre Pecaudy de Contrecoeur, the French commandant of Fort Duquesne, ordered Joseph Coulon de Villiers de Jumonville to take thirty-five troops southward to confront the approaching Washington. Tipped off by native spies, Contrecoeur intended this expedition to be purely diplomatic, not unlike the one that the young Virginian himself had exercised only six months earlier. Their intention was to deliver a message to Washington informing him that his men were now in French territory and would be viewed as hostile. As the Frenchmen out of Fort Duquesne snaked their way south toward the British, Washington himself was tipped off that this perceived war party was headed his way. He elected to gather intelligence from his own Indian allies and strike first. On May 28, the two forces met, and the results were catastrophic. Washington and his native allies ambushed the French as they slept, and after a brief firefight it was made clear that he had unlawfully attacked a diplomatic party. As the shooting ended and the officers attempted to settle the affair, the Half-King suddenly accosted the French diplomat and brutally murdered him with a tomahawk blow to the head. While it was nothing more than a ghastly affair to Washington, for Tanacharison it was a declaration of war against France.

The repercussions were sudden and swift. News traveled back to Fort Duquesne that Jumonville had been killed, and the commandant ordered swift action to be taken. In a deeply personal move Contrecoeur selected the slain officer's brother Louis Coulon de Villiers to lead the punitive force; soon after a force of over six hundred men launched in pursuit of Washington. In the weeks that followed, the twenty-two-year-old colonel prepared in every way possible given his lack of experience, and the result was a tiny, circular fort in a natural clearing that would be known as Fort Necessity. Given the circumstances, and the fact that nearly every fort in colonial America is named after a wealthy benefactor in Britain, Fort Necessity may have been the most aptly named of them all.

By mid-June Washington was resigned to his fate, and dug in awaiting the arrival of the French response. In the weeks since Jumonville's death Washington had received modest reinforcements, bringing his total number to approximately four hundred men. He was almost certain to be outnumbered, but Washington desperately hoped to retain Tanacharison and his Indian allies when the battle actually came. He would have no such luck; seeing the futility of the fort that the British had built and knowing the manpower that the French could produce, the Half-King wished Washington the best and fled. As the Iroquois and their subject peoples departed from what they believed to be Washington's doomed last stand, Shingas offered the twenty-two-year-old an interesting departing word. Washington wrote in his journal that "though King Shingas, and others of the Delawares could not be persuaded to retire to our camp with their families . . . they nevertheless gave us strong assurance of their assistance and directed us in what manner to act in order to obtain our desire . . . King Shingas promised to take privately the most subtle measures to make the affair succeed though he did not dare do it openly."[7]

On July 3, Louis Coulon de Villiers avenged his brother's death. In a rainy, hours-long firefight, Washington's provincials valiantly fought against the much larger French force, but ultimately succumbed to their superior numbers. Well hidden under a thick canopy of trees, the French officer seemed poised to overrun his overmatched adversaries. Just when the situation was at its bleakest for the British, a shout of "*voulez vous parler*?" rang from the darkness. It was the French commanding officer calling for surrender, and Washington was more than happy to oblige. Colonel Washington was grief-stricken by both his loss at Fort Necessity and the idea that his native allies had broken their promise to assist him. While it is unlikely that Washington ever knew it, history has shown that Shingas may have kept his promise after all.

Shortly after Shingas had parted ways with Washington and his men, Villiers was joined by a party of Ohio Indians, including Delawares. These guides would prove to be useful while navigating terrain, but Villiers wrote that they regularly provided him with intelligence he believed to be faulty. In his journal he wrote that they insisted "the English were coming in Battle formation to attack." This of course was untrue, and indicative of the Delawares' desire to spare Fort Necessity and keep the scales of occupation as balanced as possible. The most striking admission that Villiers would make came from the night of Washington's surrender. With his enemy pinned down and imminently beatable, Villiers's demand for Washington's surrender is completely baffling from a strictly tactical point of view. He would later claim that his thought process was entirely influenced by his Ohioan attachés. "As we had been exposed to the rain all day long, and the Detachment was very tired, and the Indians had informed they were leaving the next day, and it was repeated [by the Indians] continually that drum beats or cannon fire were heard in the distance, I proposed . . . that we offer to speak with the English."[8]

Living up to his word, Shingas appeared to have instructed his Delaware warriors to offer faulty intelligence to the French command to dissuade them from finishing Washington and cementing their occupation of the Ohio Country. The Delaware sachem knew full well how desperate the Virginia colonel's situation had become and that no help was on the way. While it did little to dissuade Villiers from initiating his attack and igniting the Battle of Fort Necessity, Shingas's role in bringing the engagement to a close is readily apparent. Despite Washington's escape from the despairing circumstances at Fort Necessity, the Delawares' scheme to counteract the French with British military opposition was a failure. In the year that followed the battle, the French would only increase their own martial strength, and they would not come alone. By the end of 1754 the Ohio Country would be flooded with longtime French allies from the Pays d'en Haut region, including warriors from the Ottawa, Ojibwa, Potawatomie, and Miami nations. These newcomers congregated around the Forks of the Ohio and made Fort Duquesne the epicenter of trade and occupation in the region. With each passing month, the British presence in the region dwindled, and the Delawares found the enticement of cheap and ready French goods increasingly difficult to resist. By the year 1755, it seemed that unless the British did something drastic, the Ohio Country would slip from their grasp for good.

WHILE GEORGE WASHINGTON WAS FOMENTING the seeds of world war in the backcountry, a council of a very different sort was being held in Albany. Based in the Stadt Huys (translating roughly to "City Hall" in

Dutch), representatives from seven of Great Britain's northernmost American colonies were meeting to discuss a radical new proposal. It was offered forth by Pennsylvania's Benjamin Franklin, and though it would ultimately fail, it was a sign of his status as one of the premiere statesmen of the New World.

The plan was called the Albany Plan of Union, and to the forty-five-year-old Franklin it was a masterstroke of innovation and initiative. It called for Britain's North American colonies to provide for their own general government separate from the empire as a whole. This new Continental Congress would devise strategy, craft policy, and provide for defense in the face of an existential French threat. The men who debated this drastic proposal of self-governance were delegates sent by Connecticut, New York, Massachusetts, Maryland, New Hampshire, Rhode Island, and, of course, Pennsylvania. They were each selected by their respective colonial legislatures to deliberate on their behalves, and from June 19 to July 11 they explored nearly every aspect of the new proposal. Franklin's proposed congress would see eleven different colonies elect delegates to work in tandem with their colonial neighbors; to show their devotion to the Crown, the president would be selected by officials in England. While Franklin believed that North America was in a better position to determine its own needs than a parliament three thousand miles away, this concession was vital to demonstrating that the new legislative body was in no way an attempt at sedition or separation.

In its conception, the Albany Plan was sound; it was devised for practical purposes to confront an imminent threat. In his mind British North America was a place of divided ambitions, not singular unity. A month earlier Franklin had printed a now-famous woodcut of a snake divided into eight pieces with a slogan that stated his case plainly: "JOIN OR DIE." He would write in accordance that "the Confidence of the French in this Undertaking seems well-grounded on the present disunited State of the British Colonies, and the extreme Difficulty of bringing so many different Governments and Assemblies to agree in any speedy and effectual Measures for our common defense and Security; while our Enemies have the very great Advantage of being under one Direction, with one Council, and one Purse."[9]

Ever the politician, Franklin had lobbied steadily for the passage of his plan, but it would ultimately fail. Even after word of Washington's debacle at Fort Necessity had spread across the colonies, the Albany Plan still faltered. The notion was generally popular at the conference itself and copies of the plan were sent back to their respective legislatures, but the delegates' optimism was quickly snuffed out. It was denied outright by the British Board of Trade and never even considered by Parliament, but even more deflating was the fact that every single colonial assembly stood firmly against it. There was a great benefit to a North American union, to be sure, but Franklin's plan for modest self-governance was buried not by a tyrannical king but by the colonies' own assembly members. While their reasons for dismissing the plan were varied, the most direct explanation was also the most obvious: to approve it would be a voluntary concession of their own power.

It seemed that the state of affairs that prevented intercolonial cooperation could be traced to the self-interested members of the assemblies themselves. Despite his frustrations, Benjamin Franklin was not without blame, and as time would tell he would become as guilty of playing the game of partisan brinksmanship as anyone else in the New World.

Yet another aspect of the Albany Congress that was often overlooked was a treaty that directly disenfranchised the Delawares. As part of the meeting, British land agents brokered a deal with the Iroquois Confederacy to purchase large tracts of land west of the Susquehanna River. As the Six Nations saw this land and its peoples as their own, they had no qualms in selling it to the British agents; naturally, the British were anxious to accept it. Yet again, though, another great disconnect of the imperial world is revealed, considering that the Iroquois themselves did not live on the land, and the sale further disaffected the Delawares and others who called it home. It seemed that the history of the Delawares was one of repeated abuses and insults, the Albany Congress just being the latest among them.

NINE MONTHS LATER, IN APRIL 1755, the single most powerful conference in the history of colonial America was underway in Alexandria, Virginia. On one side of the table were the collective governors of

British North America's most powerful colonies: Robert Dinwiddie of Virginia, William Shirley of Massachusetts, Horatio Sharpe of Maryland, James Delancey of New York, and Robert Hunter Morris of Pennsylvania. Bringing together their collective interests, they represented the first true manifestation of intercolonial cooperation in the continent's history. Across from them was a figure who had recently become the most powerful person on the continent, and whose reputation preceded him long before that pronouncement. He was Major General Edward Braddock, and the meeting known as the Congress of Alexandria was the result of his beck and call. He was a severe man and a career officer; for the governors present, he was to be the man who would engineer Britain's great counterattack against the French incursion into the Ohio Country.

In response to the events of the previous summer, there was a great distaste for open warfare among the empires involved. From the French perspective, extended combat would weaken the financial footing that King Louis had diligently procured over the last two decades. Not only would fighting prove costly, but there was always the possibility of a catastrophic defeat that could cost New France valuable tracts of land that they had spent so much to procure. Rather than resorting to a wilderness war, the initial French reaction was to simply agree to the Ohio Country as a neutral ground. While it appears to be a noble sentiment, the fact that the French already had a significant military presence in the region made this wholly unpalatable for most in the English-speaking world.

For policymakers in England, the prospect of fighting was equally unpalatable. The chief minister of the monarch was the Duke of Newcastle, Thomas Pelham-Holles, a man in an unenviable position and distrusted by his own staff. When news of Washington's defeat at Fort Necessity reached London, he had a low opinion of pursuing a broader strategy involving military action for a region as marginal as the Ohio Country. His cabinet, however, felt quite the opposite, and furtively rallied well-connected members of the military and Parliament to lobby for a forceful response. With the aid of King George's son William Augustus, Duke of Cumberland, the surreptitious members of Newcastle's cabinet devised a plan that would send a regiment of British soldiers to North America to expel the French. They would further demand that two additional regiments be created entirely from provincial communities to aid in the effort, along with a multitude of American volunteers. This amounted to a bold plan of imperial scale, but perhaps the most audacious component was that the bill was to be footed by the American colonies themselves.

Leading this bold plan was General Braddock. At sixty years old, Braddock was a career officer of modest fame, known best for his hard demeanor. After becoming an ensign at the age of fifteen, Braddock would steadily rise through the ranks of the British military until being named major general in 1754. He was in the truest sense an *empire man*; he owed his career and family name to his service to the Crown. By the time he was selected to lead the charge against the French in North America, Braddock was a respected officer in the fabled Coldstream Guards and every bit the tactician that the strategy demanded. There was more to Braddock's commission than simply battling a foreign enemy, though. As part of his selection, he was given the power to issue direct orders to the governors and the assemblies of colonial America in an almost unprecedented fashion. Until that point, the norm in the Atlantic world was to allow colonists to effectively set their own fiscal agendas, but with these new powers Braddock expected full and complete cooperation. When Braddock arrived in Virginia with his Redcoats in February 1755 he did so as a revered figure, and when he called five of the most powerful executives on the continent to a council in Alexandria that April they quickly answered the call. The cadre of governors that met Braddock came looking for a spirited strategy session marked with healthy debate, but with the general there was none to be found. The five governors who sat across from Braddock were veritable masters of their own domains, and they were rarely challenged by the attachés and sycophants that surrounded them. On this day, however, they received much more than they had bargained for in a meeting that turned out to be no bargain at all. Edward Braddock did not present his demands as a negotiation; he simply informed them of their obligations. The general plainly issued a torrent of orders, and his guests were swiftly made to feel as though they were little more than fledgling subordinates.

The colonial executives were taken aback by his boldness, but Braddock's disdain for provincial leadership was made perfectly clear. While they believed they were the most important figures in their capital cities, Braddock saw them as nothing more than agents of an empire much greater than any single colony. In this idea the general was naïve; he underestimated the powerful role that politics played in the governance of the continent. Even more than that Braddock misjudged precisely how difficult it would be to wrangle a single colonial assembly into positively voting for anything, let alone five of them. But nevertheless the sixty-year-old Braddock boldly pronounced his ambitions to the governors without the slightest hint of reservation. On the subject of his upcoming military campaign the governors were mostly in agreement with the general. The Crown's forces would attack a number of strategic posts across the American Northeast, and Braddock himself would march an army of men into the wilderness for a direct strike on Fort Duquesne and its northern posts. The men were relieved to find some common ground with the officer, as they knew that the discussion of financing the campaigns would be far more contentious.

Unlike the neophyte general, the American governors knew full well the tribulations of negotiating with a colonial assembly. Among their many duties, assemblymen controlled the purse strings of their colonies and wielded that power with the utmost vigor. It was their most meaningful political leverage in any debate, and no one knew how frustrating its calculated employment could be better than the governors in Alexandria. When Braddock informed them that the campaigns against the French would be financed through a "common fund," the executives bristled at the thought. One observer noted that the governors "gave it as their unanimous opinion that such a Fund can never be established in the Colonies without the aid of Parliament." In an age when intercolonial cooperation was almost unheard of, on this topic they were in total agreement. Their own experience had shown them that the combination of frugality, brinksmanship, and pettiness that so typified the American assemblyman would be too great even for a general of Edward Braddock's caliber to overcome. They also added "that they were unanimously of the opinion that it should be proposed . . . to find out some method of compelling them (the Assemblies) to do it . . ." In other words, perhaps it would take the weight of an empire to move the legislatures, because clearly the push of a governor was not enough.[10]

In the face of the unified governors, Braddock was flummoxed. He was not accustomed to this type of open insubordination, particularly from a party of provincial administrators. His orders had come directly from the king's own ministers, and the inability of his guests to extract even a modest sum of monies from their own colonies was utterly repugnant. The parties adjourned with little settled on April 19, and Braddock took the time to write to the politician Sir Thomas Robinson in England about their predicament. His solution was as drastic as it was foreboding; perhaps taxation was the only way to settle their dilemma. "You will be sufficiently informed, Sir . . . of the impossibility of obtaining from several colonies the establishment of a general fund agreeable to his Majesty's instructions . . . I cannot but take the liberty to represent to you the necessity of laying a tax upon all his Majesty's dominions in America, agreeably to the result of Council, for reimbursing the great sums that must be advanced for the service and interest of the colonies in this important crisis."[11]

As frustrated as Braddock had become, no one understood his outrage better than Pennsylvania governor Robert Hunter Morris. Although all colonies had their own political eccentricities, none were as cumbersome and heated as the Peaceable Kingdom. In the strictest sense Morris was not "governor" at all, but instead a lieutenant governor. As William Penn had been the founder of the colony, the official executive title was still held by his son, Thomas. As Thomas resided in faraway England, it was Robert Hunter Morris who became the proprietors' man on the ground. By 1755 Morris was in his mid-fifties and fully engrossed in Pennsylvania's unique political system, and although he had only been appointed in 1754 he was already well versed in the various pitfalls of Pennsylvania governance. Among the many challenges that Morris faced, the most pressing were his dual obligations as deputy. As a prerequisite to his commission, Morris had to commit to defending the interests of the Penn family at all costs; the most pressing among them was a pledge to never, under any circumstances, allow the adversarial assembly to tax his vast and sweeping estates.

By the 1750s a distinctive pattern had emerged in Pennsylvania that was as corrosive as it was ideological. The proprietors (the Penn family) had numerous landholdings deemed theirs by birthright. As the colony itself was held in the same regard, the Penns cunningly exempted themselves from paying any taxes on their holdings in any form. The Penns viewed this as their prerogative, but not all Pennsylvanians shared their viewpoint. The assembly became the instrument of the people, and the Penns' unwavering commitment to exemption put them directly at odds with the legislature. The result was a tiresome and exasperating back-and-forth between the anti-proprietary assemblymen and the agents of the Penn family. The assembly consisted of many prominent figures, but none was more vocal in his objections to the proprietors' tax-free lifestyle than fifty-year-old Benjamin Franklin. In this single issue Franklin had touched a nerve with working-class colonists, and his almost singular focus on the matter made him the undisputed champion of the people's assembly.

As the Penns kept their home overseas, Franklin's primary adversary had become their leading agent: Lieutenant Governor Robert Hunter Morris. By the time of the Congress at Alexandria, these two ideological heavyweights had developed a contentious relationship; Braddock's arrival, however, had forced them into an unlikely partnership. Like Morris, Franklin was present in Alexandria that spring as a chosen representative of the Pennsylvania Assembly; also like the governor, Franklin agreed that military action needed to be taken to curb a French invasion. Both men understood the danger that the expansion of New France posed, and the urgency of Braddock's upcoming campaign, and they were equally aware of the political realities awaiting them back in Philadelphia.

In the months since the completion of Fort Duquesne, Morris had petitioned the assembly for funds directly related to the defense of Pennsylvania. This would prove to be a flashpoint, as it was something never done before in the colony's history. Since his bold declaration the parliamentary trend in the capital had been as follows: Morris would request that the assembly procure funds for the defense of the colony, and the assembly would respond by offering a plan that included taxes from the proprietors' estates. Morris would then *suggest* that the body reconsider a measure that exempted Penn lands, and the motion would subsequently fail. It was a point of infinite frustration for the lieutenant governor, and his duties often left him feeling disgusted at the process. In preparation for Braddock's arrival, he had preemptively demanded specific fealty from each of the colonies that would participate in his upcoming campaign. From Pennsylvania Morris requested three thousand troops, wagons, supplies, and a collection of maps for a prospective invasion route. When he finally met with Braddock at Alexandria he had to swallow his pride and admit to the general that he hadn't acquired anything—not even the maps. "Such is the infatuation and obstinacy of the people I have to deal with . . . that even though their country is invaded, yet I could not persuade them to act with vigor at this juncture . . . I could easily have had a number of men in readiness . . . if my Assembly would have come into reasonable measures, but for want of money I have not been able to carry the King's commands in that particular execution."[12]

For Morris, the pettiness of the politics that surrounded the acquisition of funds was one that few people close to him could truly understand. For that reason he wrote to his colleague, the governor of Virginia, in search of sympathy. "They do not think themselves obliged to furnish any provisions," he wrote, "and when they do I make no Doubt they will find out some Pretence for not doing it then, their scheme being to avoid all Expence however necessary to their own Preservation." In the mind of Morris and those in the proprietary camp, the ideological rigidness of the assembly represented the worst in political brinksmanship. At a time when their colony—and, even more, their *empire*—demanded immediate action, it seemed that Philadelphia's political machine was content to deliver more of the same. For all of the pitfalls of colonial governance, though, this time the lieutenant governor was not alone. His greatest aid came not from a close ally or fellow partisan but from his public foil, Benjamin Franklin. Despite being the stalwart face of the anti-proprietary assembly, Franklin had set himself apart from many of his colleagues by taking a hawkish stance on colonial defense.

In its original conception, Penn's vision of a "Peaceable Kingdom" was rich in dogmatic Quaker subtleties. Penn was an honest broker and true to his faith, and even though his sons subsequently allowed his vision to lapse in his absence there were still some lingering manifestations of that dream. The most prominent and certainly the most visible was his trademark Quaker pacifism, and the founder loomed large when it came to defending his realm. Although not the majority, there remained in the assembly a strong current of Quakerism that held fast to Penn's founding principles of nonviolence; these religious activists stood firmly against the sanctioning of any organized military force marching under the banner of Pennsylvania. Thus, for the first eighty years of its existence, the colony was effectively left undefended and vulnerable for no practical reasons other than as a statement of ideological grace. This changed in 1747 during the War of the Austrian Succession when Benjamin Franklin joined a group that professed a specific need for some kind of organized defense in the colony. While the assembly (of which he was not yet a member) rebuked his claim, Franklin took action to create an entirely *voluntary* fighting force he called "associators." In this way, Franklin garnered outside support and proved that most colonists supported such a measure. He likewise circumvented the assembly and publicly revealed that the minority Quaker viewpoint was fading fast in the wake of major demographic changes. His fame increased greatly after this effort, and in 1751 he was elected to the assembly to great acclaim.

Like many political groups the Quaker Party was a collection of people with conflicting desires. The reality, by 1755, was that the assembly had become a sort of Venn diagram of multiple loyalties with some overlapping interests. Some members balked at Braddock's demands for three thousand soldiers on religious grounds, stating a commitment to pacifism, while others pledged their support only on the condition that the Penns pay their fair share. The speaker of the assembly, Isaac Norris, summed up the changing dynamic succinctly: "We have very much Thrown our disputes from being a Quaker Cause, to a Cause of Liberty . . ." Regardless of their reasoning, though, for Lieutenant Governor Morris it produced the same result: gridlock.[13]

Enter Benjamin Franklin. Franklin was a non-Quaker in the Quaker Party, and he knew how to walk the fine line demanded by his fellow partisans. He understood life outside of the assembly chamber and how to manipulate it to his advantage without compromising his party's founding principles. In short, he was the consummate politician, and one of the few members of his party with the immunity to bend the rules without suffering any lasting political consequences. This point is illustrated in Franklin's interactions with the general during the Alexandria Congress. According to Franklin's *Autobiography*, the assemblymen noted that Braddock only possessed twenty-five wagons for the entire campaign. After proudly boasting that Pennsylvania could provide far more due to its extensive agrarian community, Franklin claimed that Braddock assigned him the task of accumulating 150 wagons with four horses each, and as many packhorses as he could hire. Always the opportunist, Franklin placed a newspaper ad, which, he wrote, "I published as soon as I arrived at Lancaster."[14]

Where the Quakers in Philadelphia would not act, Franklin found willing and anxious participants in the Scots-Irish farmers of Lancaster, York, and Cumberland counties. As time would prove, these settlers cared very little for William Penn's expired religious objections, and were more than willing to provide for their own defense in the face of a common enemy. The advertisement that Franklin placed worked precisely as he had planned, and Pennsylvania's Frontier region supplied more than Braddock had demanded. In a show of faith, Franklin fronted £200 of his own money to compensate the families that had lent their wagons to the campaign. As a condition of their service, Franklin was able to elicit a rare guarantee from the general that no person driving a wagon would be forced into military service during the campaign. By the summer of 1755 the Quaker assembly had not contributed any meaningful military support to Braddock's great assault on the French. The maneuvering of Benjamin Franklin, though, allowed the colony of Pennsylvania to do its part in spite of its own government's efforts to obstruct it.

Aside from grappling with his assembly, Lieutenant Governor Morris also had to maintain strong ties with the Iroquois Confederacy. If there was to be a general war with the French, the various executives of North America understood that they would need to keep this polity on their side to be successful. Earlier in March, Morris had sat in council at Philadelphia with representatives of the Six Nations to reaffirm their alliance. Among the many topics discussed that day was the notion of arming the Iroquois subjects of the Ohio Country to help fend off the French who had laid claim to their area with particular emphasis on the Western Delawares. In a telling moment, the Oneida Half-King Scarouady put these thoughts to rest. "They bid them be quite easy and still," he said, "nor be disturbed at what is doing, nor meddle at all on any side . . ."[15] As a critical part of their domain over the Delaware, the Iroquois had labeled them as "women" and taken away their privilege to wage war without the Confederacy's permission. When Morris saw the strong emotional rebuke that Scarouady delivered at his suggestion, he noted that mobilizing the Western Delawares was apparently off-limits. That strategy may have been acceptable in the east, but for British agents living in the Ohio Country the warriors of the Western Delawares were thought to be a great untapped resource. In a letter to Thomas Penn, noted Frontiersman Conrad Weiser implored the proprietor to "persuade the 6 nations . . . to take the petticoat from the delawares and give them a Breech Cloath to wear . . ." In essence, Weiser was asking colonial leaders to lobby the Iroquois to allow the Western Delawares to independently wage war on the French that had invaded the Ohio Country. As time would tell, both Morris and Penn strayed from pressing this idea further in an effort to preserve the integrity of the Covenant Chain.[16]

ON MAY 29, 1755, MAJOR GENERAL EDWARD BRADDOCK'S great campaign against the forces of New France began in earnest. Assembling his men and supplies at Wills Creek in Maryland, the much-heralded savior of British North America prepared to set out with over two thousand men and a vast supply train. The trek to Fort Duquesne was certain to be difficult; there were no roads to speak of and little intelligence as to the nature of the route ahead of them. One of the few people in Braddock's camp who had ever even seen the Ohio Country was the twenty-three-year-old George Washington, then still a novice despite his previous outings. Even in the face of these challenges, though, Braddock's confidence never wavered, and he ordered his army to begin their one-hundred-mile march to the Forks of the Ohio.

Braddock could not have been prepared for what lay ahead. The ground was inhospitable, and the target was far beyond his effective reach. The supplies that he had in tow courtesy of Benjamin Franklin's wagon train were impressive, but they too were finite. Just getting to Fort Duquesne was a logistical nightmare, and once there he still had to lead his men in battle. In short, it was a daunting task for any experienced wilderness commander, and Braddock's history with the American woods stretched as far as his immediate field of vision. The task at hand was likely too great to be successful, but the pragmatic general did his best to increase his chances. Shortly after assembling in Maryland, Braddock determined that his army should not blindly navigate the forests but actually cut their own road. This would slow his progress, but it also allowed the British to control as much of their own course as possible. If his men were to follow the natural passages available to him, his French enemies would have a detailed understanding of his army's location; if they chose to ambush his forces, they could do so at a place of their own choosing. With these pitfalls in mind Braddock's army would chop, dig, and hack its way through the Ohio Country at a meager pace of only two miles per day.

Shortly after his departure from the freshly built Fort Cumberland at Wills Creek, Braddock received an unlikely guest in the form of the Delawares' sachem Shingas. By June Shingas had already met with a number of prominent British officials and had no qualms about speaking openly with the general. The sachem was willing to pledge his support to the British effort in exchange for a promise that no settlers would remain behind. Since the French had occupied the Ohio Country, the region had been flooded by their Indian allies from the Great Lakes, which were a nuisance to the Western Delawares who resided there. Shingas had no affinity for the French, but he proposed an alliance to Braddock to both honor the Iroquoian Covenant Chain and, more importantly, keep the Ohio Country free of white squatters. With these talking points delivered, Shingas awaited the general's response. Braddock's words would echo through the region for years to come: "No Savage Should Inherit the Land."

Braddock was curt and dismissive in his response. By this point Shingas had himself demanded a certain level of courtesy; he certainly had not anticipated the general's statement to be rife with disrespect. The Delawares left puzzled and bemused, and they returned a day later to pose the same question. Braddock snarled that he "did not need their Help and had No doubt of driveing the French and their Indians away," to which Shingas replied: "if they might not have Liberty To Live on the Land they would not Fight for it . . ." This exchange left the effective reality of a mutual Anglo-Delaware alliance deeply soured, and within three months it would be completely dead.[17]

As Braddock's army made its way deeper into the Ohio Country, the general grew impatient with its slow progress. To expedite the affair, Braddock split his army into two parts: the first was a 1,300-man "flying column" that would hasten their pace towards Fort Duquesne, and the other was an 800-man supply column that would necessarily lag behind. By July 9, the adjustment succeeded in pushing Braddock's heralded army within ten miles of their target and into the waiting arms of disaster. Aware that the British army was coming thanks to diligent native spies, approximately 250 French regulars and Canadian militia, along with over six hundred Great Lakes warriors, rushed to meet their attackers. As Braddock's forces attempted to cross the Monongahela River in a thin line of troops, the British collided head-on with the advancing Franco-Indian forces.

Although history would label the events that transpired as an ambush, closer examination of sources would reveal that the Battle of the Monongahela was actually a meeting engagement. In a torrid affair of fire and smoke the British and French forces unexpectedly tangled, and their native allies ran for the cover of the trees. As Braddock's men attempted to flee in confusion, the general struggled to organize the chaotic scene for a disciplined attack . . . it failed. Unprepared for the realities of warfare in the dense forest, the British found themselves surrounded by their Indian attackers. Soon after the battle began the warriors opened fire on Braddock's men from all angles, and the general's principle army collapsed into a scene of panic and bloodshed. The warriors of the Great Lakes nations decimated his command, killing numerous officers, and ultimately struck a mortal wound on Braddock himself. It was a rout in the most frightening sense of the word; 977 of his 1,300 men were killed or wounded in the melee.

Braddock himself was carried off of the battlefield alive, but barely. Earlier in the spring he had confidently announced to Benjamin Franklin that the Indians of North America were no threat to his Redcoats. He stated, "These savages may be a formidable enemy to your raw American militia; but upon the King's regular and disciplined troops, Sir, it is impossible they should make any impression." He was wrong, and his certainty cost him his life. In Edward Braddock's final moments it was revealed that confidence was nothing more than hubris, and even in his last breaths he could not accept what had transpired. Beaten and broken on the shores of the Monongahela, the general's last recorded words were: "Who would have thought it? We shall better know how to deal with them another time."[18]

Edward Braddock's defeat was not just a shock to the British world, but also to the dynamic and shifting Ohio Country. For many of the Iroquois subjects who resided there, most notably Shingas, it was a clear indication that the British had no means of protecting his new way of life. Diplomacy had been tried and failed; taking up the hatchet seemed his only viable option. In the summer of 1755 the Western Delawares had seen the best that the Covenant Chain had to offer.

Its wreckage remained on the shores of the Monongahela River.

THREE

Taking Up the Hatchet

On the morning of October 16, 1755, the family of Jean Jacques Le Roy was beginning its day in the small settlement known as Penn's Creek. Located on the western branch of the Susquehanna River, Penn's Creek was typical of communities on the Pennsylvania Frontier. Life was quiet, and success belonged to those who farmed. Approximately two dozen families had settled near Le Roy, and they each shared a similar story; they were immigrants from Europe who sought cheap land and financial opportunity in the Peaceable Kingdom. Just a year earlier the smattering of plantations called "Penn's Creek" did not actually exist, and, like most Frontier families, the Le Roys were the first Europeans to till the virgin soil on which their home now sat. Jean Jacques Le Roy and his family had immigrated to the New World in 1752 from Switzerland onboard a ship called the *Phoenix*, and like the vessel's name implied he too was looking for a rebirth on the other side of the world. His family joined him on the journey, and soon after arriving in the capital of Philadelphia he found that he was unwelcome, and that his fortunes lay in the West.

The plantations that dotted the landscape in the immediate vicinity were ordinary immigrant homesteads by eighteenth-century standards. In the preceding years the English had been the first to venture into the Susquehanna River Valley, but it was soon populated by the Scots-Irish, and eventually by the Germans and the Swiss. Life was tremendously difficult on the Frontier, but Le Roy understood that the opportunities that his family had in North America were far greater than those he had left behind in the Old World. His daughter Marie had adapted well to Frontier plantation life, and played that morning with a friend. An eldest son, Jacob, likewise flourished under his father's tutelage. Their land was fertile—so much so, in fact, that Jean Jacques was able to hire a farmhand to assist in managing the rapidly expanding enterprise. The realities of the Frontier were never far from his mind, though. Directly across the creek from his settlement was the Indian village of Shamokin, and Le Roy had learned that his new neighbors were unlike any that he had in Switzerland. From his few months living at Penn's Creek, Le Roy had seen the Delawares, Tutelos, and others that resided in Shamokin engage regularly with the new settlers; in all likelihood, Jean Jacques himself probably traded goods with them. In times of peace the Indians with whom he shared his lands were lively and agreeable, but the winds of change were shifting on the Pennsylvania Frontier.

October 16 began as an entirely ordinary day, but the expectant stillness of the countryside was soon jolted by the cracking of gunfire. Jean Jacques was still learning to navigate Frontier life, and he had not experienced anything like this yet. Now alert, Jean Jacques's mind likely went to the hired hand who was tending to the cows in the fields around his home. Five more gunshots rang out through the air, and the Le Roys leapt to their feet; it sounded as though they were directly outside. He was soon met by the unmistakable war whoops of a raiding party.

Before Le Roy could act his door burst open and eight Delaware warriors rushed forth. They were painted from head to toe in red and black, and wielded tomahawks and clubs. Jean Jacques rose to intercept the intruders and to protect his family, but the Delawares were too swift; to the shock of his children they killed Le Roy with a tomahawk blow to the crown of his head. Young Jacob next lunged toward the Delawares, but he too was "overpowered" and taken to the ground. Le Roy's daughter Marie expected her brother to suffer the same ghastly fate as her father, but to her surprise she, her brother, and her visiting friend were all snagged by the warriors and thrown from the cabin. The scene that played out next would be highly typical for Frontier families over the next year. The Delawares plundered the home and wantonly destroyed items they deemed of no value until finally setting the house on fire. The warriors next dragged the lifeless body of Jean Jacques halfway outside and plunged two tomahawks into his head; they whooped and cheered as his lower body burned into grizzled char. The gruesome and bloody display was a symbolic exclamation point on their raid. The warriors then calmly kindled a smaller fire of their own, around which they celebrated their great victory.

To Shingas, painted completely black, the raid on Penn's Creek could not have gotten a better start. The Le Roy children were told that they would be taken deep into the Ohio Country, and that their home would not be standing much longer. The self-satisfied Delawares admired their work in the form of the burning homestead, but they were soon snapped back to focus by the sound of an approaching horse. The warriors remained quiet as the sound clip-clopped nearer, and the children soon saw their neighbor, "Bastion," arrive to inspect the source of the smoke. Just as quickly as he had arrived Bastion was soon thrown from his horse, stabbed, and scalped. The warriors would keep the flesh and hair of Bastion's head as a macabre trophy to impress their comrades in their home village.

Shingas left the Le Roy homestead as a smoking ruin and proceeded to lead his band to their next target. The home of John Conrad Leininger sat approximately a half mile away, and the Delawares were swiftly upon it. When they reached the cabin the warriors found two men and two young girls, and rather than falling upon them first "demanded rum." The homeowner explained that they had none, and the Delawares then "called for tobacco, which was given to them." According to an eyewitness, Shingas and his raiders smoked a pipe in front of the frightened Leiningers and shouted, "We are the Alleghany Indians, and your enemies. You must all die!" Suddenly the Indians murdered the father with a gunshot, executed his twenty-year-old son with a tomahawk, and dragged the two girls from the home as prisoners.

For the next two days until October 18, 1755, the Delawares devastated the region. They killed fourteen people in total (including an infant) and took ten captives. Numbering among the hostages were one man, one woman, five girls, and one boy. Before departing, Shingas and his warriors were said to have laid the clotted and darkened scalps at the feet of their enemies' captive loved ones and proclaimed "that they had a good hunt that day."[1]

THE DECISION THAT THE WESTERN DELAWARES MADE to abandon the British in the fall of 1755 was a momentous one. In declaring war, Shingas and his people had elected to openly turn their backs on the Iroquois Confederacy, the colony of Pennsylvania, and even their own Delaware brethren to the east. In the immediate aftermath of what is known as "the Penn's Creek Massacre," Shingas and his warriors attempted to rally the support of the Delawares at Shamokin with little success. For the time being, it appeared as though the act of taking up the hatchet was one that occurred in the far western reaches of the Allegheny and Ohio River valleys. This was not a political posture that was made lightly; to effectively wage war, the Western Delawares that resided in the West would need a steady and reliable source of supplies, weapons, and ammunition. Without these things their war effort would likely be viewed as a failed revolution against the imperial Iroquois masters and a dishonorable reneging of their generations-old contracts with the colony of Pennsylvania.

The critical element of the Western Delawares' electing to disregard their status as "women," which the Iroquois had thrust upon them, was the French. In the aftermath of Braddock's defeat the French presence in the Ohio Country only increased, and confidence rose. As Braddock's march was described as Britain's great response to the French invasion, it was only sensible that his stunning and total defeat was reflective of British capabilities as a whole. While the colony of Pennsylvania had proven that it had no intention of arming Shingas and his people, the French would prove to be willing partners. They would soon flood the Allegheny River Valley with guns, powder, and supplies to keep Western Delawares, Shawnees, and Mingos tied to their fortunes. With the boom of trade now flourishing thanks to the demands of a war, Fort Duquesne became the beating heart of Franco-Indian relations in the Ohio Country. The sachems of the Western Delaware as well as the various other Ohioan and Great Lakes nations would learn to rely totally on the post so long as their war continued, and they never strayed too far from it.

Shingas did not have an affinity for France per se, nor did he have any interest in helping them win a war that would soon spread to five continents. The forces of King Louis were merely a means to an end for his people, the end being total autonomy for the Western Delawares as they had experienced in centuries past. Interesting insight is given in the writings of Sir William Johnson, Britain's chief Indian superintendent in the Northeast. He relays a story told by a former captive among the Western Delawares that summarizes the relationship perfectly. "The young Man that made his escape from King Shingo [*sic*] the Delaware . . . Saith they if we only Subdue the English first we may do as we please with the French, for we have them as it were in a Sheep Den and may cut them off any time. . . ."[2]

In essence, the threat posed by the British and French to the Western Delawares' homeland was far from equal. While the French had been viewed by the Ohioans as invaders over the last several months, they were never believed to be a *permanent* threat. The French had proven that they sought only trade with the natives as they had in the Great Lakes, and what little presence they had was only temporary to meet that end. The British, however, had a long history of permanently squatting on Indian lands, and Braddock's hubristic statements to Shingas only served to validate that belief. Another sachem, Ackowanothic, further confirmed this strategy later by recalling that "we can drive away the French when we please, they have even promised to go off when we pleased, provided we not suffer the English to take possession of the Lands. . . ."[3]

The unique brand of warfare that the Western Delawares brought upon the Susquehanna River Valley was one grounded in highly symbolic tradition; to the settlers, though, it was nothing short of terrorism.

Throughout the history of colonial America, witnesses told stories of terrible atrocities and "massacres" inflicted by native warriors upon unsuspecting victims, and Shingas's methodology was no different. The Indian world was a very physical one, and corporeal statements were considered the norm. While Europeans had relied on the institution of signifying agreements with written contracts and signatures, Indians had no such tradition. Rather than affixing their names to paper, the native system of diplomacy involved complex rituals of wampum belts, gift giving, and symbolic gestures. In this regard Europeans and Indians could not have been more separate, and these variances often revealed the fundamental differences between them; of these warfare was the most jarring. As seen in Braddock's defeat on the Monongahela, British soldiers attempted to align themselves in rows for volley fire in the manner customary of European battle. The Indians, however, immediately took to the trees, and easily defeated their enemy. The European custom of war was based on discipline and time-tested strategy, but it quickly fell to pieces when the opposing force played by entirely different rules. After the battle, as the men retreated for safety, they were aghast as the native warriors chased them from the field and killed the British wounded. It was in these instances of corporeal violence and postmortem mutilation that the notion of "the savage" was cemented. In a more practical sense, when Shingas and the Western Delawares raided a plantation they would often kill its residents in a gruesome manner. This was not done for the traditional reasons just explained, but mostly to drive the rest of the region into a panic. This served the raiding Delawares on a number of fronts. In the most general sense, Shingas could not have killed all of the residents of the Frontier, but he did not need to. His ultimate goal was to cleanse the region of all white residents, and if he could simply frighten them away, that was all the easier. By definition terrorism is simply political violence, and Shingas had proven to be a master strategist in this regard. By killing a person very publically and displaying the gruesome remains, the warriors were sending a clear message to settlers in neighboring areas: *leave, or die.*

THE RAID ON PENN'S CREEK SENT SHOCKWAVES throughout Pennsylvania's distant Frontier, but it was only Shingas's opening act. Two weeks later the sachem returned with his warriors to continue their murderous spree. Viewed with a bird's eye, Pennsylvania is bisected by the formidable ridges of the Allegheny Mountains. Filled with lofty peaks and covered in deciduous forest, the many ridges of the Appalachians had formed an all but impenetrable divide for much of the early history of the colony. It was only the in 1740s that Scots-Irish families began to settle the region, and the area known as the Great Cove proved to be a desirable locale for the most hard-scrabble among them.

Upon approach the Allegheny Mountains jut up from the fertile green plains of the Cumberland Valley with such abruptness that they can appear as a great wall; in this way, they were literally the division between the prosperous East and the vast Frontier. But for the residents of the Great Cove this obstacle was not a deterrent, and its earliest pioneers climbed the first ridgeline and planted their homes within the first valley they could find. And so, by 1755, dozens of families had located in this place, a veritable Garden of Eden separate from both the East and the West. Great Cove residents prided themselves on their autonomy from the Quaker elites of Philadelphia that they had grown to resent, and made a prosperous life for themselves nestled comfortably within the confines of the Allegheny Mountains. Their seclusion, though, was only an illusion, and the efforts of Shingas and his warriors were on the verge of making that alarmingly clear.

There is some debate about the date that the Western Delawares, Shawnees, and Mingos actually arrived at the Great Cove, but there is little about what transpired after they did. By Saturday, October 31, the rampage at Penn's Creek had become well known in both the Ohioan and European Frontiers, and neither side was certain of what was to come next. In the wake of Braddock's defeat the Delaware nation was largely divided; many in the East remained cautiously adherent to the British, and the majority in the West had elected to fight. But some in the Susquehanna River Valley no longer saw paying fealty to the Iroquois and Pennsylvania as a viable option, and they made their way to the Ohio Country to join the coming war. As is still the case with insurgent movements in the twenty-first century, places of political rebellion become something of a magnet for rebels themselves. Between July and November of 1755, many disaffected and ambitious Delawares made this choice, and promptly left their friends and loved ones behind to join the seditious Shingas.

Electing to move on the Great Cove and its unsuspecting residents, Shingas now led a veritable army of over one hundred Ohioan warriors. They were joined by French allies from the Great Lakes and, in some cases, even French agents out of Fort Duquesne. The goal was unchanged, but the numbers present made the expectations surrounding the raid even greater; more warriors meant more destruction. While Shingas was viewed as the public face of this new campaign of terror, it would be misleading to equate him to a European-style military officer. In the Indian world, one achieved military prowess through battlefield effectiveness, but never as a leader of men. The notion of an "Indian army" simply did not exist, but the term "war party" applied much more readily. An Indian war party was a collection of individual warriors seeking out individual glories through battle; if the achievement of that glory was facilitated by fighting as a group, then cooperation was encouraged. When Shingas led his men he did not attack with a disciplined strategy of maneuvers and salients utilized by so many European officers—he simply joined his fellow warriors in creating as much chaos as possible. For British forces this would be unthinkable, but for the Indian warriors of the Ohio Country this melee warfare was the perfect foil when battling rigid, strategy-driven opponents.

In the case of the assaults unleashed on the Pennsylvania Frontiers, Shingas and his warriors knew that they were unlikely to face any such disciplined fighting force. They operated entirely under the element of surprise and were anxious to capitalize on the unsuspecting conditions of a civilian populace. With one hundred warriors in tow, Shingas's most effective strategy would be to splinter his war party into small bands and send them raiding in all directions. The destruction of Penn's Creek was achieved by fewer than twenty men, and given the size of his war party he could spread his terroristic warfare in countless directions. To do this Shingas would need to rely on the younger warriors at his side, and there were a number of strong candidates to lead these auxiliary attacks in his stead. None, as it turned out, were more promising than Tewea.

While Shingas was viewed as the most respected member of the war party, Tewea had quickly become one of his chief seconds. It would be unfair to claim him as any sort of deputy or lieutenant, as such an idea did not exist in the Indian world, but Tewea would prove himself to be a brutal and efficient warrior who garnered the respect of his peers. Little is known of Tewea's early life, but he appears in the historical record having sold land near modern Lewistown, Pennsylvania, along the Juniata River. The man to whom he sold his title was named Buchanan, and it was he who gave Tewea the nickname of "Captain Jacobs." As was common on the Frontier, European settlers would often label natives with colloquial titles, as they could not pronounce their actual names. In the case of Tewea, a Delaware, Buchanan suggested humorously that he resembled a German settler nearby named Jacobs, and the nickname stuck. As time would tell, "Captain Jacobs" would become a name of great fear and trepidation among those same settlers.

On the morning of either October 31 or November 1, 1755—accounts vary— Shingas and his raiders began their attack on the Great Cove. The community was unaware that the strike was coming, and the results were nothing short of calamitous. The modern notion of a town did not yet exist in settlements like the ones at the Great Cove, and families typically lived on sprawling farms a mile or less apart. In many cases each of these communities would construct a fort, or "blockhouse," for protection, but most were simply modestly fortified homes of local farmers that offered little actual defensive capability. These inherent weaknesses would prove to be critical to Shingas's success, as families were often unaware of the danger until it was too late. One by one the warriors tore through the Great Cove burning barns, wantonly slaughtering livestock, and of course terrorizing its inhabitants. In the surrounding communities the satellite warrior bands produced equal devastation, giving the dramatic sense that virtually the entire Pennsylvania Frontier was set ablaze.

Perhaps the most harrowing tale of the raid came from the seventeen-year-old Hugh Martin. Martin was the son of John Martin and one of six children living in the Great Cove. Earlier in the day John had left the area for Philadelphia, leaving his family exposed to the depredations to come. Upon hearing of the surge of violence headed in their direction, his wife sent young Hugh to a nearby blockhouse in hopes that its owner could help her move her large family to safety. Hugh did just that, but he returned just in time to see his home set ablaze by Shingas's warriors. He leapt to safety behind a fallen tree, and watched helplessly as his mother and siblings, Mary, Martha, Janet, James, and William (ages nineteen, twelve, two, ten, and eight, respectively), were taken captive by the assailants. Hugh later sought out help from some settler to his east and noted that, despite walking all day, he saw nothing but smoking ruins for miles around. When the impromptu rescuers returned, there was no trace of his family left to be found. Their fate, like so many others to come, would be determined on the Allegheny River at Kittanning.

Another dramatic retelling of a similar raid came from the Woolcombers, a Quaker family living on Sherman's Creek. According to testimony, most of the Woolcomber's neighbors had congregated at a nearby blockhouse called Robinson's, but the peace-loving Quakers elected to remain in their home. Always the pacificist, the father declared the threat of Indian attack as entirely overblown and instead insisted "it was the Irish who were killing one another." This terrible disconnect from reality would prove costly, but it likely stemmed from a fizzling connection to William Penn's original Peaceable Kingdom narrative. The Indians did ultimately find the Woolcombers, and amazingly the father welcomed them in for dinner. The warriors responded by claiming that they "did not come to eat, but for scalps." When this was stated, the Quaker's teenaged son ran for the back door turning just in time to see his father's head split by a tomahawk; his mother, sisters, and young brother suffered the same fate.[4]

Still, two centuries later, the very finest account of the Great Cove attacks comes from Charles Stuart. Stuart was one of many Scots-Irish settlers who lost everything in the raid, and he and his family were fortunate enough to have been taken captive rather than murdered indiscriminately. Stuart's family was a young one; his son, William, was four years old and his daughter, Mary, was six. After the Ohioans burned his barn and killed his livestock, they proceeded to drag the captured family to their nearest neighbors' plantation over a mile away. Once there, the warriors likewise kidnapped a woman and her four children and apparently satisfied their quota of human spoils. Although Stuart could not have known it at the time, his harrowing captivity would take him all the way from Great Cove to Fort Duquesne, Sandusky, Detroit, and Montreal until ultimately finding himself in England and eventually New York following a prisoner exchange in 1757. Stuart's account of this amazing journey is a vivid testament to the interconnectivity of an imperial world, but perhaps his most shocking story came only a day after his capture.

The warriors who had raided the Great Cove left it a smoking ruin after two days of destruction. According to Stuart, he and his fellow prisoners were led away from their homes to a well-known natural thoroughfare called the Sideling Hill Gap; they then proceeded over the next day to the area of Ray's Town (modern Bedford, Pennsylvania). It was there that Stuart claims that the many differing bands of the raiding party, which he numbered at ninety, ultimately reconvened. As was typical following a raiding expedition on the scale of the Great Cove, the warriors met in council at this place to discuss the particulars of the action. In this case death tolls, scalps collected, booty plundered, and captives taken were the most pressing details.

Stuart recounts it was here that Tewea (whom he calls Captain Jacobs) returned with his warriors from raids in distant Berks County. With his reappearance, Tewea added German scalps to the grisly collection that were previously acquired at the Great Cove. Stuart was one of dozens of hostages kept at this council and also one of the most hotly resented. The warriors placed a special premium on younger, stronger captives of both sexes for their potential contributions to the villages back home, and Charles Stuart fit a profile that was undesirable. It was not his age, per se, that troubled his captors; it was that men his age tended to be renegades while in captivity and often attempted to escape. With the exception of one other man named John Condon whom he describes as an "Irish Papist," most of the prisoners were women, teenagers, and children. When Tewea returned, a sense of legitimacy was given to the council, and to Stuart's dismay it seemed that the topic du jour was to settle his fate. The warriors present determined that he and the Catholic were simply too old to take back to the Ohio Country, and their deaths would be grand entertainment to highlight an already celebratory evening. According to Stuart: "The death we were to suffer were as Follows: First our fingers were to be cut off and we were to be forced to eat them, then our eyes pulled out which we were also to eat, after which we were to be put on a scaffold and Burnt. . . ."[5]

While it was unclear whether this tortuous death was actually going to happen, Stuart claims that his life was only spared when Shingas vetoed the execution. "After the council," he said, they "waited only for Shingas as Chief Judge to give his Consent." Shingas stated that he wanted to save Stuart because he was a man of the Frontier, and that when the sachem had passed through the area previously the captive had been generous, as "their People had Frequently Called at my House in their Passing . . . between Aughwick and Fort Cumberland and had always been supplied with provisions . . . without Ever Charging them Anything for it." It seemed that, for all of the gratuitous violence and destruction Shingas had rained upon the Great Cove, in this instance Stuart's earlier generosity quite literally saved his life.

Yet still, despite all of the terror inflicted by the Ohioans, the Scots-Irish settlers of the afflicted communities did not simply cower in fear. Many of the men who had been lucky enough to be spared recouped into makeshift militias and sought out Shingas's war parties. In the vast majority of the cases the damage had already been done, and most of these militia groups gave up their chase to repair their broken communities. For them, their only course of action was more often to bury the dead than to actually capture their long-distant enemies. Although they did not have a great effect in capturing any of the warriors responsible for the destruction of the Great Cove, they did take direct action of a different sort. One after another the prominent leaders of the broken community put pen to paper and wrote incredibly detailed accounts of the ambush to their representatives in Philadelphia in hopes that action would be taken. No surprise was the fact that most of letters were sent to Robert Hunter Morris himself.

If the politics of Philadelphia were frustratingly partisan, the politics of the Frontier were downright tribal. The Pennsylvania Frontier was a melting pot of peoples from all corners of Europe, and each of them brought with them their own customs, religions, and politics. The two largest groups were the Germans and Scots-Irish, but small minorities of Swedes, Finns, and Swiss were also present. As Europe had no homogenous viewpoints on topics like religious freedom, economic opportunity, and defensive responsibility, neither did the places at which its residents settled. In short, the colonial Frontier was Europe in a microcosm, and the same issues that hotly divided the Old World equally divided the New. Before the arrival of open warfare to the Peaceable Kingdom, the politics of the Frontier were largely separate. The Scots-Irish and German minorities tended to enclave themselves and keep their political opinions to themselves; the arrival of Shingas and his warrior bands, however, changed that dramatically. The German inhabitants of the west proved to be a strong voting bloc for the Quaker Party, and this was for many reasons. The Germans themselves were not a singular group, and their political justifications were equally diverse. In the simplest sense, William Penn's long-expired devotion to religious freedom was viewed as a central tenant of their life in his colony, and his legacy loomed large in their communities. As for the behavior of the Quaker-dominated assembly, the Germans tended to be uninterested in it one way or another.

The Scots-Irish, however, were not so forgiving. At the heart of the Scots-Irish world on the Frontier was a unifying religious strand of Presbyterianism. It manifested itself in Pennsylvania in the form of an intensive commitment to community above all else. As the Germans tended to be difficult to pin down ideologically, to discover how the Scots-Irish felt about any particular issue one must only attend a church service. These congregations were the center of all Scots-Irish life, and when held the church would become a veritable ground zero for political discussions on all matters of life. The pastor of a given community tended to wield enormous power to implement local policy, and its members played an equal role in crafting it. In short, a Scots-Irish community on the Frontier was its own insular polity, and with that came a passionate desire to manage its own affairs. Following the raid on the Great Cove, it was no surprise, then, that the men of the settlements took up arms and pursued the Ohioans without any expressed permission from Philadelphia; they did not ask for it and, quite frankly, they did not feel that they needed it. This drive for self-determination also led to an intense suspicion of outsiders, and in this vein is found their political leanings in regards to colonial Pennsylvania.

In the months leading up to and since Braddock's defeat, a large amount of public scorn had been directed at Philadelphia's unproductive governance. Aside from the general discord involving accusations of Eastern "elitism," the Scots-Irish had developed an especially strong distaste for what they viewed as a wholly ineffective assembly. In the battle between the assembly and the proprietors there were no innocent parties, but despite the clear sharing of partisanship the Scots-Irish almost uniformly sided with the Proprietary Party. This was not because they shared the rigid stance that the Penns' estates should be exempted from taxation, but because they bought into the misguided belief that Quaker pacifism was *solely* responsible for the gridlock. Therefore, all across the Frontier, Scots-Irish communities expressed their aversion for Quaker pacifism as a general mistrust for the Quaker Party and assembly as a whole. Following the terrible events of October 31 to November 2 at the Great Cove, it was no surprise that local settler leaders wrote directly to Governor Morris; he was the most powerful proprietary officer in the colony, and they were some of his most valuable constituents.

One man of high standing in the region along the Conococheague River was Adam Hoops, and he penned a letter to Morris that began: "I am sorry I have to trouble you with this melancholy and disagreeable news . . . that the inhabitants of the Great Cove were all murdered or taken captive, and their houses and barns all in flames." Hoops continued by explaining that some of the local men attempted to avenge these travesties but came up empty. After listing off some more shocking events, he finished the letter with a desperate plea:

> We . . . are in as bad circumstances as ever any poor Christians were in, for the cries of the widowers, widows, fatherless and motherless children . . . are enough to pierce the hardest of hearts; likewise it's a very sorrowful spectacle to see those that escaped with their lives with not a mouthful to eat, or bed to lie on, or clothes to cover their nakedness, or keep them warm, but all they had consumed into ashes. These

> deplorable circumstances cry aloud for your Honour's most wise consideration, that you would take cognizance of and grant . . . for it is really very shocking . . . for the husband to see the wife of his bosom, her head cut off, and the children's blood drank like water by these bloody and cruel savages.[6]

This would not be the only dispatch rushed to the governor's desk. In the days that followed the attacks, he would be flooded with letters begging for action in the face of these terrible new threats. To that point, the damage was inflicted only on the very fringes of the Frontier, but a general panic had swept the entire Cumberland Valley as to the prospective reach of Shingas's warriors. In no place, though, was this anxiety expressed more defiantly than the city of Carlisle. In many ways the Frontier town was Pennsylvania's great hope for westward expansion. There were certainly other settlements beyond its borders, but Carlisle was considered to be the colony's most distant attempt at truly planting its flag in a permanent way. If Carlisle were to fall to the depredations of the Ohioans it would prove to be a crushing blow to the colony, and its most prominent residents were unwilling to remain as passive actors. In a bold and revealing set of letters, the Scots-Irish repeatedly informed the governor that they intended to take action with or without the executive's aid, but any assistance would be welcomed.

On November 2, Thomas Barton, an Anglican missionary, penned a letter to Morris claiming he had "just come from Carlisle," and that "I suppose by tomorrow there will not be one Woman or Child in the town." Even more telling was the highly unusual addition of a timestamp on the letter claiming that it had been urgently written at "three o'clock in the Morning." Despite his role as missionary, Barton finished the brief letter by claiming that he would personally see to the defense of Carlisle with or without the colony's official sanction. "I intend this morning to return to Carlisle with a Party of men to guard that Town; the Gentlemen there desire me to request your assistance without delay." Still another man named Benjamin Chambers likewise wrote to the governor stating, "I think it is in our power (if God permits) to put them to flight if you turn out well from your parts. I understand that the West settlement is designed to go if they can get any assistance to repel them."[7]

The Scots-Irish of the Frontier were more than willing to defend themselves, but they were too factional to be effective. As each community was its own entity, there would be limited cooperation among the militias to mount any meaningful defense across the vast Cumberland Valley. There was, however, one man among them who had the political connections to organize such an effort, and he too reached out to Morris. John Armstrong was as well-connected a man as there was on the Frontier, and was a true founding father of the city of Carlisle. He had worked intimately with the governor and was named as the Penn family's official land surveyor; he had a reputation for reliability and was Morris's chief agent in the sprawling Cumberland County. He was a man caught between two worlds; the Scots-Irish were his people by birth, but his political fortunes were decided by Philadelphia. Armstrong was a proprietary man to his core and had no qualms about speaking frankly to the governor.

He explained to Morris in a letter dated November 2 that "one hundred Indians were seen in the Great Cove, among whom was Shingas the Delaware King." He expressed his interest in organizing a more formal defense of the Cumberland Valley, and stated that a local leader named Hans Hamilton had already rallied sixty men to defend the upper reaches of the territory. "We have sent our expresses everywhere," Armstrong said, "and intend to collect the Forces of this Lower part, expecting the Enemy every moment."[8]

Armstrong's willingness to speak openly with his colonial superiors would prove to be an increasingly valuable asset for the proprietors. Aside from being a reliable figure with the ears of the many peoples of the Frontier, John Armstrong was also a first-rate military engineer with an eye for constructing fortifications. Armstrong had already spent a great deal of time earlier that year overseeing the construction of a supply road for Braddock's army; although the officer would never live to use it, it demonstrated Armstrong's intimate familiarity with the Allegheny Mountains. He wrote candidly to Morris that the colony should begin a concerted effort to fortify the Pennsylvania Frontier as far south as the contentious Maryland border (below referenced as "the Temporary Line"). If placed properly, these outposts would be an incredible deterrent to future Indian raids. Armstrong wrote: "I'm of the opinion that no other means than a Chain of Block Houses along or near the South side of the Kittatinny Mountain, from Susquehanna to the Temporary Line, can secure the Lives and Properties even of the old Inhabitants of this County, the new Settlement being all fled except Sheerman's Valley, whom (if God do not preserve) we fear will suffer very soon."[9]

According to a Sheriff John Potter, a civilian law enforcement officer of the Cumberland Valley, the total destruction done to the Great Cove and its surrounding communities from Saturday, October 31 to Monday, November 3 was catastrophic. He counted twenty-seven plantations completely destroyed; of the ninety-three families settled there, forty-seven were gone. For most of October the view from Philadelphia was a quiet one, and Robert Hunter Morris's greatest concern was his own legislative battles with the assembly. After reading the accounts of the attacks on the Great Cove, the governor now presided over a colony in crisis.

ON NOVEMBER 3 LIEUTENANT GOVERNOR Robert Hunter Morris had seen enough. His desk had been swamped with notes, letters, and memos describing the desecration of the Frontier, all demanding action from the capital. Only thirteen months into his tenure as de facto executive of the colony, Morris was now faced with an emergency of epic proportions. In the wake of the Ohioan raids the citizens of the Frontier were experiencing all of the emotions that followed an unprovoked act of terror: fear, guilt, denial, and most of all outrage. They demanded accountability for these actions and felt that if there was ever a time to put partisan politics aside, the fall of 1755 was the moment. Morris called upon his most trusted deputies to confront the Franco-Ohioan threat, but the proceedings were palled by an unmistakable gloom. As much as Morris and his cadre wanted to take action, they could do nothing without the cooperation of the assembly.

The lieutenant governor feverishly wrote a message to his legislative colleagues that he hoped would express exactly how dire their situation was. He wrote of the desperate pleas of the settlers and relayed the estimated cost of the damage. His letter implored the assemblymen to take action to confront Shingas, his warriors, and their French allies with as much expediency as possible; most of all, it stressed that although they had been divided in the past, circumstances demanded reaching across the aisle to defend the colony. The address was lengthy and dramatic, but Morris's overarching message was clear: Pennsylvania needed their government now more than ever before.

"His Majesty and the Proprietaries have committed the People of this Province to my Charge and Care," Morris wrote.

> I have done and still very readily do every thing in my Power to fulfil that important trust; and to that end I think it my Duty to call upon you to grant such supplies of Money and his Majestie's Service at this important and dangerous Crisis may require, and to prepare a Bill for establishing a regular Militia. . . . As the Enemy are now laying waste to the Country and Slaughtering the inhabitants there is no time to be lost . . . I earnestly recommend it to you to afford in Time that assistance which your bleeding Country stands too much in need of.[10]

The address to which Morris had affixed his official seal was direct and passionate—in his mind, exactly what the people of the Frontier had demanded—but he held out little hope for its success. Morris knew as well as anyone that the politics of Pennsylvania were as toxic as ever. Partisanship had reached a fever pitch and the combined incursions of the French and the mobilization of their Ohioan allies had virtually eliminated any hope of compromise. The language that came from the lieutenant governor's office and from the assembly were fraught with vitriol. Now with people being murdered under their watch, many Pennsylvanians hoped that these petty squabbles could be set aside. After all, if a threat of this magnitude could not succeed in bringing the Quaker and proprietary partisans together for one defense bill, what could?

If recent history showed them anything, those hoping for some sort of defensive grand bargain in Philadelphia were facing an uphill battle. As already seen in the heated debate over funding Braddock's campaign against Fort Duquesne, the assembly and governor were both in favor of providing aid; where they differed, though, was in how to pay for it. Bills would be passed by the assembly with clear demands that the proprietor's estates be taxed, and Morris would undoubtedly veto them.

It was a legalist dance that many Pennsylvanians had grown accustomed to seeing, and it left them cynical and jaded as a result. As is still common practice in circumstances of political gridlock, both parties claimed to be victims of the other's ideological inflexibility. And since "winning" is often more important than actually governing, the warring parties often lobby the people themselves to break the stalemate.

As seen in the case of financing Braddock's campaign, the assembly took their case directly to the people by expressing their own electoral vulnerabilities compared to the lieutenant governor's virtually untouchable status. As stated by Speaker Isaac Norris, "We are now to take our Leave of the Governor; and indeed, since he hopes no Good from us, nor we from him 'tis Time we should be parted. If our Constituents disapprove our Conduct, a few Days will give them an Opportunity of changing us by a new Election; and could the Governor be as soon and as easily changed, *Pennsylvania* would . . . deserve much less the character he give it, of an unfortunate Country." Such a declaration virtually dared those who disagreed with the assembly to vote them out of office, an affirmation of their own rightness and Morris's wrongness.[11]

But if there was hope for at least some middle ground in the proceedings to defend the colony, it came in the form of Benjamin Franklin. Franklin's star had risen in colonial politics after his extraordinary personal efforts to supply Braddock's march, and he was considered to be a potential broker in the coming dispute. Although he was a leading member of the Quaker Party, Franklin was no pacifist. In truth, the actual pacifist wing of the Quaker Party was smaller than ever in the assembly, and like all political parties there were often opposing viewpoints built in. Franklin represented a new school of thought that cast aside the pacifist hardliners of the party to focus their true energies on being anti-proprietary; that is, they were fully willing to oversee the creation of an official military wing, but not unless the Penn family paid their share. Because of his outstanding oratorical abilities and cunning wit, Franklin was part of nearly every committee and council that corresponded with the governor. All too often, he would be forced to affix his name to obstructionist, highly partisan legislation as a single member of a large group. In this era, Assemblyman Franklin and Governor Morris developed a public feud of historic proportions but maintained a cordial personal friendship. Again—still the case in the modern world—it is often this slight but not insignificant bond that can be the difference between a bill succeeding or failing.

Five months earlier Franklin laid his sentiments bare in a letter to his friend and colleague Peter Collinson. He wrote, "I am heartily sick of our present situation; I like neither the governor's conduct, nor the Assembly's; and having some share in the Confidence of both, I have endeavoured to reconcile 'em but in vain, and between 'em they make me very uneasy." Even later in life, Franklin spoke fondly of the governor, and saw him as nothing more than a victim of circumstance rather than an enemy of the people or his own.[12]

In 1786, he penned: "I was put on every committee for answering his speeches and messages. . . . Our answeres, as well as his messages, were often tart and sometimes indecently abusive; and, as he knew I wrote for the Assembly, one might have imagined that, when we met, we could hardly avoid cutting throats; but he was so good-natur'd a man that no personal difference between him and me was occasion'd by the contest, and we often din'd together."[13]

In another such story, Franklin recounted a time when the lieutenant governor passed him in the street and invited him to dinner that evening. After "a gay conversation over our wine," Morris laughed with the assemblymen about the fictional Sancho Panza of Don Quixote fame. In one of his most notable scenes, Panza joked that if he were to be king he would request that all of his government be "black" so that he could simply "sell them" during a disagreement. When one of Morris's other guests inquired as to why Franklin associated with the Quakers given his non-Quaker heritage, Franklin responded lightheartedly, "The governor . . . has not *blacked* them enough yet." In the weeks that followed, Franklin and Morris would come to embody the political struggles of the colony, yet these candid behind-the-scenes moments prove to be very telling.[14]

On November 4, Robert Hunter Morris was presented a bill drafted by the assembly that provided £60,000 for the defense of Pennsylvania. The sum was greater than what Braddock had required only six months earlier, and passed the chamber easily despite the pacifists that voted against it. It proved that although the Quaker Party did rule the assembly, William Penn's pacifism was losing out to changing events. This should have been cause for celebration on the Frontier as the colony approved a once-unthinkable military spending bill. Of course, Morris discovered, there was a catch. Plainly stated in the bill was a stipulation that the defensive appropriations would be funded by a general property tax including the lands of the Penn family. Once again the primary dispute that had so divided the colony reared its ugly head. To their credit, the Quaker Party did include a stipulation that the King's Privy Council in London could decide the matter if the opposition party objected, but this was a hollow attempt at compromise. In the lieutenant governor's mind, the assembly had chosen to use the murderous Indian raids as leverage for the Quaker Party to advance their agenda.

He promptly vetoed it.

The backlash was viewed as nothing less than yet another failure of governance. Morris wrote a scathing letter to the assembly in response, stating: "You have now been sitting six days, and instead of strengthening my Hands and providing for the safety and defense of the people . . . You have sent me a Message wherein you talk of regaining the Affections of the Indians now employed in laying waste the Country and butchering the inhabitants . . . I shall not enter into a Dispute of where the Proprietaries ought to be taxed or not."[15]

In the towns and cities of Pennsylvania, the people too were feeling the strain. Each day that the assembly and the lieutenant governor fought the same tired battles, Shingas and his warriors wrought more destruction. The Frontier was quickly becoming empty of settlement, and the communities that remained were beginning to fracture under the weight of assigning blame for the debacle. Among the Scots-Irish there was no doubt as to which party should absorb most of the abuse for the stalemate. While in London, an Anglican minister named William Smith published a scathing critique of the Quaker Party that became required reading across the Frontier. Published in the form of a pamphlet called *A Brief State of the Province of Pennsylvania*, Smith excoriated the pacifists in the assembly, stating that the "powers [the

Quakers] enjoy are extraordinary, and some of them so repugnant, that they are the Source of the great Confusion in the Government." Smith, who was well versed in the politics of the colony, continued by succinctly explaining precisely how the Quakers maintained their control despite being in the minority. He correctly pointed out that the Germans were their primary base of support and, using a divide-and-conquer strategy, laid out a caustic and xenophobic set of reforms designed to disenfranchise the opposition. Smith first prescribed that every member of the Quaker Party should be forced to take a public oath of allegiance to the Crown, and their German supporters should follow suit. He also recommended that the Germans of the colony be compelled to "have a sufficient Knowledge of our Language and Constitution . . . to bind them to us by a common Language and Conciousness of a common Interest." This document was celebrated in the Frontier as a cure-all for the ills of the colony; it was so effective, in fact, that a petition was soon created demanding that "no Quaker be permitted to Sitt in Assembly, in Pensilva, or any Part of America."[16]

The intensity of the debate had spilled over into the streets of Philadelphia and beyond, and in private the pettiness of the affair was beginning to wear on Robert Hunter Morris. In a letter to his distant superior Thomas Penn, Morris echoed the anti-Quaker sentiments that were consuming the Frontier. "Since Mr. Franklin has put himself at the head of the Assembly," he wrote, "they have gone to greater lengths than ever, and have not only discovered the Warmth of Resentment against your Family but are using every means in their Power, even while their Country is invaded, to wrest the Government out of your hands, and to take the whole power of it into their own." Indeed, Penn had been overseas for the length of the affair, and just as the Proprietary Party had attempted to generalize all of the opposition as pacifists, the Quakers tried to tie the Proprietary Party to the "tyrannical" Penns.[17]

Despite his habit of singling out Franklin as the source of all that ailed him, Morris was quick to seek him out when negotiating. In the weeks that followed Morris's initial veto of the defense bill, the two men discussed at length the possibility of meeting somehow in the middle. For the Quakers, the idea of having the Crown itself act as arbiter on the matter of the Penns' hardline taxation status was fair, but to Morris it was a non-starter. As part of Morris's commission he had made an ironclad agreement with the Penns that he would never allow their estates to be taxed, and he even put his own land down as punishment if he broke his word. For the lieutenant governor, it seemed that the only way to actually come to an agreement was not to present a single bill but to present two. He would claim that if the King's Privy Council took up the matter they would either approve or disapprove of a bill as a whole rather than merely striking one line item away. If the assembly were to give over two bills, the first appropriating money from a general property tax and the second on the Penns' estates alone, then the colony's defense could be funded immediately. In time, London could approve or disapprove of the second bill on its own merits. It was creative and certainly plausible; however, the many-headed beast that was the assembly never allowed this idea to manifest.

Things indeed looked bleak, but behind the scenes Franklin toiled. After furtively discussing and lobbying the more extreme voices of his party, Franklin was able to bring to the assembly a bill entitled *An Act for the Better Ordering and Regulating the Military Force of This Province.* In the long history of parliamentary proceedings, this was an outstanding measure; it was one of the rare pieces of legislation put forth by an individual member rather than a committee. But in its winding and circuitous verbiage Franklin's true political power was revealed. In essence it was like many of the other bills previously debated, but this one took special care to include specific line items that catered to the many whims of his Quaker colleagues. Participation in the military force would not be compulsory, and there would be a strict age requirement of twenty-one to participate. In short, the bill satisfied all of the issues that his more ideologically stubborn Quaker partisans seemed to be hung up on. The bill was a masterstroke for a number of reasons, but the greatest may have been that it was proof positive that the Quaker Party was no longer the party of total, unflinching pacifism. It was a practical piece of legislation that did away with many of the stereotypes that the other side had used so effectively in its public campaign against the party. But aside from its potential to defend the colony, Franklin's bill also stands as a watershed moment in the history of William Penn's legacy. Since its inception, hardline Quakerism had virtually ruled Pennsylvania—but with the easy passage of the militia bill, it was clear that the religion's traditional tenants were no longer relevant. Some of the truly pacifist members of the assembly abstained from voting for the bill, to be sure, but on the whole the Quaker Party redefined itself as willing to fight when the time came. For Benjamin Franklin, the issue was no longer lobbying his own party to support the creation of a militia but the tangled mess of financing the measure.

The political stalemate in Philadelphia was costly, but nowhere more than on the Frontier. Across the region settlements all began arming themselves regardless of the capital's consent, and in many ways these weak and disorganized militias were the only opposition that the marauding Indian warriors faced. These armed groups were often reactionary in nature and only responsive after a raid had occurred; in this way, they were entirely ineffective at *preventing* an attack. Such homegrown defense was not adhered to universally across the Frontier, though, and those left unguarded paid the ultimate price.

On the north side of Mahoning Creek near its juncture with the Lehigh River sat a community of some fame in Pennsylvania called Gnaddenhutten. It was established in 1746 by Moravian missionaries in a part of the colony that was heavily influenced by German-Indian trade and interaction. Since its creation it had become a symbol of the cross-pollination that was possible on the Frontier, and by 1755 the community had grown to its zenith. Gnaddenhutten was a place of families, both Indian and German, that stood as a shining testament to the unifying power of scripture. On November 24, however, that grace was to be spoiled by the greater political circumstances of the Pennsylvania Frontier. As the missionaries sat down for their evening supper a war band of Ohioans struck the settlement with full vigor. They burst into the mission house with guns blazing and set the building on fire. Some of the missionaries escaped in the chaos, but those not killed in the initial onslaught were surely burned to death. In total, eleven innocents were killed, and just as quickly as they had arrived the unseen attackers disappeared back into the dark regions of the Frontier. Morris was quickly flooded with letters describing the tragedy. "The Enemy is so near us, I shall be obliged to send continually Expresses," wrote William Parsons. "Pray Sir, help us for we are in great distress. . . . I imagine that my plantation and every thing there is destroyed, by which I am totally ruined."[18]

Of all the terrible abuses suffered by the people of the backcountry, none produced more collective outrage than what was being called "the Gnaddenhutten Massacre." Unlike Penn's Creek and the Great Cove, the attack on the Moravian mission came as no surprise; the Ohioans had declared war and only added to their collection of scalps. What was unconscionable for Pennsylvanians was that, even in the face of the continuing threat of Indian war parties, the Quaker and Proprietary parties continued to squabble over trivial appropriations bills. The result was the total desolation of a peaceful Christian mission and the deaths of the most innocent of residents among them. The status quo of slaughter was no longer acceptable, and the Frontier set its sights on Philadelphia. After hearing of the events at Gnaddenhutten, the lieutenant governor sat in council with his most trusted advisors and read a distressing letter. Penned by Colonel William Moore the previous day, the address informed Morris that "two thousand Inhabitants are preparing to come to Philadelphia from Chester County, to compel the Governor and Assembly to agree to pass Laws to defend the Country and oppose the enemy." Another letter was received from Berks County, written by Conrad Weiser, who warned of another mob forming there—this one made up of traditional Quaker-aligned Germans. It seemed that given the events of the last of the last three weeks, the devastation at Gnaddenhutten had brought the colony to the brink of open revolt.[19]

It was then that the glimmer of hope that Pennsylvania had been waiting for seemed to emerge. When confronted by the marching rebels, Lieutenant Governor Robert Hunter Morris shocked the political world when he revealed a sudden, one-time gift of £5,000 from Thomas Penn. This, Morris explained, should be accepted in lieu of taxation on the Penns' estates, but would equal the amount of proprietary revenue desired by the assembly. Where or when Morris received the permission to deliver this surprise "gift" is unrecorded, but he claimed that he had been enabled to do so since he first informed Penn of Braddock's defeat. The decision stunned Philadelphia's political establishment and angered those who had lost loved ones in the previous weeks. To his critics in the assembly, Morris replied: "This timely and generous Instance of the Proprietaries care & anxiety for the Inhabitants cannot fail of making the most lasting impressions upon the minds of every well wisher to this country. I have directed the receiver General to have the money ready as soon as possible . . ."[20]

The offering of a singular gift of £5,000 was a brilliant tactical maneuver by the lieutenant governor. On the most practical level, the gesture aided in financing the colony's first state-sponsored militia, but on the political level it was perhaps the most brilliant piece of gamesmanship seen in the entire affair. The assembly offered up £55,000 from a general tax that, when matched with the proprietor's share, totaled £60,000. The inclusion of proprietary monies seemed to indicate that the Quakers had forced Thomas Penn's hand, but as always the devil lay in the details. To save both face and fortune, Penn did not actually *give* the assembly anything; he merely signed over what he called "our Arrears of Quit-Rents." That unexpected twist basically meant that the £5,000 contribution would not come from Penn's existing treasury, but simply from the bad debts still owed to him in Pennsylvania.[21]

The view from the Frontier, though, was quite different. The families of the backcountry did not care about scoring political points, they cared about survival. For them, the £60,000 was a gesture that Philadelphia was finally placing the needs of its people above their own political futures. The militia bill provided for a 1,400-man force divided into twenty-five companies, and it granted the servicemen the privilege of selecting their own officers. In many ways the settlers had already informally selected their leadership, and the militia bill wisely followed suit. But even more than those particulars was the effect that the bill had on the various political constituencies of the colony; it stirred up a rapid shift in party alignment. The depredations of Shingas and his Ohioans were a great catalyst to the region, and they forced many groups to consider what their actual priorities were. The Germans, who had been singularly tied to the Quaker Party, had marched furiously on Philadelphia to demand action. For them this was what finally brought bipartisan cooperation in the capital, and with each passing day it seemed that their allegiance to William Penn's party had grown stale. More and more in the months to come the Germans and Scots-Irish would find themselves working for a common goal far more important than merely winning elections.

Politics aside, something of great importance had occurred in Philadelphia with the passage of the militia bill. For the first time in its history William Penn's Peaceable Kingdom had finally taken up a hatchet of its own.

FOUR

Into Darkness

One hundred fifty miles away from the smoking ruins of their former lives, the Ohioan captives faced the nightmarish prospects of Indian captivity. Since the war parties first struck Penn's Creek in October 1755 there had been dozens of families split by murder and kidnapping; they were quite literally the spoils of war. While their loved ones felt as though they had lost them forever, they could never have known that these captives were about to reboot their lives in another world. Some were given new names and others new families, but all would receive a glimpse of what the "other" New World truly was. It was a difficult and brutish place with limited sustenance and daily hardships, but it was also a place of community supported by deep family loyalty. The Ohio Country was to be their new home, where they would start again so long as they survived their first few weeks in captivity. Most taken were put through a rigorous and systematic series of trials and abuses to test their mettle, and the weak were weeded out in awful spectacles. If they passed their respective tests, though, they were to make their homes in the villages and outposts of the Ohio Country, with the vast majority residing along the banks of the Allegheny River at Kittanning.

The journey the prisoners took from their Eastern plantations was difficult. To them, it would have appeared as though they were wandering aimlessly west surrounded by endless, dark forest on all sides. Their Ohioan guides, by contrast, moved with near-perfect certainty, and navigated the woods with precision. To the European eye the region beyond the mountains was uncharted and intimidating in its vastness; what they often failed to see, however, was the order that had already tamed the wilderness. In the truest sense, there were no actual roads that a settler would have recognized, but to the Delawares, Shawnees, and Mingos the landscape was crisscrossed with an intricate network of footpaths. Each was a veritable freeway, and most were well-established routes that connected one town or village to another. These paths would have been difficult for the novice to discern, as they were often only a few feet wide, but in the dense forests of the Ohio Country they were essential. While they did not know it at the time, in the weeks that followed their capture the settler families were being led west on one of two primary trails: the Frankstown and Raystown paths. Although the trails were well known for their Indians captors, those warriors did little to establish them. Many had ancient origins as deer paths, and early hunting parties adopted them to better succeed in their efforts. They were not perfect—they were often circuitous and winding—but they aided in the navigation of some of the most treacherous ground the New World had to offer. The captives of the East would write about how terrible the trek was, but the Indians who guided them knew it was the best available route.

Thousands of people were held captive in the Ohio Country between 1755 and 1763, and the exact number will likely never be known. The coming of the Seven Years' War had violently churned the region into a frenzy of war, and the antagonistic empires of Great Britain and France were never far from the scene. Captives taken into the Ohio Country during this time were regularly taken to Fort

Duquesne for matters of trade and accounting, and as awful as it seemed, for historians this was a blessing in disguise. At other trading hubs, like Kuskuskies, Logstown, and Sawcunk, the natives there kept no form of record or receipt of their human cargo, causing a distinct lack of quantitative figures; the French, however, kept detailed records, and in these historians can gain a greater sense of the human traffic that passed by the Forks of the Ohio. On January 1, 1756, an officer at Fort Duquesne tallied over five hundred scalps and two hundred prisoners present at the time. As Fort Duquesne would have only had a modest sum of captives compared to the larger Ohioan villages of the region, this presents a measure by which to speculate about the total number of captives present throughout the Ohio Country. Specifics will certainly continue to be elusive, but using this metric the numbers appear to have been staggering.

The driving motivation behind taking captives for Indian warriors was not what it seemed; it was long practiced and considered a necessity of war. For most of native history peoples tended to live in small, self-sufficient communities that demanded production from each member. In the event of a war or disease, groups would need to replace their lost family and friends to keep the community functionally viable. As a result kidnapping and adoption became the norm, as did mixed-race and intertribal communities. In the modern sense, kidnapping is done for reasons of *criminality*; in this case, the captives were taken in the name of *practicality*. While it was common practice in the Indian world, no such tradition existed in Europe, and the resulting conflicts that it posed were nothing short of traumatic.

The experience of Indian captivity was common since Europeans made first contact with Native Americans in the fifteenth century, and common strands existed in the stories of the survivors, which allow certain generalizations to be made. One element that has proven typical in these "captivity narratives" is the notion of a highly ritualistic adoption ceremony; these tend to vary in length and style across the New World, but all share a basic core element. Newcomers are put through some type of trial that usually involves an element of nonlethal physical trauma. Once the torment has been inflicted, they are accepted into the community as members with little attention paid to skin color or background. The most famous example of this practice comes from one of the first ever to be documented: the adoption of Captain John Smith. An integral part of the Jamestown story, Smith seemed fated for execution until he was mercifully spared by Powhatan. This has long stood as a testament to Smith's bravery and cunning, but has recently been reinterpreted as a ceremonial adoption into the Powhatan tribe. That would be one of the first documented but certainly not the last, and still some of the finest examples come from the harrowing experiences of the survivors held at Kittanning during the Seven Years' War.

Marie Le Roy and Barbara Leininger were among the first to be captured during the attack on Penn's Creek, and their post-abduction journey took them to Kittanning. These girls, both in their teens, created a detailed journal of their experience that has proven invaluable for understanding Indian life in the Ohio Country. Upon their arrival at Kittanning they wrote that "we here received our welcome, according to Indian custom. It consisted of three blows each, on the back." She continued by adding, "They were . . . administered with great mercy . . . we concluded that we were beaten merely in order to keep up an ancient usage, and not with the intention of injuring us." What these girls were unknowingly describing was their participation in an adoption custom common to the Ohio Country known as "running the gauntlet." In this ritual a newcomer would run between two lines of warriors and be beaten with weapons; when they came out the other side, they were considered members of the tribe. The girls' experience of what they described as "mercy" was not the norm, however. Another man previously discussed, named Charles Stuart, also found himself at Kittanning and too had to run the gauntlet. Needless to say, his experience was far different. After arriving at the village, Stuart claimed that some of his fellow hostages were taken across the river to the west bank which he called "Shingas' town," but he was among the group that was to be subjected to the gauntlet.[1]

> We were obliged to Pass Between Two Rows of Indians, Containing about 100 on Each Side who were armed with various kind of Weapons such as Axes Tomahawks Cutlasses Hoop Poles, Peices [*sic*] of Wood &c, But they did not strike with the Axes, and only Used the Heads and Handles to their Tomahawks . . . I had however the

> Misfortune to receive a Blow on the Side of my Forehead with one of them which Cut me To the Bone . . . I was Knocked down to the Ground.[2]

Once integrated into the Western Delaware community, the captured girls were expected to participate in errands typical of a native woman. Especially during a time of war, when most young warriors were off fighting, native women fulfilled many of the traditionally male assignments as well as their own. In the case of Mary and Barbara, they spent most of their time at Kittanning making shoes, cooking, cleaning, clearing fields, and planting corn. As many of the men were absent, they also aided in the construction of wooden huts and chopping down trees. It was a shocking change from the world in which they came, for even though women shared in the demanding work of Frontier life they would have never found themselves in these kinds of situations. Their diet was insufficient at best, but such was the life of a native community that relied heavily on small-scale agriculture and hunting for food. Along with whatever they grew, the girls subsisted on "acorns, roots, grass, and bark." As Mary wrote so eloquently, "there was nothing in the world to make this new sort of food palatable, excepting hunger itself."

Most native villages were wholly open to travelers, and in a time of peace they would have depended greatly on wayward visitors bringing trade goods. In a time of war, though, the normal flow of Kittanning was disrupted and different rules applied. Both Mary Le Roy and Charles wrote into their accounts of numerous French officers present at Kittanning performing any number of diplomatic tasks. Its forty-mile distance from the French post at the Forks of the Ohio made it an important satellite, and Fort Duquesne's commandant would have required regular intelligence gathered at Kittanning as to the position of their British enemy. For this reason the captives both had the opportunity to see Fort Duquesne up close, and gathered helpful reconnaissance.

In Mary's case, she and Barbara lived for two months at the site performing menial chores while, she claims, "our Indian master drew our wages." Compared to Kittanning, Mary claimed to be grateful for her time at Fort Duquesne, as they gave her a half pound of bread each day, but when given the chance to stay she refused. The soldiers garrisoned there saw an obvious romantic benefit to keeping the pair of teenaged girls on-site, but the prisoners refused. When she made this determination she astutely noted: "there would be more ways open for flight in the forest than in a fort." They subsequently stayed attached to their Indian keepers.[3]

But not all of the prisoners shared Mary's impressive sense of awareness on the Frontier. So, when escape attempts were found out, the results were nothing short of horrifying. In one instance, an unnamed adult man attempted to flee for his life. He was quickly run down by a group of warriors and returned to Kittanning, where he was tied to a tree. As punishment for his transgression, the warriors attempted to burn him alive. While the Delawares struggled to kindle a flame beneath his feet a rainstorm stifled their fire; rather than giving up, they proceeded to scorch the man's flesh by repeatedly firing muskets filled with black powder onto his skin. When the man ultimately begged for a drink of water, the warriors poured molten lead down this throat, killing him instantly.

In another instance, the wife of a captive man named Alexander McAllister was chosen to be killed. She was tied to a post and scalped, then repeatedly burned by red-hot pieces of firewood. In her agony they next chopped off her ears and fingers and, seemingly to quiet her screams, forced the severed pieces into her mouth. After making her swallow the mess, they continued the tortuous burnings; she endured this torment from nine a.m. until sunset. In one of the most shocking twists, a traitorous convict who had escaped from a jail in Lancaster arrived at Kittanning seemingly to join the French and avoid incarceration. To show his commitment, he tore a piece of Mrs. McAllister's flesh off of her body and ate it in front of her. This seemed to have been the final straw for the French soldiers in the village, as an officer mercifully shot the woman in the head after this cannibalistic act. Upon her death the entertainment ceased for the Delawares, and they cut the corpse in half and fed it to their dogs. Young Mary and Barbara were forced to behold the entire spectacle.[4]

Such was the world of the Western Delawares of Kittanning. Some prisoners would never again leave the village, and still others would choose to stay voluntarily. Those that did escape, however, brought their grisly tales of torture and torment with them. By 1756 it had become clear that if the violence that terrorized the Frontier had a home, Kittanning was it.

FOR READERS OF THE *Pennsylvania Gazette* it was clear that January 1, 1756, represented more than just the start of a new year. Upon opening their papers, they saw something that only weeks earlier would have been thought impossible. In no uncertain terms, the newspaper boldly proclaimed that Lieutenant Governor Robert Hunter Morris had placed bounties on the head of Shingas. The prize for bringing the head of the man now viewed as the undisputed champion of terror in Pennsylvania was seven hundred pieces of eight—a hefty sum for the Frontiersmen rugged enough to pursue the Delawares. In time this bounty would be increased courtesy of the colony of Virginia, but the message that it sent was an unequivocal statement that Shingas was the head of the proverbial snake. Shingas's reputation was notable among his Pennsylvanian contemporaries, and men such as John Heckwelder attested to his infamy. "Were his war exploits all on record, they would form an interesting document, though a shocking one. Conococheague, Big Cove, Sherman's Valley, and other settlements along the Frontier, felt his strong arm sufficiently that he was a bloody warrior, cruel his treatment, relentless his fury. His person was small, but in point of courage and activity, savage prowess, he was said to have never been exceeded by anyone."[5]

Heckewelder's description of the sachem was filled with overblown language, but none of it was overstated. Since the passage of the militia bill in late November the residents of Pennsylvania's Frontier had begun organizing themselves into sanctioned groups for the purposes of self-defense, but still the raids came. In some cases Shingas and his war parties even ranged within the immediate sphere of Philadelphia, in spite of armed militias waiting with bated breath to strike the first blow of revenge. Calls from the Frontiers were passionate and chiding, demanding that the lieutenant governor pass a general "scalp bounty" on *all* Indians; Morris was hawkish compared to his pacifist opponents, but even he had not yet reached that point. In one instance, Conrad Weiser (Morris's chief agent among the colony's German peoples) wrote that at a meeting "they cried out that so much for an Indian scalp they would have (be they friends of enemies) from the Governor. I told them I had no power from the Governor or assembly. They began, some to curse the Governor; some the assembly; called me a traitor to the country, who held with the Indians . . ."[6]

As inhumane as this order registers in the modern world, during the 1750s it was entirely common practice. For example, during this same war a young George Washington wrote to Virginia lieutenant governor Robert Dinwiddie that his men had successfully killed and *scalped* a French commander named Douville. He lobbied for the men to receive some kind of payment for this grisly trophy, writing: "I hope, although it is not an Indian's, they will meet with an adequate reward at least, as the monsieur's is of much more consequence."[7] The ordering of a scalp bounty was more than a simple stopgap measure; it was an informal proclamation of offensive war. To 1756, the men of the Frontiers were forced into a purely defensive mode, but to be commissioned with a true scalp bounty allowed them to seek out their enemies rather than simply respond with futility. In one instance a militia leader in Northampton County declared an unsanctioned scalp bounty of his own, offering his ragtag troops "forty Pieces of Eight for every Indian they shall kill & scalp."[8]

When describing Pennsylvania's great response to the raiding warriors that had so devastated them the previous fall, "defense" was exactly their strategy. The passage of a bill providing for £60,000 was monumental in the scope of Quaker politics, but it was still a sum too small to have mounted the kind of response that the Frontiersmen demanded. It was not insignificant, and certainly provided for a strong initial response, but not enough to truly punish the Ohioans for their misdeeds. In a more ideal political setting the £60,000 spent would have been the first step in a multifaceted approach combining both defensive and offensive operations; in the Peaceable Kingdom, though, politics dictated that it would *need* to be enough. Perhaps because of its long and storied history of pacifism, or more likely its limited funding, the effort to respond to Shingas and his warriors focused entirely on defensive measures. At its heart was fortification, and the idea that a few strategically placed blockhouses could greatly dampen the Indian raids.

When considering where to build forts, policymakers in Philadelphia had options to consider. Would their primary focus be on defending specific communities? If so, how large would a settlement's population need to be to warrant the construction of a fort? If one community or another was left out, say the Germans over the Scots-Irish, what would the political ramifications be? The year 1756 already saw the colony more hotly divided than ever, and such a weighty decision as the placement of a fort would certainly arouse the animosities of those left undefended. These were not the only drawbacks to protecting specific populations, though. In most instances, Indian war parties of twenty or less never struck a major population center because they would be terribly outnumbered by the city's inhabitants; this all but ensured that places like Carlisle and certainly Philadelphia would be safe with or without protection. Another strike against defending towns, specifically, was the fact that after an Indian raid most of the victimized settlements were left abandoned. If a fort was to be built for the purpose of protection, they would not be worth much if there was no one left to defend. The safer option was to ignore population centers as a determining factor and focus exclusively on geography; while time would prove this to be far less effective, the short term political consequences were much less controversial.

Seventeen fifty-six was an election year, after all.

The decision was made in December 1755 that fortifications should be placed according to their overall effectiveness—not at defending towns but the Frontier as a whole. This strategy required that surveyors identify and report on key mountain passes and valleys used by the Ohioans to enter into populated areas and destroy them. By 1756, it was well understood that the Allegheny Mountains were a formidable obstacle to the expanding colony of Pennsylvania, but in the minds of policymakers in Philadelphia they were also a great aid. It was believed that to fully defend the Frontier a major undertaking was unnecessary, as the mountains already provided an almost impassable barrier. All the engineers needed to do was locate the key passes that the warriors used to penetrate the mountains and place forts there to stop them. They were, in effect, using the gifts that nature had provided and simply fortifying the gaps for their own defense.

The result of this strategy was initially very promising. The state would construct a small number of very formidable posts that would garrison troops. These would be completed at twenty-mile intervals covering the most vital routes of passage that Shingas and his warriors might take. They would be further supplemented with forts built by local militia leaders on the county level that would aid in closing the distance between them. Finally, individual blockhouses would be selected to add further defense; most of the time these were hardly forts at all, but simply private homes with meager walls surrounding them. To truly defend the entire Frontier, the colony of Pennsylvania required a chain of fortifications that stretched from the banks of the Susquehanna River to the shores of the Delaware River; such an effort would span over 150 miles, and its effectiveness was doubtful to say the least. Rather than attempting this enormous feat on their own, the lieutenant governor settled for focusing most of the colony's money on fortifying the West. George Croghan was a reliable agent of the Crown and knew the Frontier better than any Irishman, and was considered the king's best source of information on the Frontier. He knew the fine details of a very rough place, and Morris called upon him to construct Pennsylvania's great forts on the edge of civilization. His orders were to place the forts at strategic points identified as "one back of Patterson's, One upon Kishecoquillas, and one Near Sideling Hill." These forts were roughly fifty square feet and could house up to seventy-five men; they became known as Patterson's Fort, Fort Granville, Fort Shirley, and Fort Lyttleton.[9]

These major fortifications were hardly the best that British North America had to offer, but they were the finest that cash-strapped Pennsylvania could afford on its meager £60,000. Others began to fill in the obvious weaknesses Croghan's chain of forts lacked that were supplied on the local level, but the defense that the colony had succeeded in putting forth was far from the great barrier that administrators had hoped for. By January 17, Lieutenant Governor Morris deemed these forts ready and ordered modest numbers of troops to be garrisoned within them. But in a province with no history of a standing army and only a small amount of money available, where does one find an army? The defense of the Frontier was quite literally *of*, *by*, and *for* the people; all across Pennsylvania locals formed themselves into militias. They selected their own officers and were officially sanctioned to defend their own communities from their Indian enemies. These were the men that would garrison the forts constructed in 1755 and early 1756, and they would soon find that the defensive posture assumed by their colony would be a costly one. These militiamen were not ordered to engage the native raiders in offensive strikes, but to simply patrol the spaces between the forts. They would participate in daily marches to seek out the enemy should they appear near a settlement, but typically came up empty. While the men of the Frontier had hoped for a concerted effort to stifle the Indian threat and protect their families, more often than not they were simply chasing footprints in the snow. The Ohioan raids continued, and Pennsylvanians began to see the futility of this modest and ineffective effort.

The arrival of war in the province did alter its fortunes a great deal, and offered opportunity where most others saw only chaos. In an attempt to gain some measure of control over the ragtag militia groups that made up Pennsylvania's volunteer armed force, the lieutenant governor began handing out commissions to those whom he trusted most. Among these chosen few were three of the highest-profile men in the colony: Benjamin Franklin, Conrad Weiser, and John Armstrong. Franklin was quickly becoming the face of a populist movement in Philadelphia, and Weiser was long considered to be the voice of the German people on the Frontier. Armstrong was among the most respected citizens of the Frontier city of Carlisle and in the whole of the Cumberland Valley. Their addition to the war effort would give a sense of both legitimacy and gravitas to implementation of the militia bill, and allow for some of the blame to be spread across ethnic and partisan lines should it prove to be a failure. In the months to come, Armstrong would set himself as clear leader of the Cumberland Valley and a master of logistical discipline; Franklin, however, took a different approach. In January 1756 Franklin led a party of soldiers north to the smoking ruins of Gnaddenhutten, and their first task was to bury the dead. But after settling in Franklin seemed to flourish in his role of military commander despite being a total novice. When given the commission to recruit his army, Robert Hunter Morris believed that the assemblymen's political battles had been enough to justify his military appointment, but even for Franklin that was an unconvincing argument. He appointed his son William to a command in the militia, and oversaw the construction of a fortified post at the site.

For Franklin the daily routine was quiet enough—mostly uneventful patrols and management of supplies—but the policymaker in him soon overtook the taskmaster that he was portraying. During his tenure one troublesome incident of particular note was settled with Franklin's characteristic guile. As his army was settled among the most devout Germans of the colony, Franklin's army was often dismissive of their religious zeal. The rangers ignored their religious obligations to attend prayer service (which was not uncommon) and the local clergy vented their frustrations to Franklin. To solve the problem, the politician-turned-paramilitary threatened to cut his soldier's rum rations if they did not attend. Franklin later wrote, "Never were prayers more generally and more punctually attended; so that I thought this method preferable to the punishment inflicted by some military laws for non-attendance on the divine service." Franklin spent the cold January of 1756 among his men and heartily debated the Germans regarding their peculiar attachments to arranged marriage and pacifism, but his heart was never invested in military service. On February 2 he resigned his post and returned to his true calling: fighting in the assembly chambers at Philadelphia.[10]

THREE WEEKS EARLIER ON JANUARY 13, Lieutenant Governor Robert Hunter Morris made his return to the Frontier. In a council at Carlisle, Morris and his confidants met with George Croghan to discuss the deteriorating circumstances in the Ohio Country. In the years prior, Croghan had developed an extensive network of reliable Indian operatives willing to infiltrate war councils and report their findings; in the subjugation of Shingas and his allies, those connections would prove to be irreplaceable. In the council along with Morris were James Hamilton, Richard Peters, Joseph Fox, and William Logan. Joining them were two sachems noted as "Seneca George" and "Chief Belt." As was his lot in life, the Irish Croghan would act as both interpreter and intermediary for the length of the council.

According to a source identified as "Delaware Jo" (also known as Jo Hickman), the situation in the Ohio Country was grave. Jo traveled first to the village of Kittanning and noted a few critical points that peaked the Pennsylvania delegation's interest. First was that both Shingas and Captain Jacobs (Tewea) did in fact reside at Kittanning; while Captain Jacobs kept his home in the heart of the community, the higher-value target, Shingas, did so on the opposite bank of the Allegheny. Second was that the village was home to at least 140 warriors when Jo was present, with "one hundred English Prisoners big and little taken from Virginia and Pennsylvania." He continued by claiming that during his time in Kittanning a group of ten Western Delawares were leaving for the Susquehanna River Valley to "persuade those Indians to strike the English who might perhaps be concerned in the Mischief lately done in the County of Northampton."

This was incredibly valuable information for Morris, who upon further prodding discovered that this "Kittannin" sat only forty miles north of Fort Duquesne on the Allegheny River. As the information continued to flow Morris also learned that there were another one hundred Shawnee warriors located at Logstown on the Ohio River and they had amassed thirty prisoners of their own. Throughout all of the villages the French presence was pervasive, and they undoubtedly supported the raiding that had so troubled the colony. Delaware Jo continued that while at Kittanning he was approached by the sachem Tamaqua ("the Beaver," brother of Shingas), who offered a detailed history of French involvement claiming that they had "offered the French Hatchet" to the Ohioans as early as that spring, but were rebuked. It was only when a war party of Caghnawagos, from Montreal, and Adirondacks arrived around the time of Braddock's defeat that the residents of Kittanning agreed to wage war on the English. Delaware Jo finished his intelligence briefing by claiming that he had hoped to visit Fort Duquesne but was impeded by the thick river ice, but could confidently say: "the Number of the French did not exceed four hundred."[11]

The political landscape of the Ohio Country was certainly shifting. The presence of the French was no surprise to the lieutenant governor, but when asked whether his Iroquois allies retained *any* modicum of control over the region, the informant offered an ominous response. "There are more or less of the Six Nations living with the Shawonese and Delawares in their Towns," Jo said, "and these always accompanied them in their Incursions upon the English and took Part with them in the war." It seemed that Philadelphia was more disconnected from the true state of the Frontier than first suspected, and with that the council broke. Before parting, though, George Croghan asked why only two sachems and five warriors had actually come to Carlisle. If the local Delawares were still allies of Pennsylvania, surely there should have been more? The sachems replied, "They were most gone a-hunting."[12]

With all of the swirling reports of devastation and bloodshed on the Pennsylvania Frontiers, alarmism was at an all-time high. Compounding these worries was the looming fact that 1756 was also an election year in the colony. With the prospects of the assembly radically changing its partisan dimensions in the face of the new Franco-Indian threat, even the most basic of appointments and lawmaking was viewed with a suspicious eye. No instance highlights the supremacy of partisan allegiance over practical defense of the colony more than the creation of Philadelphia's city regiment. Although the militia bill was not in itself a blatantly partisan document, the arrangement of militias on the Frontier was a highly contentious affair. Those who held great political sway over a settlement or village unsurprisingly found themselves holding the highest of military ranks when militias selected their officers. By the modern standard, this seems like a ludicrous proposition, but even into the Spanish-American War Americans still chose their officers through political clout and blatant corruption.

In February 1756, the city of Philadelphia was no different. As part of the militia bill the city of Philadelphia was to organize its own militia. Charged with defending the capital, this armed force would be highly visible and likely see no action in the continuing crisis of Indian raids. Because of this, to command what was known as the "city regiment" would be a highly visible position, and especially beneficial to any person seeking to further their own public ambitions. In such circumstances there was a great deal of political capital to be earned, and it was no surprise that Benjamin Franklin was immediately interested in the position. Franklin was fresh off of his military foray at Gnaddehutten, which he had resigned on February 2, and already there were whispers that he would be voted on and commissioned as the leader of the city regiment.

Almost immediately the leading members of the Proprietary Party and even the hardline pacifists in his own Quaker Party distrusted Franklin's potential appointment. Members of the lieutenant governor's council expressed concerns that Franklin was going to use his very public military appointment to merely increase his own visibility. William Peters claimed that Franklin had "a design to dupe" both parties by using his commission as a personal platform rather than one merely of military service. The council went so far as to recommend that Morris block Franklin's appointment by any means within his power. Of course Morris had little to say in the matter, and Franklin was indeed selected by his men and compelled to serve. Facing tremendous political backlash if he attempted to block the nomination, on February 12 Morris begrudgingly signed Franklin's appointment.

With Morris having apparently caved to the charms of Franklin's increasingly populist political appeal, Richard Peters wrote a scathing letter to Thomas Penn in distant London. When made aware of Franklin's election and subsequent appointment by the lieutenant governor, Penn was incredulous. He wrote, "I much wonder the Governor would appoint Mr. Franklin Colonel. He should never have any commission given to him till it is certain he has changed his sentiments." All critics aside, for Franklin there was no looking back, and he in fact did make the most of his new status as *Colonel* Benjamin Franklin. As a habit the assemblyman held regular lavish reviews of his city regiment and paraded his troops to great fanfare throughout the city.[13]

In one such display, Franklin demonstrated the full prowess of this underused militia by putting on a spectacle. In the first act he marched several hundred men in two lines and had them fire empty muskets and retreat in formation to show their discipline. He next exhibited four freshly painted cannons pulled by impeccably manicured horses, and then marched the entire army once more in twelve tidy lines. Finally, as only Franklin could, the colonel himself marched alone to the cheers of his adoring city. As much as the people enjoyed it, Franklin certainly relished in the opportunity to antagonize his detractors by putting himself front and center. In a follow-up letter to Penn, the petulant Peters updated the proprietor by stating: "The City is in an infinite distraction all owing to the Officers of the Militia puffed up and now solely directed by Colonel Franklin. . . . Matters are ten times worse in the city than ever and the Antiproprietary party will gain more ground than ever by means of the Colonel who continues to evidence a most implacable enmity against the Proprietors."[14]

The city regiment became Franklin's personal political tool in the vital campaign year of 1756, and his enemies came out in droves. The greatest fear was that Franklin would use the militia to garner support for anti-proprietary Quaker candidates who would be beholden to him and that he could single-handedly take command of the entire province. Some compared him to a conquering Caesar crossing the proverbial Rubicon to conquer Rome; others simply bristled when they heard commoners speaking of how glorious his decorative militia appeared. One noted enemy, William Smith, asked "whether between 6 and 700 Men *and Boys*, a great Part of whom had never appeared at any former Muster, can with any Propriety be called a well trained Regiment of a Thousand Men?" Despite his critics, Franklin understood the persuasive power that the militia held over his constituents and never hesitated to use it. In the spring there was sure to be another political battle looming, and he would need all the support he could muster.

On April 1 the tiny settlement known locally as Rocky Spring was on edge. That morning Jean Lowry, a young mother of six who was well into her seventh pregnancy, had spent her morning completing the docket of chores typical of a Frontier wife. She and her husband, John, had carved out a life for their family the way that so many Scots-Irish had in the shadows of the mountains . . . they worked. The spring had been one of trepidation in Rocky Spring as tales of Indian raids had gripped the region. But, with their livelihood at stake, the Lowrys pressed on. Thousands of families like them had already given up and fled farther east or south into Virginia by the spring of 1756, but to abandon everything would be to start over. John and Jean Lowry had scratched out a meager existence in the Cumberland Valley, but it was theirs, and they were defiant. Their neighbors were determined to persevere, and they swore an oath to defend their community at all costs. Nearby, a man named William McCord had been proactive in this regard and fortified his home in case of an attack. Called "McCord's Fort," it was not much, but it was highly representative of the self-reliance that came with making a living on the Frontier.

In the months since the completion of the "chain of forts" along the Frontier, fears had eased a bit in Rocky Spring, but not much. Still stories abounded of war parties suddenly storming settlements and leaving them ruined. The Lowrys and their neighbors had learned to be suspicious of the elitist English that led so fearlessly from Philadelphia, believing that true security would be in their hands alone. By midday on the first of April this would never ring more true. Shortly after noon, Jean Lowry's focus on her domestic work was broken when she heard her husband shouting. He was frantically calling to rally his six children together and breathlessly motioning toward their neighbors' plantation. Jean had feared this day for months, and rushed to John's side as fast as she could. In the distance she heard the Frontier sonata of war whoops, screams, and musket fire. With everything at stake, she hurried her family into William McCord's reinforced farmhouse and began to pray for salvation "from glorious King Christ."

Immediately upon entering the home Jean rushed with her family to join the women and children of neighboring plantations on the second floor. The young mother quickly took account of her own family and helplessly waited to see what would transpire. As the war party began to assault the McCord home, Jean watched John raise his musket and fire from the first-floor window. For the families trapped on the second story, John Lowry was their only defender and was described by his wife as "a good marks-man." Within moments, the father killed an attacking Ohioan, but was himself struck down only seconds later by returning fire. Jean describes the resulting terror by writing, "Being no other Man at that time present, the barbarians rushed into the house . . . plundered the house of what they pleased, and seized two of my children." The depredations that she had only heard rumors of were transpiring directly before her eyes. Knowing that only the most vulnerable residents of Rocky Spring were left in the house, the warrior band began to shout curses at the second floor. When it was clear that the residents would not simply walk out, the attackers next began firing arrows toward the windows and ultimately set fire to the home. She continues:

> Oh how my tortur'd mind was hurry'd! Horrer of the indian barbarities and rudenesses made me think of prefering death unto a miserable life: But here I had many deaths to suffer in one: It's impossible for me to relate the thousandth part of my agony for my trembling children: But divine providence determined me to deliver myself and children up into their cruel hands, not knowing how the Lord might over-rule them and dispose of us, rather than instantly perish in the devouring flames: For now we were near suffocated with the smoke. Bursting thro' every where upon us, and terrify'd with the thundering noise of the ascending flame.[15]

Describing herself as "being big with child," Jean Lowry worried that "it was the usual indian manner to kill every woman they took in that condition." She was spared, however, and soon swept away with her children by the marauding warriors of the Ohio Country. In all, the Indian raiders killed or captured twenty-seven people from Rocky Spring, and among its victims were the most defenseless yet. To many on the Frontier this was the vilest of all of the Ohioan assaults, and it validated the sentiment that the colony's recent effort to fortify the Frontier had been entirely ineffective.

The burning of McCord's house seemed a breaking point for the men of the Cumberland Valley. Under the command of a local militia leader named Alexander Culbertson, a party of men took up arms to pursue the fleeing war parties. Three days after the initial raid on Rocky Spring, Captain Culbertson and his men came into contact with the responsible war party at Sideling Hill some thirty miles west of McCord's fort. Once there, the men reportedly exchanged fire with the Ohioans in an event that would be called the Battle of Sideling Hill. After the first volley, the Indian warriors quickly gave way and ran from the militiamen; while they did not know it at the time, this was a textbook tactic of Indian war, and the settlers fell into their waiting trap.

After pursuing the warriors, Culbertson's men found themselves completely encircled by multiple Ohioan war parties. According to one account, "In less than ten minutes our men found themselves surrounded . . . they fought for about two hours and a half . . . any then perceiving reinforcement from Shingas' party, they unanimously agreed to break the enemies circle . . . in order to make them retreat, in which they succeeded luckily."

The results of the Sideling Hill affair, like most during this period, were mixed at best. A detailed list of the settlers killed during the exchange remains, totaling twenty casualties. The damage inflicted on their Indian enemy will likely never be known, but some sources estimate that at least fifteen warriors were killed. The militiamen who reported on the affair almost all agree that Shingas and Captain Jacobs were present in the firefight, and multiple sources claimed a scalp that was brought in as a result belonged to the latter fugitive. As time would tell, Tewea was certainly not scalped at Sideling Hill and was very much alive. However, given the reward placed on both he and Shingas's heads, the Frontiersmen were likely anxious to spin yarns claiming that they had sparred with the infamous duo.[16]

Within days, the survivors of the battle and families of lost loved ones once again restarted their letter-writing campaign to Philadelphia. Stories of terrible depredations came to the desk of Robert Hunter Morris, and it was becoming evident that the forts on which they had spent so much money were failing in their efforts. The raid and destruction of McCord's fort occurred in close proximity to the outposts constructed only a few months earlier, and they provided virtually no protection for the nearby settlers. The great effort of Philadelphia to defend its Frontier was failing, and the defensive foundational strategy on which it rested was flawed. With each passing week, it seemed that Pennsylvania's officials were losing the faith and trust of their Frontiers with no remedy in sight.

AS ONE OF THE PREMIERE CITIES of the New World, Philadelphia was home to thousands of people from all walks of life. Like any major city it was a melting pot, and the residents who lived there had grown accustomed to expecting the unexpected. On its streets residents sold all manner of goods, from exotic imported fruits and nuts to homespun clothing and handmade shoes. The finest specialists on the continent practiced their crafts there, and the very best-maintained stores and shops all came to sell their wares. It was undoubtedly considered to be the political and social heart of the American colonies, and it was the bright star toward which the British Empire in the Western Hemisphere revolved. If there was a heart to this place, it would likely be considered the State House; commissioned in 1729 and completed in 1736, it was designed to physically match the spiritual promises on which the colony was founded. The picture of the Georgian architectural style, the State House would be immortalized by generations to come as "Independence Hall." Its original placement was on the outskirts of Philadelphia, and as predicted its completion pulled the commerce and trade of the existing city into its orbit. It was designed as a place worthy of the Pennsylvania Assembly's deliberations, and it succeeded in cutting a striking image. Made of brick and stone, it was a near-perfect match on its left and right sides, and at its center stood a striking bell tower that reached for the heavens. The addition of this tower only three years earlier made the structure seem more church than chamber, and that was precisely its intention.

On April 3, the State House received an esteemed visitor whose presence indicated that radical changes were afoot in the colony. That day in the warming spring of 1756 a delegation led by the Iroquois Half-King Scarouady marched nobly up its stairs and into its stately halls, all the while maintaining their dignity in the face of a city populace that regarded them with scorn and curses. On this day the Iroquois delegates would be meeting with Robert Hunter Morris himself, as well as the commission created to regulate the spending of the militia bill's £60,000. Before the council could begin, the lieutenant governor and the Half-King patiently coursed through the required gestures associated with an Indian council; Morris thought the exercises to be trivial, but he understood that his guest considered them essential. When the proceedings finally began the governor asked that the sachem be updated as to the state of the militia's organizing on the Frontier. Satisfied, Scarouady began to speak.

"You desired us in your Instructions to enquire the particular Reasons assigned by the Delawares and Shawonese for their acting in the manner they do against this Province," he said. "I have done it." As Half-King, Scarouady exercised little power within the governance of the Iroquois Confederacy, but only as a mediator and representative among the Ohioan tribes. He was given the diplomatic authority to deliver and receive messages on behalf of the Onondaga Council, but not to craft any policy of his own. For this reason it was imperative that Scarouady be present in the colonial capital, and he carried vital intelligence from the Ohioans that Morris could never garner on his own. Scarouady explained that the Western Delaware viewed the recent history of the French invasion as a reasonable justification for their recent raids on the Frontier, explaining that "the English had accused them very falsely of joining with the French after Colonel Washington's Defeat, and if they would charge them when they were innocent they could do no more if they were guilty."[17]

Now wearing a different proverbial hat, Scarouady next discussed the Six Nations' response to the seditious Ohioans. He stated that "the Council very sharply reprehended the Delawares for their cruel and unbrotherly Behaviour against the English, and earnestly urged them to repent and desist." This rebuke went obviously ignored by the warriors, and the raids continued despite the Iroquois attempt at running interference. Whether or not the Half-King knew how bad the raids had become was unclear, but the ghastly letters on Morris's desk were proof enough to the contrary. The conversation continued, and according to Scarouady the Western Delaware openly mocked their imperial overseers in response.

> When we lived among them (the English) they behaved very ill to us; they used us like Dogs . . . Now, Uncles, can this be called Brotherly Treatment? Don't you imagine such Usage must raise Ill Nature in our Hearts? And have we not good Reason for what we are doing? We don't doubt if we would let things go on as they have done but they would subdue us and make Slaves of us. Nevertheless, Uncles, we listen to what you have told us; we thank you for your Advice.[18]

The arrival of the French had empowered the Ohioans to seek their own independence through an expression of war. It was the primary function of their life that the Iroquois had stripped from the Delawares when they initially subjugated them and made them "women." Whether or not the Pennsylvania delegation understood the full magnitude of this rebellion remains to be seen, but its consequences could be found in smoking heaps across the Frontier. To that point, the war parties seemed to have all emerged from the far West, and the local Delawares had yet to join the fray. As a parting request, Morris asked Scarouady if he could visit in council with the Eastern Delawares to promote peace, to which the Half-King obliged. The council ended, and the Iroquois returned to the backcountry just as quickly as they had arrived. The nervous populace, still on edge from the most recent news of the Frontier, was relieved to see them go.

The citizens may have been at ease, but the pressure was mounting on the lieutenant governor. Since the beginning of French hostilities, executives from neighboring colonies had all issued substantial responses to their provocations. In the aftermath of the Fort Necessity debacle, Maryland had taken steps to curtail the threat by funding a militia. Even more, they did so through a number of new revenue streams, including a tax on the proprietor of the colony, Lord Baltimore, Frederick Calvert. Although the wealthy nobleman was not keen on the measure, he understood its urgency, and fought only to make it a one-time appropriation. To the south the colony of Virginia was by far the most active in combating the French invasion, and its Lieutenant Governor Robert Dinwiddie was highly critical of Morris's perceived inability to defend his own colony. Since Washington's mission to Fort LeBoeuf in 1753, and on through Braddock's defeat in 1755, the Old Dominion had been relentless in its hawkish effort to win the Ohio Country. In 1756 they even went so far as to not only build forts but also launch offensive expeditions against wanton Indian villages considered to be the most problematic to their Frontier. In short, both Virginia and Maryland faced all of the same problems that plagued Pennsylvania, but both met their respective challenges with vigor. For Morris this was undoubtedly an isolating affair, as the political obstacles that he faced with his own assembly were great but all too common in colonial America; he received no sympathy from his gubernatorial peers.

In a letter from Robert Dinwiddie to Morris, the Virginia executive stated his opinion of Pennsylvania's condition very plainly. "I congratulate you on your Assembly's being roused from their Lethargy and their voting 60,000 for the Service of the Expedition against the Common Enemy. As you are now enabled, I hope you will plan out Operations for next Spring, and I shall be ready to join in every thing for the Public Service." From the perspective of Dinwiddie, Morris's struggles were highly indicative of his effectiveness as a governor. Among the colonial executives of North America there existed a certain affection, and they often sought advice and council from one another to confront their own province's issues. For Virginia's governor there was no acceptable excuse for Pennsylvania's embarrassing condition. Since the outbreak of the conflict, Dinwiddie had regularly pushed the boundaries of acceptable norms in order to fend off the armies of New France. In one case he even accepted an influx of Acadian refugees referred to as Neutrals as a potential supplement to his own colonial militia. The move was widely criticized, with Dinwiddie describing it as "very disagreeable to our People, as they are bigoted Papists; however we have received them, as we suppose the dispersing of them . . . is intended for a general good." The politics of immigration were as fierce in the eighteenth century as they are in the twenty-first, and the religious element aggravated these animosities even further. Nevertheless Dinwiddie went forward with his plan, an indicator of his profound commitment to wartime experimentation that only made Morris appear more impotent.[19]

Even the passage of Benjamin Franklin's landmark militia bill, which stands as a watershed moment in the history of Pennsylvania, was openly dismissed by Morris's peers. Thought most offensive by Dinwiddie were the conditions of service that had been so vital to its passing, and again he did not hide his criticism. "Your Militia Law is very inconsistent with any Rules for an Army," he chided, "and I foresee many inconveniences from it; you probably think, as I do, that it is something better than none." Dinwiddie even went so far as to forward Morris copies of acts passed previously in Virginia that he felt would be suitable for Pennsylvania's use. It was an almost unbelievable reproach of Robert Hunter Morris's tenure as lieutenant governor, but in light of a war of this magnitude with the French there was no room in British North America for a weak link.[20]

In the face of mounting political pressure, Morris found himself in a political no man's land. If he continued on his current course, more settlers would die and Ohioan raiders might even be emboldened to strike at Philadelphia. Worse yet, French soldiers stationed in the Ohio Country might become equally empowered to strike in the face of the colony's perceived weakness. If he changed nothing, his purely defensive strategy would continue to fail, but if he did alter course his political opponents would spin the decision as a tacit admission of failure. This would soon be used as a propagandized tool to rally support against the Proprietary Party in the fall elections, and the Quaker grip on the assembly would become even more insurmountable. His own colony was growing restless, and bold action needed to be taken. In the aftermath of continuing Indian atrocities like the burning of McCord's fort, the lieutenant governor's councilors proposed a radical new idea: a declaration of war.

In the entire existence of the colony of Pennsylvania the enormity of such a proclamation was incalculable. Since its founding more than seventy-five years earlier, Pennsylvania's most cherished asset was its reputation as the Peaceable Kingdom. William Penn's legacy was affixed to his perceived fair and equitable treatment of native peoples—specifically the Delawares. To declare war on the Delawares now would be a stunningly sad reversal in the annals of Quaker history, but overwhelmingly cheered by the Frontier during the here and now. It was a brilliant stroke, and it would not only galvanize the West but define the Proprietary Party as the undisputed champions of defense at all costs. The Quakers would likely rally against this momentous declaration, and potentially crumble in the fall elections of 1756. It made political sense, to be sure, but what practical change would an official declaration of war against the Western Delawares bring about?

Morris's councilors had that covered, as well.

In a meeting on April 10, James Fox, James Hamilton, Evan Morgan, John Hughes, and John Mifflin addressed the lieutenant governor in council. They delivered a proposal that would both satisfy and empower the people of the West and radically change the perception of the colony's abortive defense of the Frontier: scalp bounties. When paired with a declaration of war, the promise of payment for the scalp of a dead Indian would send a clear message to the margins of Pennsylvania society, and it was as cruel as it was precise.

> For every Male Indian Prisoner, above Ten Years old, that shall be delivered at any of the Government Forts or Towns: 150 Dollars. For every Female Indian Prisoner, or Male Prisoner of Ten Years old and under, to be delivered as above: 130 Dollars. For the Scalp of every Male Indian above Ten Years old: 130 Dollars. For the Scalp of every Indian woman: 50 Dollars.[21]

As Morris and his council saw it, the distribution of funds for Indian scalps would put teeth to the war declaration. It would turn the militarization of Pennsylvania from a defensive war to an offensive one, and ready payment for these grisly trophies would reestablish trust between the people and their government. Two days later Morris and his council met once again to deliberate this momentous decision: "It was then debated whether the Governor should consult the Assembly before issuing the Declaration of War; it was unanimously agreed that his Honour should consult them afterwards, but not before."[22]

Within twenty-four hours the coming declaration was the talk of the capital. As in any legislative setting, rumors were often spread with intention rather than leaked. In the case of Morris's impending statement, it was almost certainly whispered to arouse the anxieties of the pacifist wing of the Quaker Party; whatever the case, it succeeded smashingly. On April 12 the most hardline Quakers of the assembly penned a stirring letter to the lieutenant governor, imploring him to reconsider such a drastic step. Signing the document was a veritable who's who of those politicians still passionately tied to William Penn's vision of a holy experiment. Among the signers were Samuel Powell, Anthony Morris, John Reynell, Samuel Preston Moore, John Smith, and the king of the Quakers himself, Israel Pemberton. This letter was their great manifesto, and it was written with a combination of verbose grandeur and utter resignation. The pacifist delegation knew that they were unlikely to sway Robert Hunter Morris from his determination to declare war on the Delawares, so they instead wrote an ode to Quakerism for posterity's sake alone.

They began the note by acknowledging the sufferings of their colony, claiming it was "with heart solely distressed and deeply affected with the Calamities of our Fellow-Subjects" that they wrote their letter. They next noted that they "observed the sorrowful Alteration in the State of this late peaceful Province, now become the Theatre of Bloodshed and Rapine, and distressed by the cruel Devastations of a barbarous Enemy." These words were sobering, and an unambiguous gesture to a Frontier that was fraught with angry settlers that blamed the Quaker ideology for their current sufferings. With those pleasantries out of the way the pacifists began their plea to the lieutenant governor to reconsider, and they went immediately to the source: "The Settlement of the Province was founded on the Principles of Truth, Equity, and Mercy, and the Blessing of Divine Providence attended the early Care of the first Founders to impress these Principles on the Minds of the Native Inhabitants." The body of the letter was long and divided into two calculated paragraphs, the first appealing to Morris's Christian duties, and the second appealing to his practical nature. In this second portion the pacifists reminded Morris that not *all* of the Delawares within the colony had gone to war, and that a general scalp bounty could serve to bring them necessarily to that condition.

> That full Time may be allowed for those Indians who still remain well affected toward us, to use and report the Effect of their Endeavours to reconcile our Enemies, and that proper Care may be taken to prevent our Allies being . . . injured in such manner as to provoke them likewise to turn their Arms against us . . . and that the Governor's Care . . . may carry so clear Demonstration of Christian Tenderness and aversion to shedding Blood . . . the Minds of the neighbouring Indians which may engage them heartily and sincerely to assist in the desirable work of restoring Peace and Tranquility.[23]

They had constructed a vision of settlers and Indians killing each other at random with no regard for politics or history—a dystopian landscape that saw the destruction of William Penn's Peaceable Kingdom. In a final stroke of rhetorical gamesmanship, the pacifists restated their motivations for writing to the lieutenant governor, and placed the consequences of a general Indian war squarely on his shoulders. "The Fear of God, Honour of the King, and Love of our Brethren and Fellow

Christians, are the Motives which have engaged us to make this Address. . . . May the Mind of the Governor be endued with that Wisdom which the wisest of Kings experienced to be better than Weapons of War."[24]

With the signing of the April 12 letter, the most ideologically committed members of the Quaker Party stated their case plainly and completely. They viewed themselves as the true heirs to William Penn's holy experiment, and the defenders of his legacy. Where his sons had fallen victim to the trappings of wealth in the modern world, it was they who would carry on his sacred mission. If a declaration of war was to be made, however, it would take Pennsylvania in a new direction that they simply could not tolerate. For them, no amount of political maneuvering or concessions could garner their support for open warfare. Furthermore, if the assembly was to be complicit in carrying out an act considered to be so heretical to their own beliefs, they were no longer willing to be a part of it. At stake was no less than the soul of Pennsylvania, and all eyes turned next to Robert Hunter Morris.

Presiding over a colony in crisis, Morris had little time to deliberate. On April 13 the lieutenant governor once again convened his advisory council to discuss preparations for his great pronouncement. On that day they discussed the letter sent by the pacifists and relished its timeliness; as anticipated, the Quakers responded just as the Proprietary Party had hoped they would. But soon other news from the backcountry dampened their glee. It was reported that "a great Body of the Inhabitants of the Back Counties" had begun to rally at the city of Lancaster. As seen in the previous fall, the settlers who had assembled in the West were set on marching to Philadelphia to coerce the government into action. Regardless of one's party, the idea of armed mobs besieging the State House alarmed politicians throughout the city. Morris's council was largely divided on how to handle this new predicament, but all agreed that the assembly should be informed. Morris promptly scribbled warnings to the assembly, supreme court, and city government of Philadelphia that mobs were forming in the West. He then curtly requested that they "use their utmost Endeavours to prevent the mischiefs that may attend so extraordinary a Procedure."[25]

The weight of history loomed large for Robert Hunter Morris. When he assumed the lieutenant governorship in 1754 he did so with the promise of a new administration. Now, though, he found himself being squeezed on all sides by raiding Indians, conquering French, Quaker obstructionists, and seditious Frontiersmen. He certainly dreamed of more powerful positions after Pennsylvania, and climbing the imperial ladder, but he was now faced with the very real possibility of presiding over a collapsing province. To salvage his career and spare his province, he would need to make a profound statement and leave a legacy of his own.

Finally, on April 14, 1756, he did just that. At the city courthouse, Morris's declaration was read aloud before the supreme court and a throng of citizens; it began, "A PROCLAMATION." The crowd that had gathered listened intently to the document, long and winding, as it succinctly described the colony's exhaustive attempts to make peace and pursue resolution with the Delawares. Morris's words described the "cruel, savage, and perfidious manner" in which Shingas and his warriors had "butchered great Numbers of the Inhabitants," and had decided that a declaration of war was the only solution.

> I have, therefore, by and with the Advice and consent of the Council, thought fit to issue this Proclamation; and do hereby declare the said Delaware Indians, and all others who, in Conjunction with, have committed Hostilities against His Majesty's Subjects within this Province, to be Enemies, Rebels, and Traitors . . . And I do hereby require all his Majesty's Subjects . . . to embrace all Opportunities of pursuing, taking, killing, and destroying the said Delaware Indians and all others confederated with them.[26]

The proclamation went on to offer vague exceptions to spare those Indians not allied with the Western Delawares, but to a minimal degree. Instead, it focused on the scalp bounties that would give the proverbial teeth to the declaration, and emboldened the Frontiersmen to take the war into the Ohio Country. There was no doubt that as Morris penned these words he hoped to transfer the anxieties of the mob forming in Lancaster onto the Indian peoples nearby and away from himself. In a final measure of exactitude, the lieutenant governor's message offered "one Hundred and Fifty Pieces of Eight" for each and every English captive brought back to Philadelphia alive.

Throughout the fall of 1755 and early spring of 1756, Robert Hunter Morris was virtually handcuffed by the politics of his province. He could not raise an army, build forts, or even sharpen a blade without the cooperation of the assembly. They stymied him at every turn, and when they did seek his approval he, in turn, blocked their attempts. While his neighboring executives had procured armies to stifle their own Indian threats, he could only watch his colony be laid to ruin. With this Declaration of War, though, all of that was circumvented; he need not conscript any military force to stop the Western Delawares and their allies. He simply had to turn loose a vengeful and bitter populace that was more than willing to take up the hatchet on his behalf. Morris no longer presided over a colony in collapse but a colony fighting against itself. The Pennsylvania that William Penn and the Original People had founded in the shadow of the Shackamaxon Elm seventy-five years earlier was gone. War had come, and the Peaceable Kingdom was its greatest casualty.

"The east prospect of the city of Philadelphia, in the province of Pennsylvania."Dedicated to Thomas Penn, the view of Philadelphia from the New Jersey side of the Delaware River surveyed by Nicholas Scull and drawn by George Heap was produced in 1756. (*New York Public Library*)

"View of a pass over the South Mountain from York Town to Carlisle." Published soon after the American Revolution, this illustration shows the terrain that would have been familiar to those who participated in the raid on Kittanning. Carlisle was among the most important settlements on the early Pennsylvania frontier. (*New York Public Library*)

Overleaf: "A map of the province of Pensilvania drawn from the best authorities," appeared in the December 1756 issue of *London Magazine*. It shows the 1732 boundary agreement between Lord Baltimore and the Penns, which set the southern boundary at essentially its present position. The boundary with New York is called "undefined." The western boundary is placed just west of "F. du Quesne." This is the first map of all the state of Pennsylvania itself. Kittanning is located just north of Fort Duquesne. (*Library of Congress*)

Printed for R. Bal

Baldwin in Pater Noster Row 1756.

A portrait of Benjamin Franklin rendered in 1746 when he was forty years old. This is the earliest known painting of Franklin. (*Harvard University*)

Thomas Penn in a 1751 portrait. (*New York Public Library*)

Left, a Delaware warrior drawn in the decade after the Kittanning Raid. Above, John Armstrong after retiring from active military service. (*New York Public Library*)

"A Design to represent the beginning and completion of an American Settlement or Farm," from *Scenographia Americana*, London, 1768. (*Library of Congress*)

A Delaware "fort" from Thomas Campanius Holm's *Description of the Province of New Sweden, Now Called, by the English, Pennsylvania, in America.* Published in 1702, Holm's book was based on descriptions provided by his grandfather who had visited the area in the 1640s.

A late eighteenth-century engraving of an Indian attack on a frontier family. Fear of Indian reprisals remained a theme for decades despite the reality that Indians were being forcibly driven from the frontier. (*Library of Congress*)

John Armstrong and his men were each presented with a commemorative medal struck in their honor by the city of Philadelphia. (*The State Museum of Pennsylvania, Pennsylvania Historical and Museum Commission*)

An illustration from *Travels in the Interior Parts of North America* documenting Patrick Campbell's 1791–92 visit to the frontier, shows the inexorable settlement of the Ohio Country following the defeat and removal of much of the native population. (*John Carter Brown Library, Brown University*)

FIVE

Season of War

The spring of 1756 was a season of war. For the first time in its history, the colony of Pennsylvania had made an official declaration of hostilities against an enemy. As a result, the province buzzed with excitement, and the Frontiers beamed with hope that salvation had been found at last. It was a startling turn of events that even a year earlier seemed improbable, and a decade earlier seemed impossible. But Robert Hunter Morris's public declaration against the Delawares did not make news across the whole of British North America; it was only one of many sudden calculations made in the effort to confront a new and rising threat. Although it was a watershed moment in the history of Penn's colony, it was but a small cog in the greater machine of empire preparing to fight a global war.

On May 17, the city of London was rocked when King George II issued a royal decree that Great Britain was officially at war with France. Considered to be eternal enemies, the two superpowers had tangled often over the last half century, and each time the wars seemed to expand in vision and scale. In the Middle Ages the English and French waged war over small river valleys, coastal shores, or mountain passes, but now, in the age of empires, conflicts that began as regional squabbles quickly ballooned into global events. By 1756 the British and French race for world dominance had seen the establishment of colonial holdings in North America, the Caribbean, India, and Southeast Asia; it seemed this war would be the greatest one yet, and as one commentator noted it would "set the world on fire." Historians would remember this global calamity as the Seven Years' War, while contemporaries called it "the Great War for Empire." Two centuries later, Winston Churchill would christen it as the first true World War, and given that source such a moniker speaks volumes regarding its impact on modern history.

This war would touch all corners of the globe, from the rainforests of India to the blue waters of the Caribbean, and it would it draw peoples into its midst who had little affection for either of its primary combatants. British and French administrators would lobby kings and chieftains across the planet to fight on their behalf, and the long tendrils of empire ensured their participation. In South Asia, Muslim and Hindu soldiers did battle with one another under the flag of a nation to which they bore no allegiance, and in the North American wilderness native warriors did the same. For the policymakers in Whitehall and Versailles, this was evidence of the greatness of their respective empires, but on the ground the men who did battle actually cared very little for the petty origins of a European conflict. In each theater of the war from the Ohio Country to the Philippines, from Uruguay to West Africa, the soldiers who fought took up arms for their own reasons and, more often than not, siding with the British or French was merely a matter of choosing the lesser of two evils. As illustrated in the Ohio Country, the Western Delaware only took up the hatchet with the forces of King Louis because they offered to *leave* after the war had ended . . . not exactly a stunning endorsement of France or its policies. Likewise, when Shingas and Tewea struck a Frontier village, the men who attempted to fend them off did so to save their families, not for some higher imperial calling.

When considered in that fashion, the Seven Years' War was actually many wars. They had many origins, and the differences between the stout British and eloquent French were often not found among them. In America it was the "French and Indian War," in India the conflict was called the "Third Carnatic War," and in parts of Europe it was the "Second Silesian War." To the Iroquois it would have appeared as a rebellion of their Ohioan subjects, but to those warriors it was nothing short of a revolution. The true breadth and scope of this seminal conflict cannot be fully grasped without first understanding its sheer massiveness, otherwise one would be dumbfounded when trying to follow its twisted evolution from year to year. The struggle brought together old European allies and forged new and lasting alliances, and would ultimately cease with no less than four separate official peace treaties. It was these documents that were considered sacred and official in Europe, but that is to say nothing about the countless more that remained unwritten, consecrated in distant lands around council fires and ceremonial feasts. Although the words of King George II would not reach Pennsylvania for weeks to come, they would be received with equal enthusiasm as in other parts of the British world.

> The unwarrantable Proceedings of the French in the West Indies, and North America . . . and the Usurpations and Encroachments made by them upon Our Territories, and the Settlements of Our Subjects . . . have been so notorious, and so frequent . . . and without any previous Notice given . . . a Body of French Troops, under the Command of an Officer bearing the French King's Commission, attacked in a hostile Manner, and possessed themselves of the English Fort on the Ohio in North America . . . We have therefore thought proper to declare War; and We do hereby Declare War against the French King, who hath so unjustly begun it . . . whatever Ship or Vessel shall be met withal, transporting or carrying Soldiers, Arms, Powder, Ammunition, or any other Contraband Goods, to any of the Territories, Lands, Plantations, or Countries of the said French King, the same, being taken, shall be condemned as good and lawful Prize.[1]

With these words Europe's two greatest powers called upon their newly formed coalitions to determine the fate of empire in the modern world. The British rallied alongside Prussia, Hanover, Hesse-Cassel,

Schaumburg-Lippe, and Brunswick-Wolfenbuttel; the French likewise with Austria, Saxony, Bavaria, Russia, and Sweden. It was a tangled web of alliances known as the "Diplomatic Revolution," which was bogged down with a countless array of almost unmanageable moving pieces. From the perspective of London, the alliance with Frederick the Great's Prussia was of mutual benefit. While the mighty British navy would focus on winning the colonial wars, Prussia's vaunted infantry would defend King George's interests on the continent of Europe. In exchange, the Prussians would have the backing of a major power as it moved on its longtime enemy, Austria, to conquer some highly coveted new territory. As a continental power itself, the French would likewise keep their military focus on the Old World, and rely heavily on its provincial allies to keep up the war effort overseas. In the case of Pennsylvania, it was the raiding Ohioan warriors who most demonstrated this system.

Of course with a clash of empires this vast, few in the colonies had the foresight to see the greater picture. And who could fault them? The Seven Years' War would manifest at different times for different reasons in vastly different parts of the world. For Shingas and his Western Delawares, they were not pawns on some larger imperial chessboard, and their partnership with the French was merely a means to an end. They fought with the common goal of escaping the grasp of the Six Nations and their Pennsylvanian allies, and French support merely facilitated that goal. In short London, Versailles, Philadelphia, Quebec, and even Kittanning were all nerve-centers in the Great War for Empire, yet they understood the shared conflict in immensely different ways.

Seventeen fifty-six was indeed a year of many declarations, and not all were printed in newspapers and read in public squares. For almost six months the Westerns Delawares and their Ohioan allies had been waging war on the Frontiers of Pennsylvania, and it was done directly under the nose of the Iroquois Confederacy. Since the first English colonies popped up along the Eastern Seaboard, the Six Nations had enjoyed the privilege of being the preeminent native superpower of the American Northeast. In that role they had made strong alliances with the British Empire, and were viewed as meaningful partners in the Crown's quest for imperial dominance. This diplomatic relationship made them the chief arbiters of both trade and expansion, and they profited greatly in both political and economic capital. But with the sudden appearance of the French in the Ohio Country in the spring of 1753, this status quo was challenged. The British saw the expansion of New France as a threat to their own vision, and they expected the Six Nations to be equally willing partners in curbing King Louis's armies. When the French were able to woo the subject peoples of the Iroquois into rebellion, the great Covenant Chain on which the Anglo-Iroquoian partnership was founded slowly revealed itself to be weaker than either side had previously known.

The de facto rebellion of the Ohioans was a great embarrassment to the Six Nations; in the eyes of their British allies, it challenged their outward appearance as a true ruling power on the continent. Even more, it forced them to confront the fact that they were not as powerful as even they believed *themselves* to be. The beginnings of the Great War for Empire signaled the beginnings of a new order in the New World, as well as the fading of an old one. By 1756 the Iroquois had taken the initiative to play damage control along the Frontier by meeting in councils with the seditious Delawares. Although their efforts were done in earnest, it was likely too little, too late. In February the Six Nations dispatched representatives to meet with the Delawares at the village of Otsiningo. Otsiningo was situated along the upper Susquehanna River and was actually a collection of many small villages made up of varying peoples. The most prominent were the Delawares and the Iroquoian Tuscaroras, making it an ideal spot to hold the momentous council.

Like all empires, the Iroquois was highly organized. It ran on clearly defined responsibilities for each of its member nations, and each worked in a compartmentalized fashion to maintain the suzerainty of the polity as a whole. In the months since the Ohioan rebellion began, many within Iroquoia began to single out the Seneca as having been negligent in their duties, as the Ohio Country was considered to be among them. This was stated very plainly by Little Abraham, a speaker of the Mohawk nation, to a body of Pennsylvanians. He explained, "In the Time of our Great Grandfathers, and when the Six Nations first united, it was agreed that the Seneca Country . . . were to forward the Messages to all the United Nations." He further stated that the Mohawk believed "they neglected their Offices," and "took the Affair in Hands, and sent Messenger to Otsaningo."[2]

During the council the Iroquois were granted all of the respect that they had enjoyed from their underlings for decades. The representatives of the Six Nations spoke uninterrupted, and delivered platitudes designed to both placate and subdue the rebellious Delawares. According to Little Abraham, at one point their Iroquois orator stated that "the Deputies we sent charged them to get sober, as we looked upon their Actions as the Actions of Drunken Men." This, it seemed, was a break from the traditional air of respect that so embodied these councils, and the Delaware responded in kind. In one of the most striking moments in the history of Iroquois diplomacy, a speaker representing the Delawares defiantly confronted their longtime masters, and laid out their mutinous intentions. Little Abraham recounted "that they looked upon themselves as Men, and wou'd acknowledge no Superiority that any other Nation had over them. 'We are Men, and are determined not to be ruled any longer by you as Women; And we are determined to cut off all the English, except those that make their Escape from us in Ships; So say no more to us on that Head, lest we cut off your private Parts and make Women of you, as you have done of us.' "[3]

It seemed that in this one council the Delawares had fully realized the inherent feebleness of their longtime masters. With the aid of the French, the Original People had once again regained the ability to wage war without the consent of an imperial overseer. The limitations placed on Delawares as "women" no longer needed to take precedence, and the Six Nations had proved they were incapable of doing anything about it. In perhaps the boldest declaration of the entire council, the sachems present even threatened to "cut off" the "private Parts" of the Iroquois, effectively stating that if pressed too far the Six Nations themselves could become subjects of the Delawares. While it was brash and defiant, this type of behavior was a testament to the major changes brought forth by a world on the brink of war. This newly discovered empowerment was on display for all to see, fully backed by the global forces of empire. The speech delivered that night at Otsiningo was an important one, but it was no mere declaration of war. For the Original People, it was a declaration of independence.

Just ten days after Robert Hunter Morris's historic declaration of war, he wrote to Sir William Johnson about his troubles. Johnson was one of Britain's leading Indian agents in the New World, and a true master of his craft. Given the state of Pennsylvania that spring, it was no surprise that Morris would seek his advice, as even from his home in the Mohawk River Valley of upstate New York Johnson seemed to always have his finger on the pulse of the Indian world. "You cannot conceive what Havock has been made by the Enemy in this defenceless Province," Morris wrote, "nor what Numbers of Murders they have committed; what a vast Tract of Territory they have laid waste, and what a Multitude of Inhabitants . . . they have carried in Captivity." Morris further speculated that "not less than three hundred of our People" were taken by the Ohioan warriors over the last six months.[4]

While Johnson was experienced in the potential terrors of Indian war, the lieutenant governor was still grasping its potential. He had not anticipated the utter devastation that it could bring, but since Braddock's defeat the previous July he had learned quickly. Intelligence was sparse, but Morris felt comfortable enough to single out what he felt was the source of his problems. Regarding the captives he claimed "most of them" were taken to "Shingas' Town, called Kittanning, about thirty Miles above Fort Duquesne." He continued by stating that "indeed, the main Body of the Delaware live at Kittanning and the other Delaware Towns on and beyond the Ohio, and have been the most mischievous, and do still . . . continue to murder and destroy our Inhabitants, treating them with the most barbarous Inhumanity that can be conceived." After months of raids with no end in sight, Morris's letter seemed to reveal a man at his wit's end.

The letter to Johnson was written with great candor, and revealed that the stress of the war was wilting the lieutenant governor. He claimed that after months of political squabbles and ineffective attempts at fortification, the raids had showed no signs of slowing. Furthermore, the peoples of the Frontier were growing increasingly restless, and he was unsure whether he could fend them off in the event of another march on the capital. "I have been constrained to yield to the importunate Demands of the enraged People . . . to declare the Delaware Nation Enemies and Rebels to his Majesty, and to offer large

Rewards for Prisoners and Scalps, hoping that this would engage such of our Inhabitants." Throughout his confessional Morris was sympathetic to the settlers in the West; he knew that the colony could do more to protect them. He also understood, though, that such legislative actions went through a stalwart assembly that was committed to scoring political points through calculated parliamentary obstruction. Even if he were to procure the funds to truly arm the backcountry and spur them into action, he was uncertain whether it would make a difference.

Morris explained that he saw "the Power of the Enemy to be daily encreasing" and felt that an organized effort by the colonial government to mount a retaliatory strike was unlikely to succeed. If he did have the power to authorize such a measure, it risked a disastrous defeat. But if he allowed the Frontier militia to arrange their own foray into the Ohio Country, he left open the opportunity to blame potential losses on their inherently untrained ranks. He speculated that "had I had the least Notion that they could be stopped in the midst of their furious career, I would not have gratified the People; but despairing of this . . . no Method is so likely as this to bring a Force into the Enemy's Country, and drive them from their lurking Places, and from their Towns."[5] In this most troubled time Morris could not afford to lose face, but a raid by the people, whether successful or not, could serve to bolster his image.

By the spring of 1756 Robert Hunter Morris no longer had the luxury of contending with war against just one enemy. That March, King Louis XV appointed Louis-Joseph de Montcalm as *maréchel de camp* (major general) of all forces in New France. He would be second only to the governor general of the colony, and be responsible for the conquest of North America. With this appointment would come a flood of reinforcements, supplies, and expectations. The official beginning of the Seven Years' War transformed Morris's dilemma from a localized Indian uprising to an existential crisis of empire. In the face of an invading French army fully determined to vanquish his colony, the lieutenant governor had to once again call upon his antagonists in the assembly to prepare for war. The gears of this conflict had been churning for months already, though, and—unbeknownst at the time—the great French invasion of Philadelphia would never come. Although it was unnoticed then, historians can now accurately state that Pennsylvania had already seen the worst of what a general war with New France had to offer. Their fears were not unfounded but merely misplaced.

The reality of the Great War for Empire in Pennsylvania was that the French never had a clear path to conquer much of anything. They had spent a fortune to build Fort Duquesne and its satellites, and had to concentrate their available forces in the Great Lakes and the Saint Lawrence River Valley. There were going to be epic showdowns at Fort Oswego on Lake Ontario and Fort Ticonderoga on Lake Champlain for certain, but no massive French army was ever going to cross the Alleghenies and threaten Philadelphia. Instead, policymakers of New France elected to subcontract the fighting in Pennsylvania to their Ohioan allies. Rather than using them as mere support, as they would in New York, the French relied almost completely on Shingas and his warriors to take the war to Pennsylvania. Fort Duquesne was vital in this effort, but only as a place of trade and supply. Warriors would rally at the Forks of the Ohio to receive muskets, powder, and supplies, and then venture across the mountains to wreak havoc. It was unlikely that the Pennsylvania government had any way of predicting this, and if so they would have found that they had been fighting this war for almost ten months already. In hindsight, the trepidation of a general French invasion was unfounded, but by May it was a very real concern. In accordance, Morris appealed to the colonial assembly with the greatest of urgency.

On May 10 Robert Hunter Morris called the assembly into session and delivered a message compelling them to action. "By the Latest Accounts from Europe, there is the Greatest Reason to apprehend that the French have sent . . . a Considerable Armament into America," he stated, "which, in all Probability, will be the Seat of War." He continued by explaining that the forces of New France would rely heavily on their Caribbean colonies to supply them during the conflict, and that they should take proactive steps to make that as difficult as possible. In the weeks leading up to his letter, Morris had been in regular contact with neighboring executives, discussing the idea of what he called "a General Embargo." This would effectively shut down the vast and profitable trade network between North America and the Caribbean, cutting off any supply lines that might enable New France. Most of Pennsylvania's neighboring colonies supported the measure, but all understood that unless every Governor passed a similar measure the entire boycott was likely to fail. "We shall not only Distress them, but be better able to supply his Majesty's Forces Employed in Our Defence," he reasoned.[6]

A measure on the scale of a regional boycott was ambitious, but not impossible. Given the general support that the measure had procured in neighboring colonies, the assembly would have been especially nihilistic to ignore it. The boycott, however, was not the lieutenant governor's only request, and his next demand sent the assembly into a partisan frenzy. Morris wrote that news from the Frontier had "induced me to call you Together" to pass "the Best & speediest measures . . . to Prevent . . . the total Ruin and Desolation" of the backcountry. He stated that the early bills passed by the assembly "contributed very little towards the Defence of the Frontiers," and even went so far as to describe them as "defective" and "entirely useless." He instead called for another militia bill, this one more far-reaching than the first. He demanded new funding that would "enable me to Draw the Strength of the Province" to the settlements most in need of defense. His words were sharp and biting, and would prove to be totally toxic in an already spoiled political climate.

As seen in previous correspondence, Morris was taking harsh criticism from his colleagues. Charles Hardy, governor of New York, was incredulous about Pennsylvania's apparent passivity. He wrote in a letter to Morris that "it is astonishing to think the Legislatures of these Colonies can be so Blind not to see the Necessity of such a Law."[7] Even the Superintendent of Indian Affairs Sir William Johnson noted that "these . . . Measures which Mr. Morris has Entered into is Throwing all our Schemes into Confusion."[8] Through all of this critical correspondence it appeared as though Robert Hunter Morris's tenure as lieutenant governor was eroding. He was losing the respect of his peers as an effective executive, and could not afford any further missteps. He viewed himself as an upwardly mobile player on the imperial stage with dreams much greater than his current position. To fumble now, though, with so much at stake, could derail his career and permanently damage his future prospects. Morris knew this, to be sure, and so did his counterparts across the aisle.

Two days later the assembly responded to the governor's plea with mixed results. On the positive side they were able to produce a bill "for prohibiting the Exportation of Provisions or Warlike Stores from this Province," but not without reservation. Like Morris the assembly believed that for the strategy to work there would need to be full compliance across the entire Northeast. Their concern, however, lay with Delaware, described by the assembly as "the Three Lower Counties." The assemblymen correctly believed that the "restrictions laid upon such Exportations by the Legislature of this Province" would be "rendered altogether ineffectual" if Delaware did not participate as well. This was a position of compromise that Morris could work with, but his proposal for a new militia bill was another matter altogether.

In response to the lieutenant governor's demand for a new militia bill, the assembly remained confrontational. "The Frontier of this Province is now in a better State of Defence than that of any other Colony on the Continent," they insisted. In their estimation, the whole of the backcountry was now organized into military units, which was true, and there were also many other militia units that had not yet been called to serve in any fashion—also true. They stated that the "marching of the Militia to the Frontier on every Alarm . . . would be less effectual for its Defence, and much more expensive and burdensome to the People." The assembly freely admitted that this type of martial organization was new to them, but they quickly resorted to scoring political points as a means of supporting their opposition. They coyly stated that "a considerable Sum" of the original £60,000 expenditure was "still in the Hands of the Commissioners . . . as the Governor did not point them out, when we presented the Bill, and he gave it his Assent." In short it was the same type of frustrating political brinksmanship that had so plagued Morris's first months in office. In a time of great need, Morris believed that his legislative opponents were more committed to election-year antics than presenting a meaningful defense of the province. Even more worrisome, though, was not the assembly's apparent commitment to inaction, but the fact that if they did manage to send over a new militia bill it was likely to tax proprietary lands. This would mandate a veto from Morris, and ultimately be spun as indifference on *his* part. Even under the shadow of a general French and Indian invasion, Philadelphia's partisan game was still afoot, and for his part Robert Hunter Morris had played enough to last a lifetime.[9]

Earlier that spring in a quiet letter to Thomas Penn, Robert Hunter Morris had resigned his position as lieutenant governor of Pennsylvania. Since taking the helm in October 1754 he had governed over a colony in turmoil, and was opposed at nearly every turn. In neighboring colonies he saw other strong executives crafting a colonial vision and putting it into action, but he faced obstacles that his peers could never have imagined. On May 7 the proprietor selected William Denny as his tentative replacement, but in the eighteenth-century world such changes moved interminably slowly. As a virtual lame duck, Morris was expected to stay on as executive until his replacement could arrive; Denny would not step foot in the province for another three months. In many ways, Morris's tenure as lieutenant governor had been everything that the Penns wanted, yet nothing that Pennsylvania needed. He had even been given the sole mandate of protecting proprietary interests from taxation at the point of legal reprimand, but never given the authority to promote a meaningful agenda. At the time of his commission he seemed to be an ideal peacetime executive, but the fateful twist of larger world affairs thrust him into becoming a wartime administrator. So, for the next three months, Morris would gladly tussle with the assembly and attempt to tame the Frontiers, all the while knowing that he was free from any resulting blame. His only true focus, it seemed, was salvaging what was left of his career.

Across the Atlantic, however, a battle of a different sort was underway. At the end of 1755 a great campaign against the pacifist Quakers of the assembly had been undertaken by a number of influential voices in the colony. As a result, a dramatic petition was signed and eventually circulated in London. While it was met with the expected partisan skepticism in Philadelphia, the anti-Quaker campaign caught on like wildfire in the imperial capital. All across London policymakers read of the terrible scourge that Indian war had inflicted on Pennsylvania, followed by a convenient follow-up recounting the Quaker assembly's continual inaction. The result was outrage and grief in Whitehall, with most of the aggrieved blindly associating the whole of the Quaker Party with unflinching pacifism. Of course this was a fallacy; only a small number of the Quaker representatives were *actual* pacifists. But the anti-Quaker smear campaign had its desired effect, and many across England demanded that the Quaker Party be disbanded outright. In Philadelphia such a radical maneuver was considered laughable, as most Pennsylvanians understood the complexity of the party as a whole, but in London no distinction was made. On February 26, 1756, the Board of Trade held a hearing to determine the validity of these claims, and ultimately agreed that pacifism was a position unworthy of the British Empire. In clear terms, they described the 1755 militia bill as wholly unacceptable due to its liberal terms of service, and recommended that Parliament ban the Quakers from serving in the colonial assembly outright. The Board of Trade was in no position to pursue such a venture, and they promptly forwarded their recommendation to the Privy Council.

Although the Privy Council was unlikely to ban the Quaker Party altogether, the political damage had largely been done. The Proprietary Party openly celebrated the decision by the Board of Trade as a vindication of their partisan values, and the pacifists in Philadelphia began to worry. The entire affair illustrated perfectly the notion that Pennsylvania was only part of a larger empire, and if the colony ever stepped out of line, big brother could step in and arrange a more amiable situation. Luckily for the hardline members of the Society of Friends in the colonial capital, they had powerful friends of their own in London who could rally support against the censure. While the city of Philadelphia reeled in the wake of the Board of Trade's decision, powerful Friends in Whitehall were able to rally the support of Lord Granville to their side. Granville was a major player on the imperial stage and, crucially, the president of King George's Privy Council.

Even though they swayed Granville to their side, Quakers in London worried that he alone may not be enough to guarantee their party's existence. As a fallback, they rallied for the most dedicated of the assembly's Friends to become proactive. Instead of being unceremoniously dismissed, they argued that the inflexible pacifists in the legislature should instead step down out of protest. While it seemed counterproductive, the political reality was that even if they were able to continue serving, they had likely suffered irreversible damage in the eyes of the province. Without the faith of their constituents the defenders of the Penn legacy could weigh down the entire party, and as 1756 was an election year, a full resignation might be the most expedient solution. Of course, they could vacate their posts under the dignified banner of protest, but either way it seemed that the faith, party, and province would be better off without their service. Therefore, on June 7, Speaker Isaac Norris wrote a letter to Secretary Richard Peters stating that James Pemberton, William Callender, Joshua Morris, William Peters, Francis Parvin, and Peter Worrall "have each and every of them resigned and vacated their seats in the Assembly."[10]

The news was met with outward jubilation among the proprietary ranks. Robert Hunter Morris, still acting as lieutenant governor despite having resigned the post, celebrated in private with his advisors. The proprietary assemblymen likewise toasted the pacifists' exit. In the streets of Philadelphia, newspapers relished in the scuttlebutt and the potential for political fallout. In an election year a development such as this one was major news, and many speculated that the pacifist exodus from the assembly could be indicative of a major political swing in the fall. Whether or not the pacifist resignation was a watershed moment in the storied history of Pennsylvania remained to be seen, but for Benjamin Franklin the consequences were never in doubt. In only a matter of weeks the fifty-year-old assemblyman had seen Robert Hunter Morris (his greatest political rival) and the pacifist Quakers (his most irritating colleagues) vanish from the province's political landscape. For Franklin the changes were nothing short of earth-shattering, and he planned on taking full advantage of his new found opportunity.

In the wake of the vacancies, Franklin wrote in a private letter to London: "You have pleas'd me much with the Expectation of a new Governor: All the Stiffrumps except One, that could be suspected of opposing the Service from religious Motives, have voluntarily quitted the Assembly. . . . These Changes in both Branches promise us some fair Weather, which I have long sigh'd for." Franklin further stated that the one remaining pacifist assemblyman "still endeavours to keep up a

Flame; but is become odious, and almost infamous, as you will see in the Papers. He will no longer do here."[11]

Any hope of a compromise between the Quaker and Proprietary parties was promptly squashed. On June 29 the assembly returned Morris's plea for additional funding of Frontier defense with a bill that did precisely that; as always, though, the devil was in the details. The bill sent over by Franklin and his peers did in fact provide additional funding, and unlike before it did so *without* taxing proprietary estates. In the upheaval of recent weeks, the Quaker authors of the bill hoped immediate action could be taken that would satisfy both sides. With Morris on his way out the door, it was believed that he just might sign the bill as it presently stood. Again, though, the details of the funding would make all the difference. Rather than taxing the Penn family's lands, this new bill increased revenue by placing an excise tax on liquor. An excise tax was an oft-used method of raising money by legislatures in colonial America. By placing the onus of collection on the producer and sellers of a certain product, taxes were indirectly paid by the consumer in the cost of the goods. In this case, the producers of liquors would be forced to pay more taxes, and in turn raise the price of their spirits, leaving the buyer none the wiser. The Proprietary Party had no issue with the tax itself, and likely applauded the measure as a creative way of avoiding the traditional partisan pitfalls of Philadelphia politics, but this bill carried a special caveat that brought its passage to a screeching halt.

Always looking for the political upper hand, the assemblymen included an addendum specifying that any of the new monies raised by the excise tax would be under their exclusive control. To Morris and his advisors, this was wholly unexpected. The November 1755 militia bill ordered that the allocation of the £60,000 would fall to a special commission under the lieutenant governor's control, and only they would have the authority to choose where and when the money was spent. Now smelling the blood in the proverbial water, it appeared that Franklin's Quaker Party was trying to leverage Morris's lame-duck status for political gain. The Proprietary Party bristled at this proposal, and the lieutenant governor's council immediately killed the bill. They told Morris, "You shall not give your assent to any law for prolonging the present Excise . . . or raising any money on the Inhabitants of the said Province of Pennsylvania, unless there be an enacting Clause, that all Money . . . shall be disposed of only as we, or either of us, exercising the office of Governor, or the Lieutenant Governor . . . shall direct, and not otherwise."[12]

In response, Morris once again appealed to the sensibilities of the emboldened assemblymen. He stated that their original £60,000 would be "very soon expended," and that dire consequences would follow. Still technically the executive of the colony, Morris next issued a direct threat: "I shall in that case be under a necessity of Disbanding the troops raised for the defence of the Province, and of Destroying or abandoning the several forts erected upon our Frontiers." In this statement he once again threw down the gauntlet of the bully pulpit. With the most hardline pacifists among them now very publically removed, Morris put the onus of action on the Quakers who remained. If they did not act swiftly, at best the tide of public opinion would turn against them; at worst, the tireless proprietary propaganda labeling all Quakers as extreme peace lovers would be proven true. The assembly would drag their subsequent deliberations well into the summer with no result, and the acting lieutenant governor would focus his efforts on making peace in spite of them.[13]

Since the beginning of the Delaware raids, most Pennsylvanians could recognize two distinct parties involved in the attacks. The worst of the violence stemmed undoubtedly from the Western Delawares led by Shingas and Tewea and their Shawnee allies, but they were not alone. Other raiding parties that had come from the north in Pennsylvania's fertile Wyoming Valley were far less frequent. The leading theory in the province as to this apparently weaker northern front centered on the notion that these Wyoming Delawares saw the war in a very different way. While the Western Delawares settled in the distant West as an expression of their distaste for any and all European interaction, many of the less zealous chose to instead make their lives in the Susquehanna River and Wyoming valleys. These peoples typically adhered to the original promises of their forbearers' agreements with William Penn, and saw diplomacy as a reasonable alternatives to achieving their goals. Although they did wage war during the spring of 1756, there was never a consensus among them that such rash actions were prudent. It was in these sentiments that Robert Hunter Morris saw an opportunity to bring about a peaceful resolution that could spare some of his most vulnerable communities.

Earlier in May the lieutenant governor sent messages to the Wyoming Delawares offering overtures of peace and by months' end he received a promising response. Teedyucung was considered the "king" of the Wyoming Delawares by most policymakers in Philadelphia, and he wrote back to Morris claiming that he was "willing to renew the Treaties of Friendship which *William Penn* had made with his Forefathers." Morris requested what he described as a "publick Convention," and the two parties agreed to meet in July. As an immediate gesture of good faith, the lieutenant governor rescinded his declaration of war and scalp bounty on the Wyoming Delawares, with special care to retain them in regards to their Western brethren.[14]

The council that followed was rife with symbolism and appeared as colonial America in a microcosm. Held at Easton on the Delaware River, Robert Hunter Morris was joined by his secretary, Richard Peters, and Teedyuscung was accompanied by the sachems of the Wyoming Valley. In the most practical sense, these two delegations were the only essential participants in the council, but greater circumstances made the Easton Conference a much more crowded affair. Sometimes called the king of the Quakers and widely considered to be the face of traditional Quakerism, Israel Pemberton insisted on attending the council as what could only be described as a representative of the province's pacifist legacy. When he was granted permission to appear, he stunned Morris by bringing over forty of his fellow Friends with him. Likewise, the Iroquois Confederacy demanded to be present as they *still* considered the Delawares to be their subjects, claiming that they were unable to speak on their own behalf.

The scene was nothing short of farcical. The presence of the Old Guard Quaker pacifists and Six Nations sachems outnumbered any other parties, yet they wielded the least influence of all. Even just ten years earlier these two powerful interest groups would have had total control over the conference and its results, but the coming of war had changed all of that. Now, instead of being power brokers they were nothing more than hollow guardians of a fading order, regaled in all the dignity of self-importance. Without question the dominate presence of the Easton Conference was Teedyuscung, and the stage was his for most of the proceedings. Known as "Honest John" to some of the English, Teedyuscung was Christianized and willing to work with Pennsylvania under the right circumstances. He had taken up the hatchet himself over the last few months, but always with the goal of Delaware independence in mind. For Morris he was the perfect partner; the lieutenant governor sought peace, and Teedyuscung wished for a permanent Lenape homeland in the Wyoming Valley.

In many ways he was everything Shingas was not. While Shingas too sought Delaware freedom, his primary method of achieving it was total war on the Frontier with conspiratorial French backing. His endgame was always unclear and never entirely quantifiable. Teedyuscung had the same vision, but unlike his Ohioan counterpart he never took a diplomatic solution off of the table. Both sachems had an intense desire to be free from the yoke of the Iroquois Confederacy, but Shingas saw the Pennsylvanians as an irreconcilable part of the problem. Teedyuscung, though, had the political experience to see them as a possible partner in future endeavors, largely stemming from his respect for the Delawares' shared history with William Penn's long-distant administration. In this way the history of the province loomed very large, and the differences between the Western and Wyoming Delawares were undeniably clear.

The proceedings began on July 28, and for the length of the four-day conference Teedyuscung spoke defiantly in the face of his former Iroquois masters. A decade earlier his audacious speeches would have been shocking, but everyone present had accepted that new circumstances had altered their old arrangements. "We were Accounted women," the sachem stated, "and Employed only in women's business, but now they have made men of us, and as such we now come to this Treaty, having this Authority as a man to make Peace."[15]

The Iroquois representatives were quick to chastise Teedyuscung for his insolence. "You will remember that you are our women," the representative said. "Our forefathers made you so." But even this admonishment soon faded in the face of the new political reality. The sachems in attendance understood that the Six Nations had no practical way of reining in the empowered Delawares, and soon expressed a conciliatory tone, offering to "give . . . a little Prick and put it into your Private Parts, and so let it grow there till you shall be a compleat man." From the European perspective, the politics of gender assignment that dominated the Indian world could be befuddling, but the language selected by each party was chosen with the utmost intention and care. As "women," the Delaware were not at liberty to make war or peace, and by offering "a little Prick" the Iroquois were effectively telling Teedyuscung that the great Onondaga Council would consider their requests. In one final measure the Iroquois warned, "Be instructed by us, and do as we bid you and you will become a noted man."[16]

The results of the Easton Conference were ambiguous, but all parties left with a feeling of hope. From Morris's perspective there was little settled regarding the prospect of peace with the Wyoming Delawares, but on a greater level the conference broke important new ground in the world of Indian politics. For the first time it seemed that Teedyuscung's commitment to diplomacy and politics might result in a glimmer of freedom for his kin. For all of their ineptitude in the months after Braddock's defeat, the Iroquois Confederacy still had the weight of history and precedence of their side. The Easton Conference officially revealed cracks in their imperial foundations that had been apparent to Teedyuscung for some time, and he made certain to leverage them to his own people's advantage. For the first time in months, peace seemed within reach, but more work was required. It was not exactly familiar territory to Robert Hunter Morris and his aides, but in many ways it was just politics as usual.

ON THE OPPOSITE SIDE OF THE FRONTIER, a conference of another type was beginning. On July 30, as the Easton proceedings were winding down, a force unlike any other made its way east. Although the numbers vary based on account, a war party of approximately thirty-two Ohioans made their way through the wilderness towards Pennsylvania's backcountry. Joining them was a party of twenty-three Canadian militiamen, and they were set to strike out as one unified group. Although the Ohioans had been making war since the fall of 1755, the official declaration of the Seven Years' War had radically changed the dynamics of the Ohio Country. For most of the time thus far the agents of New France could only act as facilitators of the Western Delaware Shawnee warriors' quest to wage war on the English. Now, though, active participation with the Ohioan raiders was no longer controversial but encouraged by the administration in Quebec. Fort Duquesne remained a great hub of activity at the Forks of the Ohio, and more weapons and supplies poured into the region courtesy of its northern line of forts than ever before. By the summer, the residents of Pennsylvania's Frontier counties had grown to live in a state of almost constant dread, and the raiders of this new joint Franco-Ohioan war party planned on stoking those fears.

The leaders of this new season of unified raiding were some of the most recognizable figures in their respective camps. Leading the Frenchmen was none other than Louis Coulon de Villiers, the very same officer who defeated George Washington and avenged his kin two years earlier at Fort Necessity. Throughout his campaign of terror the officer kept a detailed journal, and his diligent records have provided historians with a rare, insiders glimpse at the tactical chaos of Indian war. He stresses that twenty-three Canadian provincials were under his command on July 31, and in these very uncertain times such a statement should be held in very high regard. Coulon de Villiers was a hard and experienced Frontiersman, and Canadian to his core. Born in North America, he had served at Fort Saint-Joseph in modern Michigan and battled the Fox nation in Wisconsin; in that exchange, he witnessed both his father and brother killed. Coulon de Villiers learned a terrible lesson on that day, and that was only compounded when Tanacharison killed his other brother under the young George Washington's command in 1754. He had lived his entire life in the New World, and was willing to die to ensure that its future was under the House of the Bourbon Dynasty. When the war was officially declared, it was not hard to imagine the Canadian was anxious to take up the hatchet, fueled by a potent mix of revenge and duty.

Across from the Canadian was a leader of no less standing, and almost certainly the dominant figure in the raid. Tewea's reputation had swelled to historic proportions over the last seven months, and he was second only to Shingas in his reputation. Known more by his white moniker of Captain Jacobs, Tewea had garnered a reputation for his merciless persistence when tormenting the backcountry. Compared to Shingas, the younger sachem was physically imposing, and held fast the admiration of his fellow Delawares as an athlete, peerless in his ferocity when making war. With these physical gifts and obvious charisma, it was no wonder why even the debutants of Philadelphia trembled when they spoke his name. He had a penchant for raiding deep into the province, and it seemed that no region was too far for Tewea to strike. While he did not know it at the time, his legend was set to grow and he was about to embark on the greatest conquest of his life.

The Canadians and Ohioans had great hopes for this joint strike on the Frontier, and they had embarked out of Fort Duquesne on July 22 with important targets in mind. Sources indicate that their initial strike was determined to be on Fort Shirley in modern Huntington County, but confusion and miscommunication during their eastward trek from Fort Duquesne made that target impractical. Instead, the party settled on assaulting Fort Granville, an audacious move given its position as one of the most acclaimed posts constructed that winter. Fort Granville was so revered that Robert Hunter Morris himself visited the site before its completion and praised its readiness. As Tewea was soon to prove, there was nothing impressive about the fort at all, and his warriors would ensure that its name became famous for all of the wrong reasons.

Fort Granville was located along the Juniata River at a place where the valley tightened to a narrow pass; given the circumstances, it was well placed. It was constructed hastily and garrisoned by seventy-five men from across Cumberland County. They were hearty Frontiersmen of Scots-Irish stock, and highly indicative of the volunteer rangers designated to defend Pennsylvania's west. They were not professional soldiers and they had no formal training, but what they lacked in polish they made up for with a desire to defend their homes and families from sudden Ohioan attacks. Even so, the fort was perpetually undersupplied and undermanned, and the unfortunate souls selected to command the post spoke to this point. In April, Captain James Burd wrote to Morris, "I am convinced that unless these garrisons are re-enforced to one hundred and fifty men each . . . this part of the province will be forced." Even more, his predecessor Edward Ward claimed that of the seventy-five men stationed there, "not One man" was "fit for a Serjeant." It seemed to all parties involved that Pennsylvania's best attempt at protecting its Frontiers was barely functional, and was only one raid away from being revealed as such.[17]

Like his French counterpart, Tewea also had revenge on his mind. Only a few years earlier the sachem had called the region of Fort Granville home, and his story was one shared by many of his fellow warriors. In 1754 a Scots-Irish settler named Arthur Buchanan had ventured with his family to the Juniata River Valley. There, he met Tewea and attempted to broker a deal to purchase a settlement. It was from this meeting that the impressive physique of Tewea was first noted, and where the name Captain Jacobs was coined; it seemed that Buchanan knew of a large German who resembled the sachem and gave him that name. According to European sources, Tewea initially refused the offer but ultimately sold after a day and night of hard drinking. Buchanan's original offer was not to buy all of the Delawares' land, but only a parcel. The entire agreement was founded on a community where settlers and Indians coexisted side-by-side, but the tide of settlement quickly violated that trust. Before long, settlers flowed to the region in large numbers and began pushing the natives out. Frustrated and angry, Tewea very publically burned his entire settlement to the ground and vacated the area. It was then that he took his people west and resettled at Kittanning, where they engrossed themselves in the fiery rhetoric of the Western Delawares.

Although the French sources seem to indicate that Fort Shirley was in fact the intended target of the raid, this deep and personal history with the ground on which Fort Granville stood cannot be overlooked. When Tewea burned his village he did so in a way that sent a clear message to the Scots-Irish who had taken over his territory; settlers at the time even noted the ominous tone of his departure afterwards. With those precursors in mind, it is sufficient to say that Tewea had planned an attack of some kind in the region since he first left. With the arrival of his heavily armed French comrades, the opportunity to deliver a sudden and complete blow to Fort Granville was likely hard to ignore.

For all of its praise, Fort Granville was a soft target. Compounding the logistical difficulties that it faced on July 30 was the fact that its commanding officer, Captain Edward Ward, was not present. Known for his effectiveness, Ward was selected to lead a detachment of rangers to patrol a more vulnerable section of the backcountry. In his place was his chief second Lieutenant Edward Armstrong, and after the superior officer's departure he was left with only twenty-four men under his command. Armstrong was a man with little experience, but tremendous name recognition. Lieutenant Colonel John Armstrong was his brother-in-law, and the highest-ranking officer in the county; in the last several months he had also become Robert Hunter Morris's chief agent in charge of supplying the chain of forts along the Frontier. The elder Armstrong was a vocal proponent of building fortifications in the winter of 1755–56, and he knew better than anyone how ineffective they had been. He was the chief logistical officer of the effort, and he was bombarded weekly with desperate pleas for more weapons, stores, and powder. John Armstrong was a giant on the Frontier, and for the departing Ward to place his younger brother-in-law in command of Fort Granville was a testament to his authority.

In the afternoon hours of July 30 the Ohioans struck the unsuspecting fort. Already in a weakened state, the two dozen men and their families within Fort Granville could do little to curb the Franco-Ohioan assault. Even at full strength it was unlikely that the post would survive, but now, down fifty men, its demise was almost certain. To their credit, the Scots-Irish of Cumberland County held off Tewea from overrunning the fort in his initial attempt, and many hoped that if they could continue to hold firm into the night that the log-structure might survive the attack. To that point, in the summer of 1756 Indians raids had followed a very specific pattern. They were typically sudden and accomplished in a very short amount of time. This ambush tactic was central to the Ohioans' campaign of terror, and the warriors had little experience fighting or winning an extended engagement.

By nightfall, the Frontiersmen had indeed stood firm. In the cover of darkness, the Ohioan warriors did not fall back, however. Instead they retained their position in the trees and continuously fired on the fort. Unlike our modern understanding of warfare, where soldiers weather bursts of machine-gun fire in seemingly endless waves, eighteenth-century warfare was much more deliberate. Rather than being blasted by a steady hail of bullets, the scene around Fort Granville would have been more subdued. The Ohioans would have steadily shouted their infamous war whoops, but the gunfire itself would have been sparse, given the cumbersome nature of period muskets. Thus, for the two-dozen men inside of Fort Granville to fend off an enemy that outnumbered them two-to-one was impressive, but hardly extraordinary. The scene was likely not a continuous panic but, far more likely, an uneasy state of uncertainty broken up by random pops of musket fire.

A credit to his effectiveness and experience, Tewea refused to be deterred. He knew the land well and understood the reasoning behind its selection. The greatest strength of Fort Granville was believed to be its location along the Juniata River; in theory, the river provided a natural barrier to an enemy attack. If the opponent was a conventional army that logic would have been sound, but in the face of an irregular force like the Ohioans it was fatally flawed. At approximately midnight Tewea instructed his warriors to climb into the ravine and inch their way near the fort. When they did so, they were able to encroach within forty feet of the post, and quickly set its timbered walls on fire. Within minutes the wooden Fort Granville was set ablaze, and the inexperienced Lieutenant Edward Armstrong had to contend with both the fire and his Franco-Indian attackers. While details remain sparse, later accounts of survivors recalled the story of a young ranger pleading with Armstrong to surrender. Claiming that he spoke French, the Frontiersman asked the lieutenant if he could negotiate with Coulon de Villiers. "The first word of French you speak in this engagement," Armstrong growled, "I'll blow your brains out."[18]

Throughout the small hours of the morning of July 31 the fire kept spreading. The engagement had persisted for over twelve hours, and in a most unexpected fashion the Ohioans had implemented a textbook siege. With the outer wall of Fort Granville now severely damaged, the rangers inside faced few options. A large hole had been created by the blaze, and the efforts to extinguish had no effect. To rally his men Lieutenant Armstrong ran to the opening and attempted to snuff out the flames, but in doing so put himself in a perilous position. In a sudden flash, a musket ball whizzed through the smoldering timbers and struck him dead. Armstrong's death left Fort Granville with no commanding officer, and the Frontiersmen inside began to accept that their fate might be sealed. According to one survivor it was in this most desperate moment that Louis Coulon de Villiers shouted out from the tree line calling for surrender. Just as he had done to George Washington two years earlier at Fort Necessity, it seemed that the French-Canadian had captured yet another British fort in the wilds of North America. To sweeten the deal, Coulon de Villiers promised that no harm would come to the garrison, and personally guaranteed their safe passage to Fort Duquesne.

The Scots-Irish within Fort Granville understood the consequences of letting the province's most celebrated post fall into enemy hands, and many swore to defend it to the death. Unfortunately, though, the lack of a commanding officer left the rangers in a state of confusion, and cracks appeared in their resolve. Without consulting his comrades, a corporal named John Turner suddenly ran to the gates and heaved aside the large wooden beam that secured the doors. The Ohioans cheered as they rushed the open maw of the fort and the defeated rangers of Cumberland County could do little but throw down their arms. The warriors threw them to the ground, bound their hands, and dragged them out of the gates. In total, French records indicated that twenty-three men, three women, and an unspecified number of children were taken captive. Their fates, like so many others, lay along the shores of the Allegheny River some 150 miles away at Kittanning.

On the morning of July 31, while Robert Hunter Morris left Easton with a renewed sense of hope that a peaceful resolution could be found, Fort Granville stood broken and defeated. The fall of the outpost and the capture of its garrison stood as the greatest Ohioan victory of the entire war, and it would become a watershed moment in the history of the Frontier. Pennsylvania's great response to the campaigns of terror and bloodshed executed by the Western Delawares and their allies was now revealed to be wholly inadequate; it was clear that extreme measures would need to be taken to stem the tide of war. Before vacating the Juniata Valley, Tewea looked to place one final stamp on his greatest conquest, and proceeded to burn what remained of Fort Granville. Just as he had done two years earlier when he originally vacated the region by torching his own village, Tewea once again made a fiery statement. He triumphantly stated that he "cou'd take any Fort that wou'd Catch Fire."[19]

SIX

War Footing

Days after the burning and sacking of Fort Granville, the province of Pennsylvania had still not learned of its destruction. When they did, there would be unanswered questions surrounding the smoking ruins of the post; as the only eyewitnesses were now captives or dead, it was unlikely that the public would ever know. But the narrative of Fort Granville's fall did not end on July 31, and for the survivors it was just beginning. One of the rangers inside the post was Nicholas Barnhold, who had been injured in the fighting. When the warriors triumphantly stormed the defeated post, Barnhold and his fellows were rounded up and led into the westward forests. While most of the able-bodied soldiers were immediately tied up by the Indians, Barnhold was visibly injured and considered to be a nonthreat. After tallying the spoils of war taken from the fort, Tewea led his war party back toward the mountains, and arrogantly made the captives bear the burden of carrying the goods that had been plundered.

As Barnhold walked it was unlikely that he understood the magnitude of his capture, and desperation had overwhelmed him. He was in terrible pain from his wound but dared not to speak of it. As the hostages trekked through the mountains, a fellow captive named Brandon stated that he was too injured to continue. He showed the warriors that he was shot through the knee and could not walk. As a final appeal he also stated that he was a Catholic, and called for the French soldiers to aid him. It would do him no good; Brandon was dragged aside by the Indians and scalped. Even worse, he survived the scalping and continued to scream, allowing the warriors to make an example of him. In front of all of Fort Granville's captives they plunged a tomahawk into his bloodied scalp. Needless to say Nicholas Barnhold kept his own injury as quiet as possible. The journey to Kittanning was a six-day hike over treacherously uneven terrain. With each step Barnhold felt the sting of his wound, but also understood that it had put him at a distinct advantage. Unlike the poor souls who marched with him toward their fates, he was not restrained. He understood, to that point, that very few people taken captive over the last ten months ever returned, and escape was probably his best chance at survival. So, as the party rested at nightfall, Nicholas Barnhold ran. Through brush and brambles, into valleys and over mountains, the young militiaman fled his captors until finally reaching the relative safety of the Cumberland Valley. While his story is just one of many harrowing accounts from the Frontier conflict, his was unique, as it was the first to tell the story of Fort Granville's fall. On August 19 his tale was published in the *Pennsylvania Gazette* for all to read, and the details that he provided shocked the province.[1]

Escaping the terrible snare of Indian captivity was rare, but amazingly Barnhold was not the only one to do so. A fellow ranger named Peter Walker suddenly appeared in the Frontier city of Carlisle on August 20, and one Jonathan Rodmon was found near Fort Augusta eleven days later. In a later case two other militiamen, John Hogan and John Street, turned up in the east a whole year after their original captivity. While these escapes were certainly promising to the families that lost loved ones in prior raids, it may have offered a false hope. It was uncommon for most civilians to free themselves in a time of war, and the frequency of the rangers' success was likely due to the fact that they were young, healthy men of war. Before the fall of Fort Granville there had never been an example of *an entire* garrison being captured, and they were almost certainly more hearty and driven than the typical victim. Their stories were harrowing, but they offer us a complete account of Fort Granville's capture and their subsequent detention at Kittanning.

There was little heard from the Fort Granville captives at their initial abduction, and it can only be concluded that they were either killed or assimilated into Ohioan society. Without a doubt, though, the story of John Turner's fate is the most stunning of the lot. Turner, a native of the Buffalo Valley, was the young soldier who independently decided to open the gates of the fort to surrender his comrades. According to those who escaped, Turner was verbally and physically abused by the French and Indians throughout the westward journey to Kittanning, and regularly chided for his cowardice. Once they had arrived at Kittanning, it was decided that he should be tied to a post in front of a council house to continue the public shaming. Once he had been sufficiently decried Turner was finally put to torture. The warriors that captured Turner lit a fire beneath his ankles to roast his lower half, and as a tribute to his perceived weak constitution the women of Kittanning were allowed to repeatedly pierce his abdomen with flaming wooden spikes. He was next scalped and, still very much alive, given over to the Ohioan children. With the adults cheering them on, the young ones also stabbed at the devastated man, until he was finally killed with a tomahawk. The deathblow came from one of the young children; too small to actually reach Turner's head, a warrior lifted him into the air so that he could chop at Turner's skull from eye level.

Although rare, there were instances in which civilians were able to evade their captors and return to the east. One man named George Woods provides an important account of his time in Indian captivity. Woods claimed that during his imprisonment he witnessed the terrible spectacle of yet another gruesome execution. He recalled that shortly after his capture two warriors led a man to a tree, where they immediately tied him to it. They fastened the man in place by slicing a hole in each of his cheeks and stringing a rope through the gashes. By tying one end to the other, the man was left facing the trunk and unable to move unless he was willing to have his entire cheek torn apart. That, however, was just the start. The two warriors proceeded to threaten him at gunpoint, forcing him to circle the tree to avoid being shot. Upon reaching the other side, he was threatened by a second gun barrel, and the macabre dance continued. Woods noted that the warriors took great pleasure in this spectacle, and they ultimately sliced open his abdomen and tied his intestines to the tree, as well. It was then that they demanded the victim circle the tree a final time, killing himself by pulling his own entrails from his body. In other cases, Woods stated that his captors would often pierce the wrists of their victims, and twist until the limbs were amputated.

When Coulon de Villiers enticed the garrison at Fort Granville to surrender, he gave his word that they would not be harmed; the warriors did not feel obliged to comply. Throughout the Seven Years' War in North America, examples appear that show this clear disconnect between the French and their native allies. In the famous example at Fort William Henry, dozens of Englishmen were killed under a flag of truce. For the Ohioan warriors the captives were vital spoils of war, and no promise from any foreign officer would prevent them from collecting what they believed to be theirs. Even two centuries later, these accounts are difficult to read and their detail is striking. This is undeniable—but it is mostly because they were regularly published in Philadelphia's leading newspapers at the time. It is typically agreed that Benjamin Franklin's *Pennsylvania Gazette* and William Bradford's *Pennsylvania Journal and Weekly Advertiser* were among the province's most widely read media in 1756. These papers regularly published sensational captivity accounts during the age, and, as seen in the modern world, violence sells. But there was more than mere tabloid exploitation associated with the publishing of these graphic stories, as seen in the case of John Craig. Craig was a captive who was lucky enough to escape, and his was the first *detailed* account, published in April 1756. His story was not the first to be recorded, but it was the first to be given serious recognition by the *Gazette* and *Journal.* His vexing tale was read and discussed at length upon its publication, and suspiciously overlapped with Robert Hunter Morris's historic declaration of war against the Delawares. This was no accident; with Benjamin Franklin a vocal advocate of war, his *Pennsylvania Gazette* was the ideal editorial vessel to stir up support among the populace of Philadelphia.[2]

But for all of the attention that these captivity narratives commanded, some did have practical application. In March 1756, a teenager named John Baker reappeared at Carlisle. He had not been seen by his family for over two months. Baker was a figure of some note on the Frontier, as he was an indentured servant to the omnipresent Irishman George Croghan. Since his temporary master was the most prominent British agent living among the Indians, it was likely that the nineteen-year-old Baker shared at least a moderate understanding of the native world. On approximately January 27, Baker was traveling near the garrison at Fort Shirley when he was suddenly accosted by an Ohioan war party; it seemed that his prior knowledge might have saved his life. He was swept away to Kittanning and bore witness to any number of atrocities, but all the while he took mental notes of his surroundings. Whether it was a testament to his familiarity with Indian trails, a penchant for clever survival, or some combination of both attributes, he successfully managed to sneak out of Kittanning. Upon crossing the Allegheny Mountains, the shrewd youngster made a direct line for the city of Carlisle, and soon found himself face-to-face with its most prominent resident. He had information to share, and Lieutenant Colonel John Armstrong was anxious to hear it.

While the precise date of the meeting remains unknown, it almost certainly occurred around the time that Baker arrived at Carlisle in March. Armstrong had a reputation as a logistician, and would not have waited too long to debrief the teenager after his escape. In their meeting Baker carefully described the layout of Kittanning in detail, taking special care to note the location of the village's most high-profile targets. He remembered that the Allegheny River flowed north to south, and the village grew eastward from its banks. He described a large cornfield beside the river, and then "Gentle Hills on Giving Ground." He next pointed out the location of the homes of "Old Pisquetomen," "the Beaver," and "Captain Jacobs" on the village's large, flat plain. Despite the fact that Baker had spent most of the pivotal raiding season as a captive, he seemed to be keenly aware of the developments occurring to the east. He made a special effort to announce that Shingas's cabin—home of Kittanning's most wanted resident, alongside Tewea—was not in the main body of the village at all. He clearly marked it downstream, presumably to aid any future raids on the town and ensure his capture.[3]

John Baker's intelligence on Kittanning would prove vital to John Armstrong, and equally so to his case for attacking it. In the weeks that followed Armstrong formulated a plot to strike at the village, and lobbied to meet with Lieutenant Governor Robert Hunter Morris to discuss his plans. He continued to calculate the logistics of such a mission, and he grew more confident throughout April and May with Morris's formal declaration of war. While the assembly and executive waged their own political wars, the men and women of the Frontier felt as though they had been abandoned by their government. There was no way that they could have known it, but all the while Lieutenant Colonel John Armstrong had already drawn up plans that had the potential of ending the Ohioan raids outright. All that he needed was one more disaster to stir the Frontier into a frenzy, and with the fall of Fort Granville in July it seemed that the final piece was in place. All that he needed now was the approval of the lieutenant governor, and fortunately he knew of one who had nothing to lose by signing off on it.

Robert Hunter Morris's last days as acting executive of Pennsylvania had not gone as he'd hoped. By August 1, he was once again flooded with painful cries for help from the Frontier, and his replacement would not arrive for another three weeks. Fort Granville had been the most egregious attack that the province had experienced yet, and its effects rippled throughout the backcountry. Tewea's strike on the post not only ruined the site but also reminded the populace that they were still at war; furthermore, it showed that Philadelphia could do little to protect them. The political effects of such an action were incalculable, but judging by the reports from the Frontier the colony felt as though it was no better off than it was before any forts were even built. Morris received an update from the fiery Anglican Thomas Barton after the attack. He stated that the backcountry was now experiencing a refugee crisis, and soon it would be vacant.

> I came here this Morning, where all is Confusion. Such a Panick has seized the Hearts of People in general, since the Reduction of Fort Granville, that this County is almost relinquished, & Marsh Creek in York County is become a Frontier. . . . I should be extremely glad to have the Pleasure of a Line or two from you. Your Advice would be of service to me at this Time, when I know not what to do, whether to quit this Place, or to remain a little longer, to see whether any thing favourable will turn out for us.[4]

Barton's words may have painted a bleak picture, but his opinion was hardly unique. James Galbreath of Derry also wrote that "there is nothing heare almost Evry day but murder Commited by the Indians in som part or oather." He continued, "The name or sight of an Indian maks almost all mankind in these parts to trimble, there Barbarity is so Cruel where they are masters, for by all appearance the Devall Commitans, God permits, and the French pays, and by this the Back parts . . . will be Laid west by flight."[5]

These reports made it clear to Morris that he would not escape Pennsylvania without a fight, and he pitied the man who would inherit the mess over which he had presided for the last two years. Since the beginning of the Ohioan raids, settlers had been steadily departing the Frontier in search of a more secure location. Many had come to Philadelphia, which had placed a great burden on its cosmopolitan citizens, and still others trickled southward into Virginia. Those who abandoned the colony altogether subscribed to the general opinion that the Virginians were committed to fighting their enemies with military might, effective or not. Morris had grown accustomed to this type of flight, but after Fort Granville was destroyed even the most stalwart settlers began to wonder if staying in place was the best course of action. This is no better exemplified than in the letter the lieutenant governor received signed by "the Inhabitants of the Town & County of York."

Written with the utmost severity, the petition made it clear to Morris that his control over the West was all but gone. It began cordially, stating, "Your Petitioners are sensible that your Honour has left no measures . . . untried for the protection of our Lives and Liberties." The tone, however, changed dramatically. "You Petitioners hoped their Sufferings were at an end when a Chain of Forts were erected . . . notwithstanding this Skirmishes are made, Murders and Captivities daily committed upon the poor remaining inhabitants . . . the County of Cumberland is mostly evacuated." It continued by claiming that the entire country was now ripe to be overrun, and that even "the Metropolis" could now fall under Indian attack. The petition minced no words, and went so far as to suggest to Morris how he may fix the situation. The signers recommended that an expedition "be sent against Fort Duquesne" and that the lieutenant governor should "recommend our Complicated Distresses to the Right Honourable the Earl of Loudoun," the man currently acting as commander-in-chief all of British forces in North America. They hoped that if Loudon had heard of their plight that he would "command the Recruits now raised in this Province for the Royal American Regiment to be forthwith sent to our relief."

These statements were absurd in their conceptions, and personally insulting to Morris, but they did underscore just how much faith had been lost in the colonial government. For the petitioners of York County, as enthusiastic as they might have been, to offer such radical suggestions to the acting executive showed how desperate they had become. Big ideas aside, the signers did make one recommendation that Morris had not recoiled from; in fact, he agreed with it completely. They finished their petition by stating, "Provincials now in Pay may go against the Enemy and avenge our bleeding Cause! And you Petitioners as in duty bound shall ever pray." The Frontiers were most definitely in a broken state, but Morris's best weapon was also the backcountry's greatest asset: the men of Cumberland County were still willing to fight.[6]

It was under these pretenses that Robert Hunter Morris first began to discuss the possibility of a raid on Kittanning. Sources on the matter are scarce, but it seemed that even before deciding on Armstrong to lead the expedition, Morris had been grappling with the idea of an offensive into the Ohio Country. In his autobiography, Benjamin Franklin recalled being approached by the lieutenant governor to lead a strike on Fort Duquesne. The consummate politician Franklin declined; he thought highly of his abilities as a legislator, but he was no fool. Franklin wrote of the matter:

> And after my Return from the Frontier, he would have had me undertake the Conduct of such an Expedition with Provincial Troops, for the Reduction of Fort Duquesne . . . and he propos'd to commission me as General. I had not so good an Opinion of my military Abilities as he profess'd to have; and I believe his Professions must have exceeded his real Sentiments: but probably he might think that my Popularity would facilitate the Raising of Men, and my Influence in the Assembly the Grant of Money to pay them; and that perhaps without taxing the Proprietary Estate. Finding me not so forward to engage as he expected, the Project was dropt.[7]

Franklin was popular, but not the man for the venture that Morris had in mind. Instead he called up Armstrong, and had many reasons to justify his choice. First and foremost, Armstrong had the respect of the Frontiers. He was an Irishman by birth and was well liked by the citizens of Cumberland County. He was instrumental in creating the county, and was a founding father of its capital city of Carlisle. Upon the passage of the militia bill, it was Armstrong who recommended the now-infamous "chain of forts" that anchored the defense of the colony, and he was promptly made the commanding officer of the Second Battalion of Pennsylvania. In the Fort Granville attack his brother-in-law had been killed, and the desire for revenge may have added an extra bit of incentive to take on the incredibly challenging campaign. Perhaps most important of all, though, Armstrong was a stalwart member of the Proprietary Party. In the wake of the attack on the Juniata, Morris needed to satiate the Frontiers with a grand gesture; a raid on the village considered to be the Western Delaware capital could serve to do just that.

It should be made clear that, for all of Armstrong's strengths, he was no military genius. He had no prior military service, and his greatest martial accomplishment was building part of a road that could have supplied General Edward Braddock. Of course, Braddock never reached his target of Fort Duquesne, and as a result Armstrong's supply route became a spirited waste of time. Given the intensely partisan nature of Morris's executive tenure, it is very likely that Armstrong's position as a key Proprietary Party member in the West cemented his selection as the man that would raid Kittanning. He had already formulated a rough plan of attack based on survivors' reports, but that alone was not enough to make him the most obvious choice. The lieutenant governor had many advisors, at times probably too many, and Armstrong's intelligence gathering could have easily been handed over to a more capable officer . . . but it wasn't. John Armstrong was handselected by Robert Hunter Morris for very specific reasons, and together they would collaborate to work out the fine details.

Armstrong's selection remains a difficult topic of study for modern historians. As part of the strategic planning for the Kittanning Raid, Morris demanded "that the affair was to be kept as secret as possible." The result was at least one or more clandestine meetings with the lieutenant colonel and the executive over a period of several days. There were no minutes kept by any secretaries or lengthy quotations preserved for posterity's sake. Instead there were only partisan officials meeting behind closed doors, and as is so often the case no detailed transcription has survived. There are no recorded dates for these meetings, and likely never will be.

That is not to say, though, that we are left completely in the dark by Morris's insistence on secrecy. In one of these backroom conferences, the lieutenant governor, his council William Peters, and John Armstrong met to explore the potential effectiveness of a Frontier raid. There, Armstrong shared the intelligence provided to him by John Baker, and as a result a very crude map of Kittanning was produced. The map still exists today, and while it has been published quite frequently in the two centuries since there has been little attention paid to the scribblings found beneath it. As Morris and Armstrong weighed their options, it seems that William Peters proceeded to mark down a brief series of notes. It is in these casual writings that historians find some of the only hard evidence of the early conceptualization of the Kittanning Raid.

Writing in an unofficial capacity, Peters wrote his remarks on the map itself and labeled it "Scheme of Expedn to Kittaning." As Armstrong briefed Morris, his council recorded the details that he thought most essential. According to Baker, there were over one hundred able-bodied warriors residing in Kittanning, not including the elderly and the children. Of equal importance were the conditions of Baker's fellow prisoners, which he estimated to be around one hundred souls. If there was to be an attack on the village the commander would need to be cognizant of these prisoners; a simple total-war strategy would have been easy enough. This, however, would be unlike any other assignment yet undertaken in the whole of the Seven Years' War. It was equal parts raid *and* rescue mission, and there were a great number of innocent lives at stake. The men conjectured that for it to be successful the armed force would need to get into and out of Kittanning quickly, but Armstrong remained doubtful. Peters noted that "the Alleghany Hills will not admit any Road that can be travel'd from the Forts Shirley or Lyttleton to that Town in less than 150 Miles or thereabout." That statement carried far more weight than either the lieutenant governor or his aide probably realized, but Armstrong understood it well. If they were going to strike Kittanning, his army was going to have to do so using existing Indian trails.

Among Peters's notations were a series of questions that the three men considered to be most vital when making this raid come to life: If they were going to strike Kittanning, shouldn't it be done quickly? And how many men would be required to both fight *and* liberate captives? If such a mission was to be undertaken, where would the militiamen rendezvous? For the whole thing to work, wasn't secrecy the key? How would they rally enough support for the mission without alerting the Ohioans of their plans?

Fortunately for historians, Peters recorded their responses to these queries. At this early juncture they speculated that no less than 250 rangers would be required to undertake the raid. They would be drawn from the existing garrisons on the Frontier and launch from either Fort Shirley or Fort Lyttleton. Should he accept the mission Armstrong was given assurance that he would be amply supplied, and if possible it was decided he should build a fort in the far West, "some where betwixt the Reas Town and the Alleghany Mountain." Of course this first meeting was really more of a brainstorming session than official assignment, but the more they discussed the possibilities, the more realistic a campaign into the Ohio Country became. Although Morris was keen on the idea to begin with, he was unlikely to even be in the colony to see it through. His replacement William Denny was due to arrive in a matter of days, and it would be his to execute. The person most in need of convincing was Armstrong, and he was satisfied. The consummate bean counter, Armstrong was confident that his initial plans, along with Morris's guarantee of logistical support, made victory at Kittanning a realistic outcome.

Peters wrote that at the end of the undated session, Lieutenant Colonel John Armstrong stated: "If it is the Pleasure of the Governor and Commissioners, I desire to go personally upon this Servise."[8]

By August 16 Morris was in his final days as executive of the province, and he had secretly crafted what he hoped would be a proper retaliation against the warring tribes of the Ohio Country. It was on this date that the lieutenant governor authored a final message to his foes in the assembly in an effort to squeeze any additional funding from the body. In the days that followed the destruction of Fort Granville, Morris had received numerous memos from the various militia officers of the Frontiers claiming that they were dangerously undersupplied; given that these were the rangers that were soon to be raiding Kittanning, it was of the utmost importance that they be properly funded. "The money heretofore granted for the defence of the Province being Expended," he began, "it will be impossible to keep the troops posted on the Frontiers much longer together without their pay." He continued by imploring one final time that the House act to supply the backcountry forts, and officially confirmed the terrible rumors stemming from the Juniata Valley. "What makes this the more necessary is the number of French and Indians that are now on our Border, a body of whom, under a French Officer, have taken and Burnt Fort Granville." He further persuaded that Shingas and his warriors were presently "murdering the inhabitants and laying waste to the Country."

The colony was in crisis, and not just from Indian raids. The burden of a growing refugee populace was already stressing the capital on both social and economic levels, and ethnic tensions were steadily growing. "The People to the west of the Susquehana, distressed by the frequent incursions of the Enemy . . . are moving in the Interior part of the Province, and I am fearfull that whole country will be evacuated if timely & vigorous measure are not taken to prevent it." And with the affixation of his signature, Robert Hunter Morris addressed the colonial assembly for the last time. He offered a spirited case for action, fully knowing that none was going to come; whether deservedly or not, it seemed that a single £60,000 appropriation was to be his greatest legislative accomplishment. By August that money was running dangerously low, and he was liberated in the thought that after two years in office it was no longer his problem to solve.[9]

ON AUGUST 20, THE CITY OF PHILADELPHIA was alive with excitement. William Denny had arrived to become the new lieutenant governor of Pennsylvania, and the streets were buzzing. Outside the courthouse, thousands had gathered to welcome the new executive to the colony, and the Delaware River was filled with ships flying triumphant flags. The crowd at High Street anxiously awaited the first appearance of their new lieutenant governor, and when he appeared on the balcony guns fired off in salute and church bells rang out across the capital. William Denny waved politely to the Philadelphians and gave them a playful smile, but he was likely not what most had been expecting. He came from a military background—that was well known—but he cut an unimpressive figure. He was short and rotund with soft features and an unmistakable large nose, but his affable demeanor compensated for his lack of physical prowess. Denny was not comfortable with all of the fanfare associated with his arrival, but he was a good sport. In truth, by the time of his debut, he had already had enough of Pennsylvania's unique political climate.

He had crossed the Atlantic on a ship called the *Stirling Castle* and made landfall at New York City. Once there, he was hurriedly met by Robert Hunter Morris's commissioner, Richard Peters, likely seeking to gain favor with his new boss. As he made his way across New Jersey, he was informed of what awaited him in his new province; the details were soon to be validated. Denny was a very private man with a penchant for austerity, and he hoped for a *quiet* arrival to the executive mansion in Philadelphia, but he was soon to be disappointed. By the time he reached Princeton, he saw an unexpected welcome party consisting of the king of the Quakers, Israel Pemberton, and his allies. This was presumably the same group of sycophantic Friends that had inserted itself into the Easton Conference only three weeks earlier. After talking briefly with Denny, they proceeded to follow him into Philadelphia and cheer his arrival. It was flattering, but there was more to the ballyhoo than met the eye. The closer he came to the Delaware River, the de facto border between Pennsylvania and New Jersey, the more sarcastic the cheers became. The procession continued to grow and soon included Quaker assemblymen, and before he knew it their true motives were revealed. They were not so much applauding Denny's arrival as they were Robert Hunter Morris's exit. Once in Philadelphia the shouts of welcome were half genuine, and the rest a playful jeering at the outgoing executive; according to those present, the fatigued Morris was celebrating his impending departure as loudly as anyone.

After playing to the crowd at High Street, the introverted Denny soon fled to the seclusion of the gubernatorial mansion to sooth his nerves. He was selected at the behest of the Duke of Cumberland, and was made a lieutenant colonel after accepting Thomas Penn's offer. At forty-seven, Denny was a seasoned military officer but a man of modest presentation; these somewhat awkward attributes made him an ideal candidate to uphold the Penn family's highest obligation. Upon accepting the gubernatorial promotion, Penn briefed Denny on his most pressing duty: do not sign any law that taxed proprietary assets. For all of his personal shortcomings, Denny was a practical man. He valued a solitary life and wanted to dispense with troublesome matters as expediently as possible. When told that he was forbidden from signing any bill that taxed Penn lands, and briefed on the recent quarrels of his successor with the assembly, Denny balked. He seemed to be genuinely conflicted over the matter, and refused to view himself as the puppet figure that Thomas Penn had taken him for. He would sometimes talk openly of his distaste for Penn's refusal to use his own personal fortune for the greater good of the colony, often to his detriment. Richard Peters, a chief ally to Denny but a dyed-in-the-wool proprietary loyalist, wrote to Penn informing him of Denny's statements.

> I know not what to say about the Governor . . . He sometimes talkes in a serious manner so indifferently as to the Proprietors and expresses such unfavourable sentiments of their measures . . . that I

> am at my wits end with respect to his future conduct. He is a triffler, weak of body, peevish and averse to business and, if I am not mistaken, extreamly near if not a lover of money . . . I see so little judgment, and difficulty of access, and such a dread of visits tho' from men of influence and character, so little enquiry into the nature of matters before him. . . . He effects not to know you he says he is appointed by the Crown.[10]

To ease in the transition and passage of power, Robert Hunter Morris worked with Denny for the first days of his tenure. They discussed any number of issues ranging from the obstinance of the assembly to the proposed Kittanning Raid, and Denny's aversion to the rigors of partisanship became clear. Morris noted that his successor was distant and uninterested, and worst of all he was not keen on playing by the rules of the Proprietary Party. Morris wrote:

> He is extreemly slow and formal in everything else as well as business which he seems to hate and from that cause things are much in arrears and will be much more so soon. He sees no body, has no company at his house, dines & sups alone, goes not out, in common conversation with those he ought to trust he is over cautious expressing his fears about being over heard & shutting up the windows and doors even when the subjects are known to all the town, at other times when with men he ought to fear he is quite open concealing nothing and most of all so after a hearty glass. His inclinations are in favour of the Assembly, frequently complains of having his hands tied by instructions, is full of an unmeaning distinction between the King's affairs & the Proprietors as if the Proprietary government was not the Crowns.[11]

Both Morris and Peters harbored serious doubts regarding the political acumen of William Denny. In their correspondence to England they each pointed out his personal faults and claimed that he harbored some fondness for the colonial assembly. In time it would be revealed that Denny would indeed protect the interests of the Penn family within the colony, and he would openly communicate with his legislative counterparts, but he was no friend to the House. In the minds of the most powerful assemblymen, Denny was a welcome change. They knew that he would be an agent of the proprietors, but they also recognized that it would be hard to top the venom and animus that existed between themselves and the departed Morris. Case in point: in prior administrations, it was customary for the assembly to grant a salary of £1,000 to the executive. In the heat of their battles with Robert Hunter Morris over the past two years, though, they had rescinded that gentlemen's agreement. Their resentment was so great for the lieutenant governor in his final months that the House granted him nothing, and they made no effort to hide it. When Denny arrived, the assembly approved a stipend of £600 as a gesture of good faith, and Speaker Isaac Norris welcomed him personally. He wrote, "We heartily congratulate him on his Accession, and hope from the excellent Character we have received of him, his Administration will be as happy for the Province as we shall endeavor to make it easy and comfortable to himself."[12]

The office that Denny had assumed was a contentious one, but he soon discovered that uncooperative Quakers were the least of his worries. On August 20, John Campbell, the Earl of Loudon and commander of all British forces in North America, welcomed Denny by delivering crushing news. One week earlier the forces of Imperial France had besieged and captured Fort Oswego on Lake Ontario, and effectively neutralized the Crown's presence on the Great Lakes. French General Louis-Joseph de Montcalm had scored a decisive blow in the new global war, and it was a costly one. "I must put you on your Guard against every ill Consequence of such an unhappy event," Loudon wrote, "and as you may now expect the weight of the French Indian power on your back, I must caution you to put your Frontiers immediately in the best posture of defence you are able."

Lord Loudon's letter to Denny was harsh and abrupt, and conveyed a tone that expressed the utter urgency of the time. As the British kept their base of operations on the Atlantic Coast and the French in the Saint Lawrence River Valley, Loudon understood that the war on the Frontier would likely determine who was winning in the North American theater of the war. He considered it of the utmost necessity that all of His Majesty's colonial governments cooperate to neutralize the threat; given Pennsylvania's reputation for legislative discord, it is no wonder, then, that he chose to single out Denny directly. "I must in the strongest manner, and from motives of the most interesting nature, demand your Assistance and that of your Province." He continued by explaining that he demanded total cooperation from the colony, and threatened that "if Obstructions to the Service shou'd arise within your Province . . . I must at this Time undertake to Advance it."[13]

Denny barely had time to settle into his new role before being faced with a seemingly existential imperial crisis. If the capture of Fort Oswego was any indication, he would need to rally the colony into action in a way that didn't seem possible judging by his understanding of its recent history. When the post on Lake Ontario fell, Montcalm took with him over one hundred cannon and a shocking 1,700 prisoners. Numbering in those ranks were mostly soldiers, but a great number of noncombatants were also taken captive, including women and children. Furthermore, the capture of Fort Oswego had a chilling effect on the region as a whole; the tenuous alliance that the British had with many of the Western Iroquois nations fell to pieces upon the defeat. It seemed that for every loss that the Crown suffered, it was simply another reminder to their native allies that the French were winning the war. With each of Monsieur Montcalm's conquests, the forces of King Louis could boast that they offered a much more attractive partnership to regional Indian powers. As it stood, Pennsylvania's native alliances were meager at best, and they could not afford to lose what little they had.

Fueled by urgency, Denny immediately set out to corral the assembly into action. On August 24 he penned, "You cannot but have observed that His Majesty, in His Declaration of War, hath Assigned the French encroachments . . . of the Ohio Country . . . as the principal cause of his entering into this just and necessary War." He further instructed the House that "it is particularly incumbent on you to exert yourselves in the Support of such measures as have been or shall be concerted for carrying on the same with Vigour." He reminded the assemblymen of the "Devastations, Cruelties, and Murders" that had plagued the Frontiers, and that the original sum raised in November 1755 had become "quite exhausted." Without a new supply bill, Denny waxed that the men who garrisoned the forts "must be immediately disbanded," and that the people of the backcountry would be left "defenceless to a savage and merciless Enemy, unless fresh supplies are raised for their support."[14]

While Denny wrote the speech with uncharacteristic fire and passion, it was unlikely that he was prepared for the political fallout. In his first foray into the game of Pennsylvania politics, the new lieutenant governor soon learned how fickle it could truly be. With no immediate response issued, Denny proceeded to write the assembly for a second time. In this instance he was sure to include the details provided by Lord Loudon, and made it known that their inaction would greatly hinder the imperial war effort. He wrote, "If the Country is to be saved, it must be the dispatch and vigour of your resolutions. . . . May heaven prosper your Councils; and permit me to remind you that it is your duty to enable me to protect the people and support His Majesty's Government at this Critical conjuncture."[15]

When the assembly finally did respond to his wishes on August 31, they did so in a characteristically coy manner. As it was one of their earliest negotiations with Denny, the response was written with the purpose of defining themselves as superior in the relationship. "As soon as we heard and considered the Governor's Speech, and before we received his Message with the Letter from Lord Loudon, we resolved to give a Sum of Money for His Majesty's Service," they wrote. But, they explained, with a sum as great as £60,000 there would need to be certain caveats in place. First, they asked that Denny present a detailed budget showing precisely how these new funds would be used, to which the executive consented. Done as a show of goodwill on Denny's part, the House next declared that the money would only be signed over if a commission *of their members* were in charge of dispersing it.[16]

Along with protecting Proprietary assets, Thomas Penn had also instructed Denny that all spending should be controlled by a commission under his own supervision, not by the assembly. This has been the case with the first bill signed the previous fall, and it was a modicum of power that the legislators were trying to wrest away from the freshman governor. With this demand, Denny stood firm; he did not care for all of the proprietor's self-serving regulations, but like a good soldier he followed his orders and vetoed the bill. Ultimately, after more sparring, the assembly realized that they had lost the political high ground, and under mounting pressure agreed to supply the Frontiers. If the threat had been of Ohioan raids and not mobilized French armies, it is unlikely that the House would have relented. As seen over the last year they were willing to stand firm while Shingas, Tewea, and their Ohioans burned the backcountry. But now, in the wake of Montcalm's victory at Fort Oswego, their political scorecard had to be set aside. In one final act of defiance, they very purposely cut Denny's proposed figure of £60,000 in half, and supplied only £30,000 to the defense of the colony.[17]

This was only the first of many chinks in the political armor of the Quaker Party. With the fall elections looming, the emergence of the Seven Years' War had made their ideological foundations a terrible liability. Even though the genuinely pacifist members of the assembly were at a historic low in terms of representative proportion within the party, the political machinations of the proprietary wing had hidden that fact. As the average citizens of the Frontier waited in panicked reservation for some kind of help from the capital, Denny's apparent victory had put many of the Scots-Irish firmly on the side of the Penn family. The Proprietary Party had succeeded in roundly painting the whole of the crumbling Quakers as unwavering pacifist zealots, and it appeared that the party's grip on the colonial legislature was slipping. With the arrival of the Seven Years' War, a great political upheaval seemed poised to occur.

AUGUST 20 WAS BECOMING A POPULAR DATE in the colony of Pennsylvania. Along with the ascension of William Denny and Lord Loudon's report on Fort Oswego, Lieutenant Colonel John Armstrong also toiled to piece together an army to march into the Ohio Country. His goals were clearly outlined, but he was having a great deal of trouble achieving them. That evening he sat down to pen a letter to Robert Hunter Morris, still governor as far as he knew, updating him on the status of his campaign. "This Night I expected to have been at Fort Shirley," he began, "but am much disappointed." For Armstrong, a man of no military service but a wealth of logistical experience, the delays he was suffering were a cause of great anxieties. He was supposed to have rallied his troops at Fort Shirley; instead, his would-be army was still spread out across the backcountry. His schedule had suffered wounds that were largely self-inflicted, and a testament to the pitfalls of working with a non-professional army. He was begrudgingly writing from his home in Carlisle, which he had hoped to leave days earlier.[18]

As agreed upon throughout the month of August with the outgoing Morris, Armstrong was to lead 350 men to Kittanning. They would be divided into seven companies and be composed of fifty men each. On paper this sounded foolproof, but putting it into effect proved to be far more difficult. First, Morris and Armstrong had decided that it would be most prudent to pull the men that garrisoned the Frontier forts away from their posts to fill their ranks. As proprietary men they were both well aware that creating a conscript draft in colonial Pennsylvania would be impossible, and by using existing militia they could keep the Quaker Party in the dark as long as possible. Should their political opponents have discovered the raid in its formative stages they would certainly have attempted to inject themselves into the proceedings, and that was a risk that neither executive nor officer was willing to take. There were drawbacks to this strategy, and they manifested quickly. First, by robbing the "chain of forts" of its garrison Armstrong had left the Frontier virtually undefended. There was no great rebuttal for this complaint, except to use the modern colloquialism that the most effective defense was a good offensive. By moving through the Ohio Country on established Indian trails, Armstrong's force could serve as a magnet for roving Franco-Ohioan raiding parties moving eastward. It was not ideal, but it did take the pressure off of settlements in the backcountry.

Secondly, the figure of 350 men was more than likely to be a suggestion than a reality. As the earlier militia laws were based on funding an entirely volunteer militia, no one was compelled to serve against their will. In a perfect setting the men of Cumberland County would have jumped at the chance to seek revenge, but the realities of Frontier life proved that reaching those figures would be extraordinarily difficult. At summer's end, families were harvesting crops and hunting in preparation for winter, and leaving home for an untold number of days or even weeks was a difficult proposition. In order to build a public militia to be sent on a secret mission, Armstrong would require the charms of an officer corps that could woo potential rangers away from their plantations and swell their ranks. He would lead one of his expedition's seven companies himself; that was a given. But filling the remaining six vacancies required the experienced eye of a true Frontiersman, and the thirty-eight-year-old John Armstrong was just that.

His earliest selections were easy to make. As the bulk of his army would be made up of militiamen presently serving in posts west of the Susquehanna, Armstrong called upon the officers already in command to lead their men. They included his brother George Armstrong, Hanse Hamilton of Fort Lyttleton, Edward Ward from Fort George but originally from the fallen Fort Granville, and Hugh Mercer at Fort Shirley. Each brought with them a unique skill set and vast array of experiences, and as a whole they were highly representative of the Frontier experience in colonial America. Hamilton had sparred with Shingas and Tewea at the Battle of Sideling Hill earlier that spring, and Ward was certainly anxious to avenge the capture of his garrison at Fort Granville. Perhaps the most compelling of them all was Hugh Mercer, whose personal history is outdone only by his exploits later in life.

Born in 1726 in Aberdeenshire, Scotland, Mercer was the son of a Presbyterian minister. At the age of fifteen he began his formal education at the University of Aberdeen and graduated with a degree in medicine. It was upon the completion of his degree that Mercer was first attracted to military service, an unthinkable prospect given his erudite upbringing. At nineteen Mercer joined the forces of Charles Edward Stuart's Jacobite Army as a battlefield surgeon. Duty bound, the young man served until the fateful Battle of Culloden in 1746, when the consequences of his decision soon came to bear. In the wake of the defeat Mercer was both a fugitive and traitor, and booked safe passage to the New World, where he attempted to rebuild his life. Once there Mercer settled in the backcountry of Pennsylvania, and soon found himself embroiled again in the politics of empire. In 1755 he served again as a surgeon in General Edward Braddock's march to Fort Duquesne, and the shocking aftermath of the defeat compelled him to greater service. He had never seen such violence and brutality as that inflicted by the Indian enemy, and Mercer promptly determined to serve in a more active role. By 1756 he was a captain and held command over the rangers of Fort Shirley. Although it was relatively minor, his past battlefield experience at Culloden and the Monongahela made him a strong candidate for the position. In the future Mercer would become a close ally of George Washington and die in the service of liberty during the American Revolution. His first true command though would be against Kittanning, and the experience would stay with him for the rest of his life.[19]

The selection of his brother George was also an easy one. Although nepotism had initially spurred George Armstrong's promotion, he had served with Captain Ward at Fort George and was well suited to the wilderness. The two remaining companies would be led by less *conventional* commanders, and they would prove vital in both recruitment and discipline. The men chosen to round out the expedition's officer corps were Cumberland County sheriff John Potter and the Reverend John Steel, each a veritable giant of the Pennsylvania Frontier. From Shingas's earliest raids on the Great Cove, Steel and Potter had set themselves apart as vocal defenders of the region. While colonial authorities decried retaliation from the backcountry, it was the sheriff and "the Fighting Parson" who led the cries of war. The pair were the picture of Frontier grit, and their reputations as genuine firebrands made them natural choices to rally support for the campaign. There was more to the men than their hotheaded demeanor, though, and in many ways they were unique products of the untamed west.

At the heart of any Scots-Irish community on the colonial Frontier were the twin pillars of self-reliance and faith. As the Scots-Irish valued their rights of self-determination more than most of Pennsylvania's ethnic enclaves, the role of sheriff epitomized a community's ability to handle its own affairs. Potter would have been *chosen* to fulfill the role by his peers, and that spoke to his character as a man that could be trusted under even the most difficult of circumstances. Presbyterianism was another element of Scots-Irish society that would be deemed essential; as a veritable commander of his pulpit, John Steel had presided over many of the most influential debates in his region. As is the case for so many marginalized groups in American history, the sanctuary of the church offered the Scots-Irish the privacy to transform it into a de facto assembly. Within the confines of the church, critical decisions would be debated and ultimately decided. Steel was known as a fiery and passionate speaker who was a sensationalist extraordinaire, and his sermons were considered extreme by the modest Quakers of the East. On the Frontier, he was the undisputed champion of the unique brand of outraged defiance that so defined the Scots-Irish experience, and John Armstrong desperately needed his talents.[20]

Armstrong's assembled force was rich in its symbolism. Comprising officers and rangers mostly born in Europe, they had come together for a common cause of defending a land that their forbearers never dreamed of. Stories such as this one have long fascinated modern historians as to the charms of the Frontier, but not everything was as it seemed. Armstrong's men were not assembling to march into some foretold destiny and had no guarantees of triumph; in truth they were not certain if they would even return at all. From the earliest preparatory stages of the expedition, Armstrong and Morris's vision was too grand for its own good. They would be asking men to leave their families and march into a region where few settlers had ever been. Once there they would need to do battle with an Indian enemy of which they knew very little but for scant bits of intelligence, and they were not even that certain of where their target actually was located. As Armstrong wrote to Robert Hunter Morris that night in Carlisle, these were the uncontrollable elements that would have driven the statistically minded colonel mad.

Along with the inherent difficulties of the mission, Armstrong had been receiving regular reports from his subordinates that only added to his grief. Each company was to have three officers and fifty men, but Armstrong soon found that to be a laughable figure. Sheriff John Potter reported that he had only forty-seven men, and the Fighting Parson's company had been whittled down to a meager thirty due to widespread desertion. Captain Ward was already operating at a tremendous loss due to the number of men that had been captured at Fort Granville, and the remaining posts were not much better off. His force remained unassembled and spread thinly across the Susquehanna River Valley, and by his best estimates Armstrong would be lucky to start his march with even three hundred rangers under his command. Those absent, whom Armstrong referred to as "strays," would simply need to be left behind. Of their arrival he wrote, "We shall not wait longer than this day."[21]

For as much of a nuisance as his recruitment drive had been, Armstrong at least took solace in the fact that he was adequately supplied. He wrote to Morris that "there is not one Shilling laid out on this Occasion that does not give me Sensible uneasiness . . . the good end proposed shou'd fail of being obtained." In truth his army was far from flush, but the colonel understood that the trek to Kittanning would require a certain amount of rugged poverty. His men were given muskets and cartridge pouches; some wielded tomahawks, and others carried scalping knives. They each had a canteen to drink from, as the march was certain to be treacherous in the late-summer heat, and there was no shortage of enthusiasm among the present ranks. Armstrong did have one complaint, though—he had no tents. He had ordered them from the commissioners in Philadelphia, but they never came. Always the party man, Armstrong even took this in stride, writing: "They were probably right in keeping back the Tents, as they might have proved an incumberance." It was almost certain that his men would have disagreed with the colonel's sentiments, especially if a sudden rainstorm was to come upon them. Instead the expedition settled for blankets, one per ranger, as their protection from the elements. This fairly minor detail would prove to be enormously important in the weeks to come.[22]

Despite the drawbacks already suffered and those others still certain to appear, Armstrong saw no reason why he should not leave Kittanning in ruins. If not for "the want of Experience and fewness of Our Numbers," he wrote, he saw victory as a near certainty.

With nearly all preparations completed to move forward with the campaign, Armstrong next relayed some vital intelligence to the capital. According to the colonel, one of the escapees from Kittanning, named Peter Walker, passed on information that was vital to the security of the colony. Walker had stated that "not less than 120" of the French and Ohioans raiders who attacked Fort Granville returned to the Allegheny River Valley safely, and only one Frenchman was wounded. Furthermore, Walker impressed upon Armstrong that Shingas and Coulon de Villiers "designed very soon to attack Fort Shirley with four hundred Men." These numbers were undoubtedly inflated, but the warning still held true. With the rangers now preparing to launch, all of the forts west of the Susquehanna would be left with only a skeleton garrison to defend them. Unless Armstrong could rally his men and march within a few days, he would be forced into a terrible dilemma: either he marched with great urgency toward his target, or he would necessarily have to hold back to defend Fort Shirley. As far as Armstrong was concerned, he had already made up his mind. "As Fort Shirley is not easily defended, and their Water may be taken possession of by the Enemy, it running at the Foot of a high bank Eastward of the fort . . . I am of Opinion, from its remote situation, that it can't serve the Country in the present Circumstances, and if Attacked I doubt will be taken if not strongly Garrissoned."[23]

Armstrong added further that "Lyttleton, Shippensburg, and Carlisle . . . are the only Forts now built that will . . . be Serviceable to the Publick." The colonel gave his regards to Morris and stated that he hoped to begin his march to Fort Shirley as soon as possible, but made no promises of steady communication with the capital. Living in Cumberland County had imprinted a healthy paranoia into its residents, and John Armstrong knew that prying enemy eyes were all around him. "I dare not venture any thing of consequence now with a single Messenger," he wrote ominously, "so many Indians being in the woods."[24]

One week to the day from William Denny's ascension to lieutenant governor, August 27, he finally sat in with the provincial council. Present were eight of the most trusted proprietary agents in the colony, as well as the now–former executive Robert Hunter Morris. Their meeting was one of the utmost importance, and despite being the new chieftain, Denny was still second in the room to the more experienced Morris. As the men exchanged pleasantries, Morris presented Denny with the previously described letter by John Armstrong written on August 20. The colonel's correspondence was read aloud to the room, and the new governor looked quizzically at his colleagues for some explanation as to what he was hearing. Amazingly, it was not until that very moment that William Denny had ever heard mention of an impending raid into the heart of the Ohio Country. Morris explained that "Shingas and Jacobs, the two heads of the Enemy Indians lived at Kittannin[g], a Town about twenty Miles above Fort Duquesne."

He continued by stating that "from thence the Indians were fitted out for their Incursions on this and the Neighbouring Provinces and the Prisoners and Plunder carried there." To this, Denny was likely stunned; he had been acting lieutenant governor for an entire week, and had never been briefed on a major military operation coalescing within his colony. Morris stated "that the Affair was to be kept as secret as possible, and the Officers and Men ordered to March to Fort Shirley, and from thence to set out for the Expedition."

As a lifelong soldier, Denny quietly accepted the furtive nature of the mission. He knew the dangers presented by an intelligence leak, as well as the lives at stake should the Ohioans have heard of the impending attack. As the meeting continued Morris undoubtedly explained the many benefits of the proposed raid both on and off the battlefield. If Kittanning were to fall, one of the major capitals of the Ohioan world would be eliminated. The warriors would likely have to regroup at another village, which would subsequently prove injurious to it as well. With only finite resources on hand, the dozens of Kittanning's residents would be moved to Kuskuskies or Logstown and subsequently drain their supplies. Moreover, support for the Quaker Party's unique brand of politics was at a historic low, and should the Kittanning Raid be a success it could prove to be a major boost in the upcoming fall elections. If Armstrong and his Frontiersmen were victorious, their triumph could usher in an unexpected proprietary majority in the Pennsylvania Assembly, and grant the party near-total control over the colony's affairs. As Morris stated, the raid "will be of great use to the public, as it will raise the spirits of the people and serve to remove that dread and panic which has seized the generality." For Denny, Morris, and the other power brokers of the Proprietary Party, the stakes surrounding the Kittanning Raid suddenly became much higher.[25]

SEVEN

The Raid

On the morning of August 30, Lieutenant Colonel John Armstrong and his three hundred militiamen marched from Fort Shirley. For nearly a year the Pennsylvania backcountry had been victimized by Shingas and Tewea's raiding Ohioans, and the men of Cumberland County were poised to strike back. It was one month to the day that Fort Granville had been attacked, and for the first time in its history the colony of Pennsylvania had sanctioned an army to march into enemy territory under its own flag. A generation earlier William Penn's Peaceable Kingdom would have wept at the thought of such a venture as the Kittanning Raid, but the greater circumstances of an imperial world left them with few alternatives. For John Armstrong's civilian army the march ahead of them was a trek into the unknown; many settlers had gone into the Ohio Country against their will, but few had ever returned. If the mission laid before them was a success, the reign of terror inflicted by the Ohioan warriors and supported by New France could be brought to a sudden and violent end. With steady resolve, the men of the Pennsylvania backcountry mobilized and began their march.

John Armstrong was a voracious consumer of intelligence, and he wanted as much information as possible before he started his march. For this reason he had dispatched the companies of Captains George Armstrong and Edward Ward ahead of the army days earlier to investigate the ruins of Fort Granville. He made tentative plans to regroup with the advanced companies on September 3, where the reunited force would continue their march to Kittanning. It was this desire for information that also persuaded Armstrong to petition the young indentured servant John Baker to join him on the expedition; Baker was one of the few captives to escape Kittanning, and now, only five months later, he agreed to return. The colonel was grateful for the young man's brave service to his province, describing him as "our best assistant." For the nineteen-year-old Baker the favor was a great one. In joining the campaign there was no guarantee of safety, and if captured he would likely be tortured to death in a most brutal way by warriors still resentful of his previous escape.[1]

By September 3, Armstrong was pleased to find that his army was proceeding on schedule. In the aftermath of the previously messy three weeks, the colonel was pleased to have his force arrive at Beaver Dams safely. Once there, he reunited with his brother's and Ward's companies, and his men settled in for the night. Beaver Dams was located on the North Branch of the Juniata River, just a short distance from the abandoned Delaware village of Frankstown. It was at this location that Armstrong took account of the ruined Fort Granville, and contemplated the events that had claimed his brother-in-law's life a month earlier. The leaders of the advanced companies reported that the damage to the fort was total—that it had been entirely destroyed. The army set out early the next morning.

Almost immediately, though, the expedition stalled under the fears of an Indian ambush. Before setting out, a small scout party returned to inform the colonel that they "had discovered the Tracts of two Indians about three Miles on this side of the Allegheny Mountains." From the beginning, the officers understood that to be spotted in any form by a stray war party could doom the secrecy on which the campaign was founded. If there were in fact spies in the area, it would not be long before other warriors would arrive to confront them. Armstrong was cautious, and recounted: "From the freshness of their Tracks, their killing of a Cub Bear, and the marks of their Fires, it seemed evident they were not twenty-four Hours before us, which might be looked upon as a particular Providence in our Favour that we were not discovered."[2]

It was determined that the area was clear. John Armstrong next needed to make a decision as to the route that he would use to approach Kittanning, and there were two distinct options available to him. The most prominent routes west for any enterprising Englishmen were well known and heavily traveled Indian paths, and each had their own unique quirks. The first was the Raystown Path, and the second was called the Frankstown Path. Armstrong himself had traveled the Raystown Path a year earlier when constructing the abortive auxiliary supply road for Braddock's army; he knew it was a shorter distance to Kittanning, but over very treacherous land. The colonel again relied on his past Frontier experiences, and decided that even though it was longer, the Frankstown Path was the better option. As his army marched it would be doing so under constant threat of Indian attack, and in the event of an ambush he wanted to ensure that his men would be fighting on good, level ground. The captive-turned-guide John Baker agreed, and claimed that there was really no *easy* way to reach their target. With a short deliberation, the Frankstown Path was chosen as the more secure option. This route was not without its own dangers, however. The Frankstown Path was a veritable superhighway of the Ohioan world, and it was heavily traveled. If a raiding party was to venture to the east, it would in all likelihood use the Frankstown Path and subsequently collide head-on into the Pennsylvanians. With security being his greatest concern, and remembering the cumbersome terrain of the Raystown Path, Armstrong remained steadfast in his decision, and on September 4 they proceeded west.[3]

The march was slow, and the days were routine. Averaging approximately two miles per hour, the three hundred rangers marched in a narrow line that stretched for over one hundred yards. All the while they trudged west, the force roughly shadowed the western reaches of the Susquehanna River, a route well known to Indian travelers. By September 5 the expedition had reached what many migrating Delawares had called "the Canoe Place," named as such because it was the farthest one could travel by water on the Susquehanna River. Once the Canoe Place was reached, the travelers would need to abandon their watercraft and proceed toward the Ohio Country settlements on foot. It was also at this location that the Frankstown Path diverged and became known as the Kittanning Path. Given the size of their force and the many pack animals that came with them, moving via water was not a realistic possibility for Armstrong, and his men made the eighty-mile journey from Frankstown to Kittanning on many a sore foot.[4]

The Pennsylvanians camped for the night at one of the few locations that any of them had ever heard of—a place called "the Forty-Mile Lick." It was located roughly forty miles from Kittanning, and had a notorious history: it was here that returning warriors would stop to groom their captives, cutting the prisoners' hair and altering their physical appearances before bringing them into their home village. While Armstrong made no note of that fact during his march, it was likely his army was traveling the same route that so many unfortunate souls had over the previous eight months. From this location the colonel dispatched "an Officer, with one of the Pilots and two Soldiers" to move far ahead of the army and reconnoiter the village of Kittanning itself. It would be a dangerous assignment, but Armstrong needed whatever meaningful intelligence he could gather; should the scouts be discovered, it would mean almost certain death.[5] While the commander never mentioned the names of these rangers, a secondary account of the expedition identifies them as James Chalmers and Thomas Burke.[6] On the evening of September 5 the army made camp, and John Armstrong led his men in prayer service.[7]

The expedition continued on their trek and on September 6 stopped to fill their canteens at a natural water source known as Shaver's Spring. Named for the Indian trader Peter Shaver, the location was an overdue godsend to Armstrong's men. While little remains of the Indian trails or the Pennsylvanians' presence there, Shaver's Spring is one of the few landmarks that can still be found today. A plaque was erected over the site in 1963 by the James Le Tort Chapter of the Daughters of American Colonists. Thirsty travelers be warned, though; the spring has since been covered up, and the plaque most humorously sits in the basement of the Hadley Student Union Building on the campus of Indiana University of Pennsylvania.[8]

By September 7 the men of Cumberland County had been marching for a week. The land was rough, and consisted of a steady rhythm of hills followed by plunging valleys. These were not mountains, by any measure, but the fact that they were covered in thick forest made navigation a difficult affair. The trees of the Ohio Country were endless and uncut, many ancient with trunks of a circumference measuring over fifty feet. Even in the daytime the leafy canopy above them was so dense that it blocked out the sun almost entirely. It was a place like they had never seen before, and as the sun set the edginess returned. Suddenly every cracking branch and rustling leaf was an ambush waiting to strike, and even the most experienced Frontiersman was fraught with unease. Finally, no more than ten miles from their target, Armstrong's four-man scouting party arrived back at camp. The colonel was puzzled by their early return, and wrote: "We met them on their Return, and they informed us that the Roads were entirely clear of the Enemy, and that they had the Greatest Reason to believe they were not discovered; but from the rest of the Intelligence they gave, it appear'd they had not been nigh enough the Town either to perceive the true Situation of it, the Number of the Enemy, or what way it might most advantageously be attacked."[9]

Night was falling, and John Armstrong was able to gather nothing of value from his scouts. He did not know the location of the village, the number of enemy combatants within it, or even their state of readiness. The scout party had not laid eyes on Kittanning at all, and likely did everything possible to avoid it. The only bit of helpful information that they provided to their commander was that they had seen no Indians during their ranging. Armstrong had no idea how far they had even traveled, but it indicated to him that the trail was probably clear for at least a few more miles. And so, they advanced.

As midnight approached on September 7 one of Armstrong's advance scouts hurried past his fellow rangers to meet with the colonel.

Less than five miles from Kittanning, he stated that he had seen a fire blazing along the path only a short distance ahead. He claimed that "he perceived a Fire by the Road side at which he saw two or three Indians a few perches distant from our Front." With this news, the expeditionary force was poised to confront its first Indian enemy of the entire campaign. Since the beginning, the army had feared an Indian encounter at every turn on the wilderness trail, and now in the black of night it seemed that the time had come. For Armstrong it could not have happened at a worse time. His men had been on a forced march all day and had tallied over twenty miles that day; the last thing he needed was a sudden engagement only a few hundred yards from his intended destination.

Armstrong sent the scout back to once again spy on the unsuspecting Indian party, and the figure was confirmed as "not above Three or Four Indians at the Fire." His men were tired, but they were anxious for a fight. Given their superior numbers the colonel's fellow officers suggested they could "immediately surround and cut them off," but Armstrong demurred. He knew that if a single one of the unsuspecting natives had escaped "it would have been the Means of discovering the whole design," and he decided to take a more cautious route. Rather than simply overwhelming the men and hoping they were alone, Armstrong decided to *sneak around* the four-man party. This was accomplished by ordering the rear companies of his army to move backwards, subsequently allowing the most forward companies to retreat. The entire concept of rerouting an army of three hundred to simply bypass a party of four seemed excessive, but not to the disciplined Armstrong. In his estimation, the entire raid depended on the element of total surprise, and what better than an attack under the cover of darkness. If the army waited too long they would be faced with a daytime assault, which was less than ideal. As Armstrong wrote, "the light of the Moon . . . wou'd not admit of our staying until the Indians fell a Sleep."[10]

To expedite the process Armstrong elected to stash his most weary horses, as well as the army's goods and blankets, in a nondescript gully nearby. To protect the supplies he assigned a force of thirteen men under the command of a Lieutenant James Hogg to "watch the Enemy but not attack them till break of Day, and then if possible to cutt them off." These orders seemed to be predicated on the main body of the army beginning their attack in the early morning hours; if the main assault had already begun, there was no harm in Hogg attacking the small Indian party by dawn, as the trap had already been sprung. Not much is known of Hogg other than the fact that he was a member of Captain George Armstrong's company and was likely recommended as a good candidate for the job to Armstrong's brother. Whatever the case, Hogg and his men stayed behind and quietly watched the small gathering of warriors in the forest while the rest of the army pressed on.[11]

After making the decision to circumvent the Indians on the path ahead, Armstrong was faced with the terrible burden of stepping off the well-defined path. That meant taking an army (now only 290 strong) into the forest with no sense of direction in the blackest part of the night. As if the slowness of the campaign had not tried the colonel's patience enough, he next had to watch his men meander through the dense foliage of the forest floor, grasping blindly for whatever lay ahead. In the small morning hours of September 8, Armstrong's frustration was palpable, and his description equally vivid: "a Circuit off of the Road, which was very rough and incommodious on Account of the Stones and fall Timber, in order to prevent our being heard by the Enemy at the Fire place. This interruption much retarded our March; but a still greater Loss arose from the Ignorance of our Pilots, who neither knew the true Situation of the Town nor the best Paths that lead thereto . . . ."[12]

For much of the next two hours Armstrong's seven companies tripped and stumbled their way through the wilderness. In the darkness of night the men relied on the soldiers to their front to warn them of downed trees and snaring vines, but few had any sense of where exactly they were going. Finally they began to descend a great hill, and at the bottom they found the shores of the Allegheny River. At that hour of the day they could not have perceived the size of the river, and if they could they would have seen a waterway unlike any they had seen since leaving the main flow of the Susquehanna River. Just forty miles south sat Fort Duquesne with two hundred French soldiers, and an untold but undoubtedly larger number of native warriors from across the

Northeast. In the darkness they saw only white strands of moonlight broken by the gentle current of the river, and heard nothing but the rushing of its southward current. For all of the wonderment that the Cumberland County men must have experienced at being some of the few Europeans to ever see the Allegheny River, it quickly passed. They had marched for over a week using all of the prescribed trails, and they were now on the banks of the Allegheny. But one question loomed large in their minds: *where was Kittanning?*

In the general confusion of those tense minutes, Armstrong had attempted to make careful notes of their location. His best guess put them "about one hundred Perches below the main Body of the Town." The estimate was accurate, and after he directed his army to proceed quietly north he began to hear the ominous precursors of Indian settlement. "To which place," Armstrong wrote, "rather than by the Pilots, we were guided by the Beating of a Drum and the Whooping of the Warriors at their Dance." The colonel was critical of his guides throughout the expedition, especially then, but in fairness they were hardly at fault. Few Europeans had ever been to Kittanning, and even fewer ever returned to describe it in detail. As for Armstrong and his men, they certainly understood that they were now in uncharted territory, and they would need to exercise extreme caution.

While the army slinked along the river, the drumbeats and whoops began to intensify. These were no acts of war, though, but the simple routines of daily life in an Ohioan village. Kittanning was a settlement of families, friends, and neighbors, and although their perceptions of war were the stuff of nightmares, the village itself had a life outside of combat. On their approach to the village, Armstrong noted that they suddenly heard a man who "whistled in a very singular manner." At this, all three hundred Frontiersmen paused, "at which we immediately sat down." Armstrong continued "after passing Silence to the rear, I asked one Baker . . . whether that was not a Signal to the Warriors of our Approach?" The young Baker had been held at Kittanning for weeks, and he set his commander at ease. "He answered no, and said it was the manner of a Young Fellow's calling after a Squa [Squaw] after he had done his Dance . . . "When the colonel signaled for his troops to continue, the same man "clean'd his Gun and shot it off before he went to Sleep." The tension must have been enormous for the rangers, as even these basic comings and goings of Ohioan life had shaken their resolve.[13]

When the Pennsylvanians first laid eyes on Kittanning, it was not what they expected. As they had moved along the eastern side of the Allegheny, the cluster of villages were spread out all before them no more than half a mile away. For all the bluster and commotion that they had heard over the last hour, by the time they actually looked on Kittanning things had gone quiet. Just as their speculative map had shown, the main part of the village had a large cornfield on the floodplain near the river's edge. Above it were a collection of logs and bark homes, and across the water there seemed to be a smattering of other cabins. None of these details surprised Armstrong, as he had studied the map for weeks, but the location of the residents did. Rather than sleeping in the center of the village the colonel watched as several men rested beside fires *within* the communal field of corn. Armstrong once again asked the escapee, Baker, what he was seeing. "Gnats," Baker said. As Armstrong explained, "the Night being warm and that these Fires wou'd immediately be out, as they were only designed to disperse the Gnats." It was a small comfort for the Delawares, but an important one. The small insect swarms were known as "ponkies" to the natives, and they would have been brutal in the summer heat; only the smoke from a burning fire could keep them at bay. Just forty miles north, another village called Ponks-utenik (modern Punxsutawney) on the Mahoning Creek was so infested by the creatures that its name literally translated to "town of the flies."[14]

With the peoples of Kittanning clearly asleep and their situation unchanging, the commander ordered his men to rest as well. They had marched over twenty miles that day, and a raid at that precise moment could not be done at full strength. Instead, the colonel believed that a strike just before daybreak while the Delawares and Shawnees were still asleep would be just as effective. "All this time we were Obliged to lay quiet and hush," he wrote, "till the Moon was fairly set." They would attack at dawn.[15]

ON THE MORNING OF SEPTEMBER 8 the village of Kittanning was quiet, and with the exception of a few chirping birds and the flowing Allegheny there was not a sound to be heard. The residents of Kittanning slept in their cabins and in the cornfield, and across the river the same was occurring. The western shore of the Allegheny had some secrets of its own, though, and neither John Armstrong nor his officers had any sense of what it held. Along with the cabin of Shingas, the smattering of cabins that comprised west Kittanning also held a small party of French agents who had arrived earlier that day from Fort Duquesne. As Kittanning only sat a mere forty miles north of Fort Duquesne, its commandant Jean-Daniel Dumas would have been given regular intelligence briefings on the activities of the village. Whether there for combat purposes or merely in logistical support, the presence of these French soldiers is a testament to the global reach of empire during an imperial war.

Since John Armstrong was unaware of the French presence in Kittanning that morning, it had no impact on his decision to attack the village. Just before dawn he had ordered "some proper Hands . . . immediately dispatched, and the weary Soldiers . . . roused to their Feet . . ." Armstrong was an officer who valued contingencies, and his quick study of the landscape informed his next preparatory maneuvers. When viewed from above, Armstrong saw that Kittanning had two natural features that made it highly defensible. The first was the Allegheny River that flowed on its western edge, and the second was a high, tree-covered ridge that provided cover to its east. The cluster of villages lay directly between these two natural obstacles, which had sheltered its location. Armstrong was a neophyte when it came to military matters, but even he recognized that this blessing of nature could just as easily entrap the Indian residents if done correctly.

Still operating under the cover of darkness, the colonel ordered a portion of his men to leave the main body of the army and assume control of the hill overlooking the town. In his estimation, this would maximize the damage inflicted by the raid, as it would block the escape of Kittanning's residents. He explained this methodology in detail:

> A proper Number of sundry Officers were ordered to take the End of the Hill, at least one hundred perches, and so much further, it being day Light, as wou'd carry them Opposite the upper part or at least the Body of the Town. For the lower part thereof and the Corn Field, presuming the Warriors were there, I kept rather the larger Number of the Men, promising to postpone the Attack in that part for Eighteen or Twenty Minutes, until the Detachment along the Hill should have time to Advance to the place Assigned them.[16]

Upon its completion, this preemptive flanking maneuver had effectively divided Armstrong's force into three separate components. The main body army was to push directly into the village proper, the hilltop companies were to attack in delayed support, and thirteen soldiers under the command of Lieutenant James Hogg remained in position some six miles west. With all of the pieces in place and the pinkish hues of dawn washing over the Allegheny River Valley, the Pennsylvanians began their assault. According to one participant, "the form in which we made the attack was, our captains stood all in rank, each company behind their captain."[17]

When constructing an analysis of the Kittanning Raid, sources typically cite two men. The first is Lieutenant Colonel John Armstrong himself, and the second is one Robert Robison. While Armstrong wrote his account immediately following the raid, Robison described his experiences decades after. Given that fact, his details must be taken with a degree of skepticism, but as many of the key events match Armstrong's account they will be considered as reliable. According to the colonel, his men were ordered to rush forth, and "the Attack was begun in the Corn Field . . . a party being also dispatched to the Houses, which were then discovered by the light of the day." On this detail the two sources agree, as Robison recalls that Armstrong shouted, "'Every man do for himself!'" And then "we rushed down into the town."[18]

Immediately upon reaching the outskirts of the village, the rangers encountered their first enemy. The morning silence was splintered by the sudden outbursts of barking dogs, and an Indian man emerged from his cabin to investigate. When he stepped outside he saw the onrushing Pennsylvanians and "held his hand, as shading the light from his eyes." He covered his face with good reason, because within seconds five soldiers fired on him, and he soon ran for cover. By Robison's account the man was unharmed, but he fled while shouting "'*Shewanick*,'" which the rangers believed "signifies white men." By all accounts, these were the opening shots of the Kittanning Raid. The village seemed simple enough—log cabins, huts, and an utterly unprepared population. But within minutes Armstrong's men soon found the great complication of the attack. The rangers were surprised when in the smoke and haze a white woman emerged from one of the homes. She was a prisoner and young, and emerged from the cabin with her hands in the air. Robison writes, "The guns were firing so fast she got frightened, and ran back to the house again, where she got a grain of swan shot through her arm." It must have been a chaotic scene. From the earliest planning stages with Robert Hunter Morris, Armstrong had made the rescue of captive settlers a priority of the mission. Now, in their first attempt, his rangers had been so consumed in the wildness of the attack that they actually fired on their first hostage. All was forgiven, though, as Robison said "she then made out a second time and was received by us."[19]

While the initial melee in the town had begun, the remaining half of Armstrong's men had taken to the cornfield along the river. This was most likely a rout, as the Delawares were asleep among the stalks and could not see the approaching Frontiersmen. At worst, the Pennsylvanians probably pounced upon them as they slept, but in all likelihood the surprised natives arose and ran for the safety of the town. The colonel stated, "Our Men with great Eagerness passed thro' and Fired in the Corn Field, where they had several Returns from the Enemy." He also noted that, at the same time, warriors on the opposite shore also began to fire their guns toward the raiders.

It is of great importance to note that Armstrong's attack on Kittanning was not designed to be a battle. In a traditional battle, two armed forces square off in an organized encounter; even in the case of a meeting engagement this holds true. Braddock's defeat was certainly a one-sided affair, but it was still fought under these unwritten rules. The attack on Kittanning, however, met neither of those standards. It was a surprise attack on an unsuspecting settlement, no different from the types that Shingas and Tewea had been leading on the backcountry for

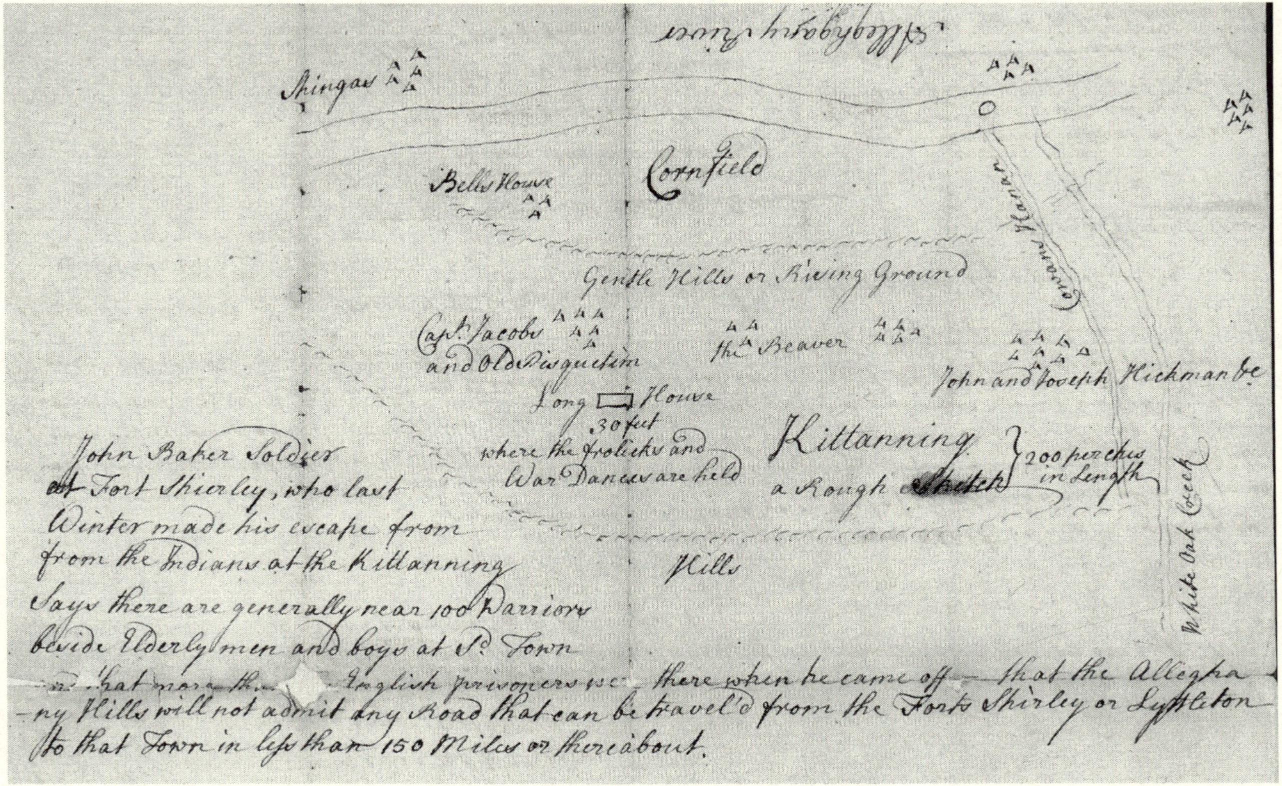

John Armstrong described his plan to raid Kittanning to the Pennsylvania governor and commissioners. The map was drawn using information from a soldier who escaped captivity in Kittanning. The Allegheny River is at top. Shingas's settlement is located in the upper left opposite the large cornfield between the river and Kittanning. The settlements of Captain Jacobs (Tewea), the Beaver (Tamaqua), and "Delaware Jo" Hickman are identified from left to right, as well as the village's Long House. (*American Philosophical Society*)

months. It was a *raid* in every sense of the word, and by September 1756 that seemed to be the default nature of Frontier combat. For this reason it is very difficult to paint a timely, tactical analysis of the event, for its entire foundation was based on surprise, shock, and awe. But as the fighting developed into a back-and-forth affair, a battle was precisely what it became.

It was in these early stages of the raid that the major players began to emerge, none more famous that Tewea himself. According to Armstrong, "Captain Jacobs immediately gave the War-Whoop, and with Sundry of other Indians . . . cried the White Men were at last come, they would have Scalps enough." There must have been a fascinating divide within the cluster of villages that made up Kittanning. Despite being the far more powerful sachem, Shingas's residence on the western bank of the Allegheny kept him away from the chaos of the raid. He is never mentioned in the sources, either Indian or Pennsylvanian, as having participated in the battle; even more, there was no evidence that his participation was ever sought. Instead, Tewea appears as the dominant war chief on that day, and a rallying point for his fellow warriors. This may have been due to Shingas's absence from Kittanning at the time, but sources are unclear as to his whereabouts. The colonel recognized his adversary's leadership role, and elaborated that Tewea "at the same time ordered their Squas and Children to flee to the woods."[20]

The next phase of the battle, which was undoubtedly the longest portion of it, came when the warriors had taken cover within their wood and bark cabins. As previously mentioned, eighteenth-century firefights tended to be much more deliberate than most contemporary battles. Because of the lack of automatic weapons and the tedious nature of period muskets, engagements were slow-paced exchanges of single-shot fire. In this, however, is found some startling revelations, particularly on how European tactics and technology had changed Indian warfare. Ever the astute observer, Armstrong noted that many of the traditional-looking Delaware cabins in Kittanning were equipped with fairly standard European defenses. The colonel noted that some of the dwellings had built-in portholes for firing, a technique common in European posts but not typically in their Indian counterparts. Unlike previous raids on McCord's Fort and Fort Granville, the Ohioans had effectively turned the tables on the Frontiersmen. Whereas before it was Shingas, Tewea, and their war parties firing from out in the open, now the Pennsylvanians found themselves there. From the safety of their fortified cabins, the residents of Kittanning could draw the battle out at length and suffer minimal casualties. Armstrong was astonished, and claimed "from the Advantage of the House and the Port Holes, sundry of our People were wounded, and some killed." He recalled "the Indians always firing, whenever an Object presented it self, and seldom mist [missed] of Wounding or killing some of our People." Such was the nature of the colonial Frontier, a place of conflicting worldviews and blended new ones.[21]

The back-and-forth firefight in Kittanning had lasted for hours, and John Armstrong found that "returning the Fire upon the House was ineffectual." As his men had settled into their positions behind the trees and cabins, it was clear that their efforts to remove the entrenched enemy were only wasting ammunition. It was then that the colonel gave a new order, one that drew on his past experiences on the Frontier and probably some deep-seated emotions from the death of his brother. Recalling the fall of Fort Granville, Armstrong directed his men to torch the buildings. He "ordered the contiguous Houses to be set on Fire; which was performed by Sundry of the Officers and Soldiers, with a great deal of Activity . . ." The decision to set fire to the Indian cabins was exactly the change that Armstrong needed. As the raid itself was predicated on surprise, the firefight that developed chipped away at its effectiveness. The attack had been organized to strike fast, retreat quickly, and leave nothing behind. The militiamen stood to gain nothing from a prolonged siege, and the burning of the cabins put a ticking clock on Tewea's defensive strategy. "Presently after," Armstrong penned, "a brisk fire begun among the Houses, which from the House of Captain Jacobs was return'd with a great deal of Resolution." It was a great moment for the colonel, and a strong statement to his martial effectiveness which he had yet to show. But the joy was not to last; shortly after the blaze began, Armstrong was dropped by a musket ball that sunk into his shoulder. According to Robison, upon being struck Armstrong shouted: "Is there none of you lads, that will set fire to these rascals that have wounded me, and killed so many of our men?" In his account the commander makes no reference to this query, but in the aftermath of being shot Armstrong's words will certainly remain a mystery.[22]

Thus arrived one of the critical points of the raid, and its fine details remain contentious. According to Robison, after Armstrong was shot the fires had begun to spread at a rapid rate. Now consuming most of the heart of the village, Tewea became a vocal agitator to his attackers. Keeping up his fire from within his cabin located in the center of the village, the Pennsylvanians began to shout for his surrender. One man, listed as a private named John Ferguson, snagged a flaming piece of bark and held it against Tewea's dwelling. Done in an apparent response to Colonel Armstrong's earlier challenge, the young man "swore by the *Lord God* that he would, he goes to a house covered with bark, and takes a slice of bark which had fire on it, he rushes up to the cover of Jacob's house and held it there until had burned about one yard square, then he ran, and the Indians fire at him the smoke blew about his legs but the shot missed him . . ."[23]

With his home burning, Tewea remained defiant, claiming "he was a Man and wou'd not be a Prisoner, Upon which he was told in Indian he wou'd be burnt. To this He answered, he did not care for, he wou'd kill four or five before he died, and had we not desisted from exposing ourselves, they wou'd have killed a great many more, they having a Number of loaded Guns by them."[24] In another account, written by James Smith many years after the event, the scene is remembered in a more dramatic fashion. Smith claimed that "Jacobs could speak English, our people called on him to surrender; he said that he and his men were warriors, and they would all fight while life remained. He was again told that they should be well used, if they would only surrender; and, if not, the house should be burned down over their heads; Jacobs replied he could eat fire."

Whichever description was most accurate remains to be seen, but the outcome was not in doubt. With his home burning, Tewea continued to cajole and jeer the militiamen who had surrounded him. Considered second only to Shingas among the village populace, Tewea's defeat would have been headline news. Eventually, when the flames overtook the cabin, the man called Captain Jacobs ran from the flames along with his wife and son; they were all shot dead on the spot. What followed was undoubtedly one of the most spectacular sights in the whole of the event. As the Indian cabins burned, stores of gunpowder held within began to ignite; one by one the cabins began to explode into black clouds. As a consequence of using Kittanning as a starting point for its raids to the east, New France's agents had been steadily filling the village with stores of gunpowder and ammunition. In the colonel's estimation "they had a sufficient stock of ammunition for ten Years War with the English." There was so much, in fact, that individual warriors began to store the powder within their homes. The result was an explosive display unlike any other in the history of the Ohio Country. Robison stated, "Their guns took fire, and went off like a platoon, their magazine blew up at the same time," adding that the blast was "heard at fort Pitt," a mistaken reference to Fort Duquesne.

The explosions were grand in scale, and the aftermath was gruesome. As Armstrong recounted, when Tewea's cabin finally blew up there "was thrown the Leg and Thigh of an Indian with a Child of three or four Years Old, such a height that they appeared as nothing an fell in the adjacent Corn Field."[25]

Armstrong's Kittanning Raid had succeeded in neutralizing one of the most violent leaders in the whole of the Indian world. But, as with many aspects of Frontier combat, even this fact is debated. According to Armstrong himself, an Indian man was killed at that pivotal moment, but he did not go so far as to verify that it was Tewea.

> As the fire began to Approach and the Smoak grow thick, one of the Indian Fellows, to shew his Manhood, began to Sing. A Squa [Squaw], in the same House, and at the same time, was heard to cry and make Noise, but for so doing was severly rebuked by the Men; but by and by the fire being too hot for them, two Indian Fellows and a Squa sprung out and made for the Corn Field, who were immediately shot down by Our People, then surrounding the Houses it was thought Captain Jacobs tumbled himself out at a Garret or Cock loft Window, at which he was Shot.[26]

There are a few legitimate reasons why Armstrong would deny his greatest military achievement. Firstly, it should be stated that other sources do identify the native man who was killed as Tewea. Robison describes the scene in a similar way, writing, "Jacobs . . . sprung out, Jacob's squaw wielded a tomahawk round her head before she jumped the fence, Jacobs fell first, then his wife, and then his son, in proportion seven feet high." Even in the moments following the raid, some of the prisoners who were rescued confirmed that the body belonged to the war chief, stating that he famously wore the late Edward Armstrong's boots, which he had claimed at Fort Granville. Still, the question remains: why would the colonel not take credit for this triumphant event? In all likelihood, John Armstrong understood that news of Tewea's death would be received with great acclaim in the East, and he deliberately downplayed the event as a final slight to the dead sachem. Perhaps the animosity that he harbored for the murder of his brother-in-law was so great that this was his final measure of revenge.

The circumstances surrounding Tewea's demise continued to develop in the months that followed. In a letter written by the Anglican Reverend Thomas Barton two weeks after the raid, the minister recounted the matter in a much different way. "I shall . . . observe to you, that the famous Captain Jacobs fought, & died, like a Soldier. He refus'd to surrender when the House was even on Fire over his Head; And when the Flame grew too violent for him, he rush'd out into the Body of our Men flourishing his Tomahawk, & told them he was born a Soldier, & would not die a Slave."[27]

Barton himself was not at Kittanning, and only heard of the event secondhand, yet he painted a vivid picture. In his tale, Tewea is almost heroic, and suffers a death that is nothing short of glorious. Even stranger, five months later the good Reverend wrote to Thomas Penn, this time offering an account of the event that is radically different: "One Mr. Callender, who at that Time bore only a Lieutenant's Commission, distinguish'd himself by the most uncommon Bravery & Resolution. It is asserted that when Jacobs took to a House, out of which he kill'd & wounded Many of our Men-Callender undertook to fire it, which he accomplish'd at the infinite Hazard of his Life . . ."[28]

As puzzling as Armstrong's deference was, Barton's actions are well understood; they are best understood, though, with a brief explanation of Pennsylvanian politics. As an Anglican minister, Barton was highly representative of the elitist Philadelphia political machine; the man whom he erroneously ascribes as having burned Tewea's cabin was one of his congregants. Barton was not a Quaker by faith, but he did align with the Quaker Party on a strictly political level. In the east there was a general sense that natives were worthy of respect and capable of restraint, and Barton's writings were likely part of this agenda. On the inverse was the more conservative Proprietary Party view, embodied in the Scots-Irish, that the Indians were savage marauders that needed to be eliminated. While Barton was indicative of the former, Armstrong and his raiders were most definitely subscribers of the latter.

Politics aside, on the morning of September 8 the village of Kittanning was mostly in flames. Although the fighting was still ongoing, if John Armstrong's raid had accomplished nothing else, Tewea was a dead man.[29]

With thick black smoke filling the Allegheny River Valley and most of the Indian combatants killed or having fled, Lieutenant Colonel John Armstrong had seen enough. He ordered his forces to leave the main portion of the town and proceed to the crest of the hill that overlooked the site. Beneath them the destruction was rampant, and the explosions of gunpowder had reduced Kittanning to ruins. As Armstrong had his shoulder wound dressed, he recorded that his men cheered enthusiastically as the village stores continued to explode. "During the burning of the houses which were Near thirty in Number we were agreeably entertain'd with a quick Succession of charged Guns gradually firing off as reach by the Fire, but more so with the vast Explosion of sundry Bags and large Cags of Gunpowder."[30]

Although the Cumberland County men were pleased with the results of their historic raid, the celebration was soon muted by the vulnerability of their situation. They were deep into enemy territory, and well aware that their conquest had been noisy and many Ohioans had fled. Reinforcements had to be coming, and they could not afford to stay in place too much longer. Armstrong had rallied most of his troops above the town, and it was there that he first met a group of white captives liberated by his army. In total, the Pennsylvanians had rescued eleven people, but only came away with seven. When the raid began, many Ohioans ran into the trees dragging their hostages along with them; most of the one hundred captives held in the town disappeared deeper into the western fringes of the Ohio Country. The ones that were fortunate enough to be recovered had a great deal of information to share with the colonel, and he took serious note of their warnings. They told Armstrong, "That very day two Battoas [bateaux] of French Men, with a large party of Delaware and French Indians, were to Join Captain Jacobs at the Kittanning, and to set out early the next Morning to take Fort Shirley . . ." This news gave the commander great pause. His men had succeeded in raiding the unsuspecting village, but they certainly could not stand up to a large French force *and* a full native war party. With his men tired and satisfied, Armstrong decided that they had accomplished their intended mission and began his retreat.[31]

Like most large-scale engagements, the whole of the fighting at Kittanning was not confined to the village proper. In fact, there were actually three separate segments that encompassed the whole of the event. These alternate skirmishes were small and self-contained, but bear out further examination to properly evaluate the entirety of the affair. Throughout the firefight that had occurred in the village center, numerous reports determined that the Ohioan warriors had been shooting from the western bank of the Allegheny River. It is unlikely that these wayward riflemen actually killed any of the militia. The warriors only fired individual rounds, and did not employ the volley-style fire that typically produced reliable casualties. They were mentioned by most sources, however, and that is enough to make it a point worthy of study. While the natives kept no records of the affair, they were not alone on the western shoreline. The morning of the raid, a party of French troops had arrived at Kittanning just before Armstrong's seven companies. The only sources that speak to the French involvement in the affair come from two men, neither of whom was at Kittanning on September 8. The first is the noted Louis Antoine de Bougainville, and the second was a lesser officer named Nicolas Renaud. As they were not present that day, their information comes secondhand from Dumas, the commandant of Fort Duquesne. According to Renaud, the French officer in Kittanning that morning is only identified as Monsieur de Normanville, and he arrived with "*avec soixante hommes*" (with sixty men). Furthermore, Renaud went on to specify that the commander had been wounded in the thigh during the exchange of fire.[32]

The identity of this officer can be narrowed down to two distinct figures. Throughout the French occupation of the Allegheny River Valley, a pair of men named de Normanville were present at Fort Duquesne. Likely brothers, both Joseph Godefroy de Normanville (b. 1727) and Jean-Baptiste Godefroy de Normanville (b. 1736) saw considerable action at the Forks of the Ohio. Although sources only identify the Kittanning officer by surname, previous experience heavily favors that the elder Joseph was at Kittanning during the battle. A year earlier, in 1755, Joseph Godefroy de Normanville was instrumental in gathering intelligence as a scout during the approach of Braddock's ill-fated army. He had also proved invaluable for his ability to retain the trust and support of many native warriors leading up to the Battle of the Monongahela. Eleven years older than Jean-Baptiste (who was barely twenty), Joseph's previous successes made him a natural candidate to command several dozen men upriver at Kittanning.[33]

Bougainville adds a new layer to the story. In his writings it is made very clear that the French soldiers did not fight Armstrong's men at all. Instead, they only served in a supportive role aiding in the relocation of women, children, and captives. The Frenchman writes: "In the first days of September a corps of 300 English came to burn the village of Attigue. This party arrived without having been discovered and made his attack at the beginning of the day. A French officer who was in this village held firm to help the Indians to secure their women and their children." He also added that the majority of the Indians chose not to pursue the retreating Pennsylvanians because "*Ils n'ont pas été poursuivis sur-le-champ parce que les Sauvages manquaient de poudre, deux barils en ayant sauté pendant l'action.*" (They were not pursued immediately because Indians lacked powder, two barrels having exploded during the action.) Even though these two French officers were only reporting what they had heard after the fact, the inclusion of highly verifiable details lends great credence to their testimony. The indication by Renaud of de Normanville's apparent leg injury indicates that at least some of Armstrong's men must have fired back toward the western bank, intentionally or not. It is unclear whether the French soldiers from Fort Duquesne participated in any meaningful way during the Kittanning Raid, but they were most certainly present at the time.[34]

The clarification of their role in the affair offers great insight into New France's relationship with the Ohioans in the summer of 1756. Although they raided Fort Granville together in July, the French more often relied on the warriors as auxiliary raiders in support of their war against Great Britain. Rather than entering into a traditional military alliance with the Ohioans, the administrators of New France were more inclined to simply encourage the raiding parties as a means of destabilization and distraction. By furnishing weapons and supplies to the Western Delawares, they could drain their enemies' resources by facilitating attacks on the colonial Frontiers. This strategy was a rousing success, as Maryland and Virginia spent great sums of money to combat their own Indian threats. In the case of Pennsylvania, a simple glance at the highly divisive political, social, and financial turmoil leading to the Kittanning expedition illustrates this point perfectly.

While the fighting was in full vigor across the river, many Ohioan men ushered their families away from the fray. According to the French sources, several French soldiers helped the panicked Delawares and Shawnees gather their families to flee. The hectic scene was mostly the elderly, women, and children, but some of those taken deeper into the wilderness were indeed European captives. Two of them, Marie Le Roy and Barbara Leininger, were among the unlucky few. Le Roy and Leininger were among some of the earliest prisoners to be taken to Kittanning after the raid on Penn's Creek. They had been held in captivity for almost a year, and Armstrong's men were viewed as their salvation. It was almost certainly a mournful sight for the teenaged girls to be dragged away, leaving their rescuers far behind. Fortunately for them, they ultimately survived their captivity and left a detailed narrative. The Kittanning Raid is featured prominently: "In the month of September Col. Armstrong arrived with his men and attacked Kittanny Town. Both of us happened to be in that part of it which lies on the other side of the river. We were immediately conveyed ten miles farther into the interior, in order that we might have no chance of trying . . . to escape. The savages threatened to kill us."[35]

Their case was not unusual. Before the raid began, estimates placed over one hundred captives on site, but only a handful were saved. They were housed on the western bank of the river, an unfortunate twist of fate that virtually guaranteed a continuance of their imprisonment. The girls later stated they were brought back to Kittanning after the fact, and that the "town had been burned to the ground." In the aftermath they were taken south to Fort Duquesne, "where we remained for two months."[36]

Six miles east of the main battle, a second vital component of the Kittanning Raid occurred. Upon his original approach to the village on the night of September 7, John Armstrong dispatched Lieutenant James Hogg to watch a party of Indians along the main trail and guard the army's supplies. With thirteen men under his command, Hogg placed his forces between the Indians and a large quantity of goods, including a few horses and dozens of rolled blankets. These items were vital but too cumbersome to take into the village, and the location became known as "Blanket Hill." Like the raid during which it took place, the circumstances undertaken at Blanket Hill are muddied by conflicting reports. A quick study, however, can produce a clearer image of what occurred there.

According to Armstrong, Hogg had received bad intelligence from his pilot that there were only four Indians around the fire. He refers to this scout's faulty information as a "fatal Mistake," and recalls that Lieutenant Hogg proceeded to attack them based on those figures. With thirteen men in his own party, Hogg believed he could easily overtake the four warriors, but soon discovered "a Number considerably Superior to his." At about the same time as the main assault on Kittanning began, Hogg and the Ohioans also began to fight. The "warm Engagement" lasted for more than an hour, and three of the men in Hogg's detachment were killed; the lieutenant himself was wounded twice. Claiming that three of the enemy were also killed at the outset, the injured Hogg "was obliged to Squat in a thicket" until help arrived from the main body of the Pennsylvanians. It would never arrive, and hence the controversy begins. Armstrong continued by stating that despite his efforts to hide, the remainder of Hogg's men placed him on a horse and fled the scene.

They soon encountered another group of four warriors, and Hogg, "as a Brave Soldier," ordered them to fight off this new threat . . . but they refused. Instead, they all ran into the forest and left their wounded commander to fend for himself. The colonel stated that "the Indians pursued, killing one Man and wounding the Lieutenant a third time through the Belly." With that, Lieutenant James Hogg perished, and Armstrong placed the blame squarely on his "cowardly Sergeant." As a result, all of the horses, blankets, and supplies kept in the nondescript gully were lost.[37]

Yet another retelling of the Blanket Hill skirmish emerged fifty-five years later in the deposition of Robert Robison, and it differs greatly from Armstrong's official report. Robison relates that Hogg's men "crawled near the Indians" at dawn, and most of the warriors ran. He then states that the Indians soon returned, and Hogg was killed almost immediately. "Shortly after they began, we began at the town," he writes, "and they heard our firing which discouraged the Indians greatly . . ." According to Robison, the rangers at Blanket Hill began to shout "your town is on fire, you dogs you," and were able to escape in the confusion. This story is hardly worthy of charges for cowardice and desertion, but given that neither Armstrong nor Robison was present during the skirmish, one must consider the sources. Robison claims that his version of the events was told to him by prisoners liberated from Kittanning; this is clearly possible, as freed captives had already passed on information to the militia while the raid was ongoing. Armstrong, however, says the report that he wrote came from "a Sergeant of Captain Mercer's Company and two or three other of his Men," who "had met with Lieut. Hogg, who lay wounded . . . by the Road side."[38]

Given that Armstrong was told this story by three separate witnesses, his version seems to be the most plausible. Although it was a secondary action, the skirmish at Blanket Hill is a vital part of the Kittanning Raid and is worthy of study. Today, a blue Pennsylvania Historical and Museum Commission marker honors the site, and one can still gain of sense of just how unforgiving the terrain would have been by visiting it.

The final part of the Kittanning Raid occurred in the midst of the heaviest part of the fighting. Shortly after Tewea and his warriors took shelter in their cabins, Captain Hugh Mercer was shot. The ball tore through his arm and broke his right wrist, rendering the officer useless in the firefight. To escape the scene and set the fracture, Mercer retreated to the ridge above Kittanning, where the rangers of his company were waiting. In the early morning hours before the raid began, Armstrong dispatched an undisclosed number of Mercer's company to assume the hill overlooking the site; when Mercer arrived wounded they feared the worst. Whether it was because the fighting had settled into a long engagement or because they feared some further retaliation, the soldiers in Mercer's company informed the commander that they were leaving. From above the village they were not directly involved in the fight, but they could easily see the action below and the warriors firing from across the river. Thus, as the main body of Armstrong's army continued the fight below, Captain Hugh Mercer's company deserted the field.

It is not known how vigorously Mercer protested the retreat, but given his terrible injury he had little choice but to follow. For a detailed explanation of the events that followed, historians once again rely on Robison's testimony a half century later. Robison claims that of all the companies, Mercer's was the least prepared for combat. "His company was chiefly composed of traders, who persuaded their captain that there would not one living man of us ever get home."

Back on the main path out of the town, the men's route of escape was soon cut off by a party of Indian warriors. There is no way to be certain, but given the general vicinity in which the encounter occurred it is very probable that this was the same war party that had decimated Lieutenant Hogg's force a few hours earlier. "His men, unfortunately, fell in with the Indians that lieutenant Hoge [*sic*] had been fighting with that morning," Robison recalled. "They fell upon his company and broke it, killing about twenty men." Whether this attack was an ambush or a meeting engagement, it soon devolved into a melee. Mercer's company quickly broke ranks and jumped from the path, and many were killed in the process.[39]

Unlike James Hogg, though, Mercer seemed to have the loyalty of at least *some* of his rangers. Mercer, on horseback, was guided to safety by Thomas Burke and a young officer identified as "ensign Scott." Burke was one of the original scouts selected to first reconnoiter the town days earlier, whose premature return caused Lieutenant Colonel Armstrong so much grief. In this escape Mercer's damaged arm fell painfully from its sling, and he needed to dismount his horse to fix it.

Relying on his previous medical training Mercer knew precisely how to secure the limb to ensure that it could heal properly; he did not count on what happened next. In the process of stepping off of his horse, the officer was overcome with pain at the exact time that a lone Ohioan warrior came upon his small group of survivors. Mercer fainted into unconsciousness and rolled into the weeds while Burke and Scott snagged the unmanned horse and rode away. According to Robison, "the Indian came about six feet from him, and seeing Burke and Scott riding, he gave out a halloo and ran after . . ." Drifting in and out of consciousness, Mercer heard two gunshots issue in the distance. He then rolled deeper into the forest and elected to rest there until nightfall.[40]

Some of Mercer's company were later able to meet up with the main body of Armstrong's force, which is when they relayed the information gathered from the dying James Hogg. They were able to travel with strength in numbers, but unfortunately for Hugh Mercer he was on his own. He had seen the aftermath of Braddock's defeat and inspected the mutilated bodies left behind by the French-allied warriors there. It was those terrible scenes that convinced him to leave medicine and become an officer; now alone in the wilderness, he was determined to avoid suffering that same grisly fate. What transpired over the next fifteen days was nothing short of epic, if Robert Robison's tale is to be believed. Electing to travel only by night, the injured Mercer survived on a diet of wild berries, freshwater clams, and "one rattle snake, and to eat it raw."[41]

When Mercer finally reached the foothills of the Allegheny Mountains "he saw one day what he through to be an Indian." Sensing the danger present, Mercer darted to hide behind a tree and was spotted by the strange figure in the woods. The mystery man also took cover, and after an awkward moment "he found it to be one of his own men." The two soldiers must have been thrilled to be reunited, but both were grievously injured; according to Robison, Mercer's new comrade soon had to "lay down unable to go any further, with an intention never more to rise." He went on to say that just seven miles after losing his partner, Mercer himself gave up home and finally fell to the forest floor. A sudden change of luck, however, would spare him a lonely death in the wilderness.

"At this time there was a company of Cherokee Indians in kings pay, and being at fort Littleton captain Hamilton sent some of them to search along the foot of the Alleghany mountains to see if there was any signs of Indians on the route, and these Indians came upon captain Mercer, able to rise, they gave him food, and he told them of the other, they took the captains track and found him, and brought him to fort Littleton, carrying him on a bier of their making."[42]

When Mercer finally returned to the east, he was glorified as a hero. In total, he had spent fifteen days alone in the wilderness of the Ohio Country, and his exploits immediately became lionized. His story was told in the September 30 edition of the *Pennsylvania Gazette*, and was delivered with the spirit of good humor. Among the details it included was that, "coming near Fort Shirley, he found a Piece of dry Beef, which our People had lost, and on Trial rejected it, because the Snake was better."[43]

LIEUTENANT COLONEL JOHN ARMSTRONG'S ARMY came to Kittanning in seven organized companies, but left in a rabble. According to his estimates, after six hours of continuous fighting he suffered seventeen killed, thirteen wounded, and nineteen missing. The worst of the damage was suffered by Mercer's doomed company, of which seven were killed, one was wounded, and nine were missing. Mercer himself was among them, and his harrowing tale was a testament to the condition of the retreating army. For Armstrong the victory was bittersweet; he had successfully razed Kittanning to the ground, but not all of the men of Cumberland County were coming home. Among the dead was the nineteen-year-old John Baker, the young captive who voluntarily returned to Kittanning after narrowly escaping just six months earlier. Although those lives could not be replaced, there was a glimmer of hope in the aftermath of the raid. The militia was able to free eleven prisoners from their bondage, but over ninety were unable to be saved.

The near-total loss of Mercer's company troubled Armstrong, especially because four prisoners were among their ranks. By the time that the Pennsylvanians reach Fort Lyttleton four days after the attack, only seven captives numbered among them. These liberated persons were not nameless figures, and special care was taken to correctly identify them. They were taken from all across the Pennsylvania Frontier and one woman was from as far away as Winchester, Virginia. Among them were most notably Ann McCord and Martha Thorn, both of whom had been captured during the raid on McCord's Fort. Another was Thomas Girty, a survivor of the Fort Granville attack and the brother of the soon-to-be-legendary Simon Girty. As for the four people attached to Mercer's company, a woman and three children, they were never identified and never heard from again.[44]

The damage inflicted on Kittanning was catastrophic, and the village never recovered. By Armstrong's estimates, he had destroyed at least thirty cabins and stated, "It is impossible to ascertain the exact Number of the Enemy killed in the Action." He does, however, speculate that "there cannot be less than thirty or Forty killed and Mortally wounded . . ." These are figures that will likely forever be lost to history, and they should be considered as purely speculative. The rangers left a terrible scene in their wake, the details of which the colonel was certain not to spare. "As much Blood was found in Sundry part of the Cornfield, and Indians seen in several places crawl into the Weeds on their Hands and Feet, who the Soldiers, in pursuit of others, then overlooked, expecting to Scalp them afterwards; and also several kill'd and wounded in crossing the River." With that last note, Armstrong was deadly serious. He claimed that his army left Kittanning with "about a dozen of Scalps" but "four or five are missing."[45]

Considering these factors, the Kittanning Raid could be viewed as a success. Tewea was almost certainly killed on that day, and that is verified by the fact that he is never mentioned in the historical record afterwards. Along with the majority of the village the rangers also managed to burn up an untold volume of French supplied goods, weapons, and ammunition that would have been used in future attacks in the east. In the larger context of the Seven Years' War, Armstrong's raid was one of the lone bright spots in a period known by the British as "the Years of Defeat." Most importantly, though, was the completion of its primary directive: *action*. From its earliest stages the Kittanning Raid was designed to show that the colonial government of Pennsylvania was capable of defending its citizens. There surely could have been more Ohioan warriors killed, and many more captives freed, but in the end the maneuver was a calculated political effort to alter the developing narrative across the Pennsylvanian backcountry. Angry Frontiersmen had directed their rage at Philadelphia over the previous year for its proven inability to protect its residents, and the Kittanning Raid was designed to silence those critics.

As Lieutenant Colonel John Armstrong finished penning his official report on September 14, he made one final request to new Governor William Denny. He asked that Robert Hunter Morris, and the "Gentlemen Commissioners for the Province," be provided a copy of his letter recounting the destruction of Kittanning.[46]

EPILOGUE:
Victory

On January 5, 1757, John Armstrong stood proudly in front of a large crowd gathered in the city of Philadelphia. That day Mayor Attwood Shute had honored him for his service to the colony, and the ceremony was a great spectacle. He had gotten accustomed to these very public displays of gratitude over the last four months, but the grandest gesture yet was still to come. Thomas Penn, the lord and proprietor of the colony of Pennsylvania, came to the city to personally thank the colonel for his service. Having traveled all the way from England, Penn presented Armstrong with a decorative sword and lavishly embellished belt. It was the greatest honor of his life. Along with the aforementioned gifts, John Armstrong and his men would be flattered further by having a medal struck in their honor.

Despite the fact that the Kittanning Raid had been executed almost wholly by the Scots-Irish of the Pennsylvania backcountry, the celebration was a distinctly cosmopolitan affair. A local watchmaker named Edward Duffield designed an engraving that would adorn the Kittanning Medal. On the front was an image of the raid itself, and it read: "Kittanning Destroyed by Col. Armstrong, September 8, 1756." Although they were pleased, the rangers who participated likely scoffed at Duffield's design. It portrayed a village made up of Frontier-style log cabins, and showed an officer directing a soldier to shoot at a native warrior who was subsequently plunging into a river. Most laughably, the entire scene was backwards; as the attack had happened on the eastern bank, the Allegheny should have been on the opposite side. On the inverse was the Philadelphia coat of arms, and a not-so-subtle inscription reading "THE GIFT OF THE CORPORATION OF THE CITY OF PHILADELPHIA." The veterans were then told that Lieutenant Colonel Armstrong and his officer corps would be granted silver versions of the celebrated medallion . . . his men, however, would only receive copper. Despite its obvious motives, the minting of this medal is widely recognized as one of the earliest examples of the practice in the history of colonial America.

It had truly been a strange four months since his return from Kittanning. Armstrong and his men were instantly fawned over by the news media of the capital, and they published glowing editorials to celebrate the expedition as much as possible. On September 30, the *Pennsylvania Gazette* published a ten-stanza poem entitled "Ode to the Inhabitants of Pennsylvania" in honor of his raid, making sure to promote the colonel's achievements. It was filled with details of the raid, and clearly gave it pride of place in the midst of the ongoing imperial war:

> Still shall the tyrant scourge of Gaul With wasteful rage resistless fall On Britain's slumbering race? Still shall she wave her bloody hand And threatening banners o'er this land, To Britain's fell disgrace?
>
> And not one generous chieftain rise (Who dares the frown of war despise, And treacherous fear disclaim) His country's ruin to oppose, To hurl destruction on her foes, And blast their rising fame?
>
> In Britain's cause, with valor fired, Braddock, unhappy chief! expired, And claim'd a nation's tear; Nor could Oswego's bulwarks stand The fury of a savage band, Though Schuyler's arm was there.
>
> Still shall this motley, murderous crew Their deep, destructive arts pursue, And general horror spread? No—see Britannia's genius rise! Swift o'er the Atlantic foam she flies And lifts her laurell'd head!
>
> Lo! streaming through the dear blue sky, Great London's awful banners fly, In British pomp display'd! Soon shall the gallant chief ad-

> vance; Before him shrink the sons of France, Confounded and dismay'd.
>
> Then rise, illustrious Britons, rise! Great Freedom calls, pursue her voice, And save your country's shame! Let every hand for Britain arm'd, And every breast with virtue warm'd, Aspire at deathless fame!
>
> But chief, let Pennsylvania wake, And on her foes let terrors shake, Their gloomy troops defy; For, lo! her smoking farms and plains, Her captured youths, and murder'd swains, For vengeance louder cry.
>
> Why should we seek inglorious rest, Or sink, with thoughtless case oppress'd, While war insults so near? While ruthless, fierce, athirst for blood, Bellona's sons, a desperate brood! In furious bands appear!
>
> Rouse, rouse at once, and boldly chase From their deep haunts, the savage race, Till they confess you men.
>
> Let other Armstrongs grace the field! Let other slaves before them yield, And tremble round Duquesne.
>
> And thou, our chief, and martial guide, Of worth approved, of valor tried In many a hard campaign, O Denny, warmed with British fire, Our inexperienced troops inspire, And conquest's laurels gain![1]

It was indeed an unexpected honor, and the rumors continued to fly. One week after the publication of "Ode," the *Gazette* published a report that Armstrong's rangers had voluntarily given up their collected scalp bounties. "An Instance of Generosity this," the article claimed, "which shews that those Gentlemen did not go against the Enemy, from a mercenary Motive, but from a Regard for the Service of their King and bleeding Country." There is no evidence to suggest that the militiamen ever declined compensation, and it likely never happened. In point of fact, the volunteer army of Cumberland County consisted mainly of poor farmers, and most had suffered terrible losses as a result of previous Indian raids on their settlements. This point is illustrated by the city of Philadelphia's decision to offer cash rewards to the men who were lost during the campaign.

On October 5, the city council meeting of minutes read that it should "contribute to the relief of the widows and children of those who lost their lives in that expedition" and "that this Board will give the sum of £150 out of their stock in the Treasurer's hands, to be paid out in pieces of plate, swords, and other things suitable for presents, to the said officers and toward the relief of the said widows and children."[2]

On January 24, John Armstrong penned a letter to the city of Philadelphia for their gracious reception. He said "the kind of acceptance of our past services by the corporation gives us the highest pleasure and furnishes a fresh motive for exerting ourselves on every future occasion for the benefit of His Majesty's service in general and in defense of the province."[3]

Despite the glorious fanfare that occurred in the first months after Armstrong's return from Kittanning, the affair left some lingering questions. For all of the destruction that the Kittanning Raid had wrought, the colonel himself was still not fully satisfied with the result. Always the statistician, Armstrong believed that they could have done more to retrieve more captives if not for the incompetence of his wilderness guides. He wrote:

> Upon the whole, had our Pilots understood the true situation of the Town and the Paths leading to it, so as to have posted us at a convenient place, where the Disposition of Men and the Duty assign'd them cou'd have been performed with greater Advantage, we had, by divine Assistance, destroy'd a much greater Number of the Enemy, recovered more Prisoners and sustained less damage that what we at present have; but tho' the advantage gained over the our Common Enemy is far from being satisfactory to us, must we not dispise the smallest degrees of Success that God has pleased to give, especially at a time of such general Calamity, when the attempts of our Enemys have been so prevalent and successful.[4]

Armstrong was by nature a practical man. As such, he could not shake the feeling that perhaps the Kittanning Raid had not been as wildly successful as his fellow Proprietary Party members made it seem. In the aftermath of the attack, the newspapers continued to speak of raids on the Frontier. In fact, by the end of 1757 the frequency of the Ohioan raids would actually *increase*, though casualty figures did drop. More than that, when the rangers were originally drawn from the garrisons of Forts Granville, Shirley, and George they were never replaced.

Amazingly, after the Kittanning Raid it seemed that the colony was willing to throw away what previously stood as its greatest defense achievement. The men were subsequently reassigned to posts farther east, and the famous "chain of forts" was simply left to rot. Of all the shortcomings of the expedition, however, none troubled Armstrong more than his failure to rescue captives held on site. Despite their roundly applauded return, the men of Cumberland County only brought seven prisoners home with them. How could they possibly face the families of the ninety people left behind and honestly declare victory?[5]

In these sentiments the colonel was not alone. One of the greatest critics of the raid was the aforementioned Thomas Barton, and he held nothing back. On February 28, 1757, the minister wrote that "since the Reduction of Kittanning under Colonel Armstrong, we have not been much disturb'd. . . . But, alas! I fear the approaching Spring will again make us tremble. We have a great deal to do, & but little done . . ." In this opinion, the notable anti-proprietor was correct; the immediate aftermath of the Kittanning Raid was the winter of 1756–1757. Given that raids tended to naturally diminish in the winter, how was anyone to know if Armstrong's assault actually had any meaningful effect on the Ohioan raiders? Shingas was still alive, and he would continue to inflict pain on the backcountry in the months to come. When his warriors struck, they still did so with vigor and with plenty of French-supplied powder. Aside from the physical demolition of the village and the death of Tewea, one would not be remiss to suggest that Kittanning had not really been the end of anything.[6]

With the fall elections looming, the Kittanning Raid placed the Quaker Party in a very difficult position. By all standards, the affair had the public perception of a rousing success, and they would have been foolish to attempt to minimize it. As hard as it was to do, sometimes a political party must simply take its medicine and give the other side a tip of the proverbial cap. The Quaker Party seemed to celebrate the raid as much as anyone, but the fact that they were already facing a historic lack of support made them mindful of their approach. It was apparently decided that, rather than simply accepting the raid as a victory for the proprietary faction, they should try to monopolize the celebration and commandeer the political capital gained. It was for these reasons that Benjamin Franklin's *Pennsylvania Gazette* became one of Armstrong's greatest cheering sections. The publication of the absurdly melodramatic "Ode to the Inhabitants of Pennsylvania" further underscored this fledgling stratagem. But Franklin's media gamble was not directed at the Penn-aligned Proprietary Party alone. Since the beginning of his time in colonial politics he had been waging a two-front war against the proprietary faction and the pacifist members *of his own party*. In embracing the Kittanning Raid, it underscored that his new wing of the Quaker Party was fully supportive of military action, so long as the Penns paid their fair share. As time would tell, this tactic would pay dividends in the fall elections. Away from the political arena, though, some were still willing to speak the truth in private despite their positive public demeanor. Again, one need look no further than the Reverend Thomas Barton. In one of the most impressively candid statements of the entire period, he summed up his position perfectly: "Tho' the killing of a few Indians & burning their Huts at the Kittanning is an Action not very considerable in itself, yet it is the best that has yet appear'd for this Province, And will I hope in the End countervail the Expence the Government has been at to maintain it."[7]

THE ELECTIONS OF OCTOBER 1756 HAD PROVEN to be a watershed moment in the history of Pennsylvania. The Quaker faction had successfully rebranded itself as the anti-proprietary party, and Benjamin Franklin was its ideological and legislative leader. Through their actions at the polls, the citizens of the Peaceable Kingdom had greatly bolstered Franklin's wing of the party, and reduced the religious Quaker hardliners to only twelve seats. For the first time in the history of the province they were no longer the undisputed power brokers of the assembly, and their delegation had reached a historic low. Stripped of their power and badly embarrassed, four of the remaining Friends resigned their seats in protest as a result. Since the summer of 1756 a total of ten hardline, pacifist Quakers had vacated the House, and Benjamin Franklin's newfound rule was virtually uncontested. The dreams of the Proprietary Party of achieving a voting majority in the assembly were unrealistic, but even they relished the dismissal of the nonviolent defenders.[8]

The results of the fall elections sent shockwaves through the colony. The political boundaries that had existed between East and West became suddenly blurred, and the province was ripe for a partisan realignment. With the Quaker Party now in the hands of the pragmatic Franklin, many Friends declined to run for future offices, and many more petulantly swore off participating in elections altogether. Perhaps the greatest weapon that Franklin had at his disposal was his recent history; the passage of the militia bill was viewed as his crowning achievement, and it proved that he could live up to his promises. Since its earliest time Pennsylvania's politics had been effectively divided between religious pacifism and military force, but that had changed. With both parties in favor of raising a provincial army, the colony could now choose their partisan affiliation on fresh criteria. Initially, the Proprietary Party saw the election as a sweeping rebuke of their opposition, stirred forth by the success of the Kittanning Raid, but they soon found that they had lost their greatest bargaining chip in the process. Suddenly Benjamin Franklin's rebooted Quaker Party was able to launch an intensely populist campaign centered on taxing the rich, and evening the playing field with the tax-evading Penn family. In characteristic fashion, Franklin relished his newfound power. Just days after the victory, Franklin wrote to a friend:

> The Proprietors . . . are greatly incensed at some Parts of my late Conduct. I am not much concern'd at that, because if I have offended them *by acting right*, I can, whenever I please, remove their Displeasure, *by acting wrong.* Tho' at present I have not the least Inclination to be in their good Graces on those Terms. I have some natural Dislike to Persons who so far *Love Money*, as to be *unjust* for its sake: I despise their *Meanness*, (as it appears to me) in several late Instances, most cordially, and am thankful that I never had any Connection with them, or Occasion to ask or receive a Favour at their hands.[9]

Although Franklin walked the streets of Philadelphia with a renewed vigor, his shine was soon to wear off. Before long the same tired debates began, and the old political wounds were torn open. When the assembly passed bills which taxed Penn family estates, the lieutenant governor promptly vetoed them. It was a frustrating and cumbersome exercise, but unlike before the elections had tipped the scales in Franklin's favor. Thus, in 1757, Franklin was selected by his peers to represent the Pennsylvania Assembly in London with the goal of nullifying Thomas Penn's birthright. The British Empire had never been a monolith, but was a patchwork quilt of different governance styles and philosophies. In the case of Pennsylvania, a "proprietary colony" was established under the control of one family, the heirs of William Penn. Could Pennsylvania's charter be revoked, it could be restructured as a "Royal colony," thus placing control of the province in the hands of the king and colonial assembly. Most importantly, though, this action would strip Thomas Penn and his collaborationist governors of any meaningful authority. For the next five years Benjamin Franklin fought that fight and ultimately lost, but his European residency had greatly directed his fate. He soon became the talk of London, and spent much of the next two decades solidifying his reputation as "the first American." By the time he returned to Philadelphia in 1775, the debate over proprietary vs. anti-proprietary rule had been replaced by another issue altogether: revolution.

THE SEVEN YEARS' WAR RAVAGED THE PENNSYLVANIA FRONTIER for another two years after Kittanning burned. There was not another raid mounted into the Ohio Country for another two years, until General John Forbes undertook his legendary march in the summer of 1758. With over seven thousand men at his disposal Forbes began construction on a permanent road across the southern portion of the colony that led directly to the Forks of the Ohio. His campaign was slow moving, but was viewed as a juggernaut. With Fort Duquesne clearly in its sights, great unease began to spread among the French-allied Indian nations of the Ohio Country. In advance of Forbes's inevitable arrival at Fort Duquesne, the diplomat missionary Christian Frederick Post paid a visit to the region's most famous resident. In September, under the guns of Fort Duquesne, Post and Shingas met to discuss the potential for a complete cessation of hostilities between the British and the Western Delaware.

Although Shingas had been painted as the face of terror on the Frontier, he never viewed war as a final step. All along he had claimed that total Delaware sovereignty was his ultimate goal, and if achieved that he would lay down his hatchet. His initial attraction to the forces of New France was not based on their policies or worldview, but on the fact that they swore that they would not settle in the Ohio Country after the war had been won. If the British could match that promise, he claimed that he would be more than willing to lay down the hatchet. Shingas was a wanted man, and with the army of John Forbes barreling down on the region, he was naturally skeptical of Post's sudden outreaching. According to Post, Shingas replied, "Brother, you very well know that you have collected all your young men about the country . . . and now they are standing before our doors. You come with good news and fine speeches. Brother, this is what makes us jealous, and we do not know what to think of it; if you had brought the news of peace before your army had begun to march, it would have caused a great deal more good. We do not so readily believe you."[10]

Shingas had good reason to be skeptical. Since the destruction of Kittanning he had bounced from one Delaware village to the next, from Logstown to Sawcunk to Kuskuskies. There was a bounty on his head, and to willingly disclose his location was to risk capture and death. But Post came with proof of his goodwill; a year earlier, Teedyuscung, king of the Wyoming Delawares, had made peace. Shingas was told that he could do the same, and in doing so rebuild a life for his Western allies. The only caveat would be to lay down his arms and abandon the French at Fort Duquesne. Over the next month, Shingas reluctantly agreed, and sent his brother Pisquetomen across the mountains to finalize the agreement. Weeks later, a council of over five hundred Indian delegates from more than a dozen nations met in council with Lieutenant Governor William Denny. Joining the executive was a collection of influential Quakers who had dedicated their public efforts to the cause of peace. Known as the Treaty of Easton, it was at this time that Pennsylvania attempted to right the perceived wrongs that had plagued the Delawares for generations. They offered land grants as a de facto *mea culpa* for the great swindle of the Walking Purchase and promised to negotiate directly with the Delawares instead of deferring to the crumbling façade of imperial Iroquois rule. They further promised that the Ohio Country would remain a land exclusively for the Ohioans, and forbade the settlement of any British citizen on its lands. On October 26, 1758, the Treaty of Easton was consecrated, and the terrible Indian war that had plagued the Peaceable Kingdom came to an end. With the cessation of hostilities in place, the army of General John Forbes descended on Fort Duquesne with no fear of an Indian ambush. Knowing that the post would never survive the attack, the French commandant evacuated the site and destroyed the fort. On November 25 the British occupation of the Ohio Country began, as did the eventual conquest of New France. Before it was even a month old, it seemed that the promises made at the Treaty of Easton had been broken.

For his part, Shingas appears in the historical record only intermittently from that moment on. While there is some evidence to suggest that he may have participated in the attack on Fort Pitt during the Indian uprising of 1763, it remains purely speculative.

WHILE HE LACKED COMMAND EXPERIENCE AT THE TIME, John Armstrong's raid of Kittanning was the beginning of an illustrious military career. He went on to be commissioned a colonel in command of Pennsylvania's 1st Battalion, where he served in the army of John Forbes during its capture of Fort Duquesne. At the outset of the American Revolution Armstrong lent his exceptional engineering talents to defending the city of Charleston, South Carolina. He was named a brigadier general, and was a standout among the ranks of George Washington's Continental Army. After returning north he went on to lead troops at the Battles of Brandywine and Germantown; in the year 1777, at sixty years old, he finally retired from active military service. Never one to rest, John Armstrong was selected to serve in the Continental Congress from 1777 to 1780, and later in the Congress of the Confederation from 1787 to 1788.

As a reward for his military service, John Armstrong was granted a tract of over 550 acres of land along the Allegheny River. The patent read, "In testimony and Memorial of the Services of Colonel John

Armstrong in his arduous and successful Expedition against the Indians at the Indian town and Settlement of Kittanning on the Allegheny which was the first instance of carrying the War into the Indian Country and gave a check to their Incursions into this Province." By no coincidence, he was awarded the land on which sat the burned-out remnants of the once-flourishing village of Kittanning. He was subsequently asked what he wished to name his grant, and he penned a single word.[11]

"Victory."

NOTES

PROLOGUE: A POLITICAL WAR

1. Kenny, *Peaceable Kingdom Lost*, 13.
2. Soderlund, *Lenape Country*, 11.
3. Ibid., 170.
4. Betts, *Rank and Gravity*, 46.
5. Zimmerman, "Benjamin Franklin and the Quaker Party," 292.
6. Ibid., 306.
7. Anderson, *The War That Made America*, 70.
8. Ibid.; Betts, 107.

CHAPTER ONE: THE ORIGINAL PEOPLE

1. Sipe, *The Indian Chiefs of Pennsylvania*, 217.
2. Treaty of Carlisle, November 1, 1753, FranklinPapers.org.
3. Harper, *Promised Land*, 18.
4. Weslager, *The Delaware Indians*, 31.
5. Ibid.
6. Anderson, *The War That Made America*, 5.
7. William Penn to the Committee, August 16, 1683, in Soderlund, *William Penn and the Founding of Pennsylvania*, 316.
8. "Names Which the Lenni Lenape or Delaware Indians Gave to Their Rivers, Streams, and Localities . . . from a Ms. by John Heckewelder," in *Transactions of the Moravian Historical Society*, vol. 1, 23.
9. Soderlund, *Lenape Country*. In this monograph Jean Soderlund masterfully elaborates on the amount of control that the Lenape possessed over the Delaware River Valley.
10. "From the 'Korte Historiael Ende Journaels Aenteyckeninge' by David Pietersz, 1630–1633, 1643 (1655)," in Myers, *Narratives of Early Pennsylvania, West New Jersey, and Delaware, 1630–1707*, 16–17.
11. Tuckerman, *Peter Stuyvesant*, 176.
12. Lovelace to Carr, September 26, 1671, *Pennsylvania Archives* 5, 602–603.
13. Deed of Sale to Andros, *Pennsylvania Archives* 5, 673–675.
14. William Penn to Robert Turner, in Cope, *Passages from the Life and Writings of William Penn*, 235.

15. Penn to the Indians, August 18, 1681, in Cope, *Passages from the Life and Writings of William Penn*, 246–247.
16. Ibid.; Soderlund, *Lenape Country*, 11.
17. Timothy J. Shannon, *Iroquois Diplomacy on the Early American Frontier*, 26.
18. Ibid.; Anderson, 7.
19. Moretta, *William Penn and the Quaker Legacy*, 145.
20. Ibid.; Harper, *Promised Land*, 48.
21. Pencak and Richter, *Friends and Enemies in Penn's Woods*, 106.
22. Ibid.; Anderson, 14.
23. The Walking Purchase of 1737, as quoted in Harper, *Promised Land*, 67.
24. Harper, *Promised Land*, 81.
25. Canasatego's Speech to the Delaware, 1742, *Colonial Records* 4, 578–580.

CHAPTER TWO: INVASION

1. Barr, "Victory at Kittanning?".
2. "The Treaty of Logg's Town, 1752," *Virginia Historical Magazine* 13, 167.
3. Anderson, *The War That Made America*, 9–10.
4. Journal of George Washington, November 24, 1753, in Kopper, 7.
5. Tanacharison at Logstown Council, January 28, 1754, *Colonial Records* 5, 734–735.
6. Ibid.
7. Journal of Colonel George Washington, 1754, in Toner, 123.
8. Villiers' Journal, as quoted in Dixon, "A High Wind Rising," 46.
9. Benjamin Franklin to Richard Partridge, May 9, 1754, FranklinPapers.org.
10. Braddock Council, April 1755, as quoted in "The Carlyle House and Its Associations," Spencer, 8.
11. Ibid., 10.
12. Morris to St. Clair, February 10, 1755, *Pennsylvania Archives: Papers of the Governors* 2, 356–357.
13. Zimmerman, "Benjamin Franklin and the Quaker Party, 1755–1756," 297.
14. Sparks, *The Works of Benjamin Franklin*, 183–185.
15. Scarouady to Robert Morris, Philadelphia, March 31, 1755, *Colonial Records* 6, 342.
16. Conrad Weiser to Thomas Penn, May 1755, as quoted in Wallace, "Conrad Weiser and the Delawares," 148.
17. Bond, "The Captivity of Charles Stuart, 1755–1757," *The Mississippi Valley Historical Review* 13, no. 1: 63–64.
18. Ibid.; Sparks, 192.

CHAPTER THREE: TAKING UP THE HATCHET

1. "The Narrative of Marie Le Roy and Barbara Leininger," *Pennsylvania Archives* 7, 429.
2. *The Papers of Sir William Johnson* 2, 439.
3. "The Speech of Ackowanothio, 1758," *Pennsylvania Archives* 3, 549.
4. Testimony of Robert Robison, as told in Loudon, *A Selection of Some of the Most Interesting Narratives of Outrages Committed by the Indians in Their Wars with the White People*, 161.
5."The Captivity of Charles Stuart, 1755–1757," 61–62.
6. Adam Hoops to Robert Morris, November 3, 1755, as quoted in *The Indian Chiefs of Pennsylvania*, 289– 290.

7. Thomas Barton to Robert Hunter Morris, November 2, 1755, *Colonial Records* 6, 675–676.
8. John Armstrong to Robert Hunter Morris, November 2, 1755, *Colonial Records* 6, 452–453.
9. Ibid.
10. Robert Hunter Morris to Assembly, November 3, 1755, *Colonial Records* 6, 672.
11. Isaac Norris to Robert Hunter Morris, September 29, 1755, *Colonial Records* 6, 637.
12. Benjamin Franklin to Peter Collinson, June 26, 1755, FranklinPapers.org.
13. Sparks, *The Works of Benjamin Franklin,* 179–180.
14. Ibid.
15. Robert Hunter Morris to Assembly, November 6, 1755, *Colonial Records* 6, 684.
16. William Smith, *A Brief State of the Province of Pennsylvania,* as quoted in Zimmerman, *Benjamin Franklin and the Quaker Party, 1755–1756,* 309.
17. Robert Hunter Morris to Thomas Penn, November 22, 1755, *Colonial Records* 6, 739.
18. William Parsons to Robert Hunter Morris, *Colonial Records* 6, 737.
19. Council at Philadelphia, November 24, 1755, *Colonial Records* 6, 729.
20. Robert Hunter Morris to Assembly, *Colonial Records* 6, 783–784.
21. Robert Hunter Morris to Assembly, *Colonial Records* 6, 731.

CHAPTER FOUR: INTO DARKNESS

1. "Narrative of Marie Le Roy and Barbara Leininger," 409.
2. "The Captivity of Charles Stuart," 66.
3. "Narrative of Marie Le Roy and Barbara Leininger," 411.
4. Ibid., 410.
5. John Heckewelder as quoted in Sipe, *The Indian Wars of Pennsylvania*, 287.
6. Conrad Weiser to Robert Hunter Morris, November 19, 1755; Brunner, *The Indians of Berks County, PA*, 41.
7. Washington to Dinwiddie, April 7, 1756, *Writings of Washington*, vol. 1, ed. J. C. Fitzpatrick, 302.
8. Ibid.; *The Indians of Berks Country, PA*, 421.
9. *Pennsylvania Archives* 2, series 1, 536.
10. Sparks, *The Works of Benjamin Franklin*, 202.
11. Carlisle Council, January 13, 1756, Thwaites, *Early Western Travels, 1748–1846*, 84–87.
12. Ibid.
13. Thomas Penn to Richard Peters, May 8, 1756, as quoted in Brands, *The First American*, 269.
14. Richard Peters to Thomas Penn, April 25, 1756, as quoted in Brands, *The First American*, 268–269.
15. *A Journal of the Captivity of Jean Lowry*, 3–4.
16. Edward Shippen to Robert Hunter Morris, April 24, 1756, *The History and Topography of Dauphin, Cumberland, Franklin, Bedford, Adams, and Perry Counties*, 106.
17. Scarouady to Council, April 3, 1756, *Colonial Records* 7, 70–71.
18. Ibid.
19. Robert Dinwiddie to Robert Hunter Morris, January 2, 1756, *Colonial Records* 7, 31–32.
20. Ibid.
21. Lieutenant Governor's Council, April 10, 1756, *Colonial Records* 7, 78–79.

22. Lieutenant Governor's Council, April 12, 1756, *Colonial Records* 7, 83–84.
23. Quakers to Robert Hunter Morris, April 12, 1756, *Colonial Records* 7, 84–86.
24. Ibid.
25. Provincial Council, April 13, 1756, *Colonial Records* 7, 87.
26. Declaration of War, April 14, 1756, *Colonial Records* 7, 88–90.

CHAPTER FIVE: SEASON OF WAR

1. His Majesty's Declaration of War Against the French King, May 17, 1756.
2. Little Abraham to Council, May 13, 1757, *Colonial Records* 7, 520–522.
3. Ibid.
4. Robert Hunter Morris to Sir William Johnson, April 24, 1756, *Colonial Records* 7, 97–100.
5. Ibid.
6. Morris to Assembly, May 11, 1756, *Colonial Records* 7, 120–122.
7. Charles Hardy to Robert Hunter Morris, 9 May 1756, *Colonial Records* 7, 97-100; 123-125.
8. Sir William Johnson to William Shirely, 24 April 1756, *Colonial Records* 7, 116-117.
9. Pennsylvania Assembly to Robert Hunter Morris, May 14, 1756, *Colonial Records* 7, 126.
10. Isaac Norris to Richard Peters, June 7, 1756, *Colonial Records* 7, 148–149.
11. Benjamin Franklin to Peter Collinson, June 15, 1756, FranklinPapers.org.
12. Commission to Robert Hunter Morris, June 29, 1756, *Colonial Records* 7, 177–178.
13. Robert Hunter Morris to Assembly, June 29, 1756, *Colonial Records* 7, 179.
14. Teedyuscung to Robert Hunter Morris, as quoted in Thompson "An Enquiry Into the Causes of the Alienation of the Delaware and Shawanese Indians from the British Interest," 88–89.
15. Ibid.
16. Easton Conference, July 31, 1756, *Colonial Records* 7, 218.
17. James Burd to Robert Hunter Morris, April 19, 1756, and Edward Ward as quoted in Betts, *Rank and Gravity*, 65–66.
18. John Armstrong to Robert Hunter Morris, August 20, 1756, *Colonial Records* 7, 230–233.
19. Ibid.

CHAPTER SIX: WAR FOOTING

1. Betts, *Rank and Gravity*, 70–71.
2. Steele, *Setting All the Captives Free*, 391.
3. Map of Kittanning, published in Hunter, "Victory at Kittanning," 384.
4. Thomas Barton to Richard Peters, August 22, 1756, *Pennsylvania Archives* 2, 756.
5. James Galbreath to James Hamilton, August 10, 1756, *Pennsylvania Archives* 2, 740.
6. Petition to Robert Hunter Morris, August 1756, *Colonial Records* 7, 231–232.
7. *Autobiography of Benjamin Franklin*, 207.
8. Scheme of Expedition to Kittanning, published in Hunter, "Victory at Kittanning," 385.
9. Robert Hunter Morris to Assembly, August 16, 1756, *Pennsylvania Archives* 2, 750–751.
10. Richard Peters to Thomas Penn, October 2, 1756, as quoted in Wainwright, "Governor William Denny in Pennsylvania," 174–175.
11. Robert Hunter Morris to John Penn, as quoted in Wainwright, "Governor William Denny in Pennsylvania," 175.
12. Isaac Norris to William Denny, August 23, 1756, *Colonial Records* 7, 227–228.
13. Lord Loudon to William Denny, August 20, 1756, *Colonial Records* 7, 234–235.

14. William Denny to Assembly, August 24, 1756, *Colonial Records* 7, 228–229.
15. William Denny to Assembly, undated, *Colonial Records* 7, 235–236.
16. Assembly to William Denny, August 31, 1756, FranklinPapers.org; Ibid.; Wainwright, 173–174.
17. Minutes, September 18, 1756, *Colonial Records* 7, 256.
18. John Armstrong to Robert Hunter Morris, August 20, 1756, *Colonial Records* 7, 230–233.
19. Brady J. Crytzer, *Fort Pitt: A Frontier History*, 18–19.
20. Ibid.; Betts, 80.
21. John Armstrong to Robert Hunter Morris, August 20, 1756, *Colonial Records* 7, 230–233.
22. Ibid.
23. Ibid.
24. Ibid.
25. Robert Hunter Morris as quoted in Barr, "Victory at Kittanning," 29.

CHAPTER SEVEN: THE RAID

1. John Armstrong to William Denny, September 14, 1756, *Colonial Records* 7, 257–263.
2. Ibid.
3. Paul A. W. Wallace, *Historic Indian Paths of Pennsylvania*, 49–54.
4. Betts, *Ranks and Gravity*, 86.
5. John Armstrong to William Denny, September 14, 1756, *Colonial Records* 7, 257–263.
6. Robert Robison's Account, as printed in Loudon, *Interesting Tales*, 162.
7. Hanna, *Wilderness Trail*, 262.
8. Betts, *Rank and Gravity*, 573–574. William W. Betts Jr. has written a dutiful biography of John Armstrong, which details his long military career. Betts served on the faculty of IUP for four decades.
9. John Armstrong to William Denny, September 14, 1756, *Colonial Records* 7, 257–263.
10. Ibid.
11. Hunter, "Victory at Kittanning," 386.
12. John Armstrong to William Denny, September 14, 1756, *Colonial Records* 7, 257–263.
13. Ibid.
14. Betts, *Rank and Gravity*, 574.
15. John Armstrong to William Denny, September14, 1756, *Colonial Records* 7, 257–263.
16. Ibid.
17. Robert Robison's Account, as printed in Loudon, *Interesting Tales*, 162–163.
18. Ibid.
19. Ibid.
20. John Armstrong to William Denny, September14, 1756, *Colonial Records* 7, 257–263.
21. Ibid.
22. Robert Robison's Account, as printed in Loudon, *Interesting Tales*, 162–163.
23. Ibid.
24. Ibid.
25. Ibid.
26. John Armstrong to William Denny, September 14, 1756, *Colonial Records* 7, 257–263.
27. Thomas Barton to William Smith, September 23, 1756, as quoted in Myers, "Pennsylvania's Awakening," 408.

28. Thomas Barton to Thomas Penn, February 28, 1757, as quoted in Myers, "Pennsylvania's Awakening," 410.
29. Myers, "Pennsylvania's Awakening," 412–413.
30. John Armstrong to William Denny, September 14, 1756, *Colonial Records* 7, 257–263.
31. Ibid.
32. Journal Militaire Tenus Par Nicolas Renaud, *Rapport de L'Archivist de la Province de Quebec, 1928–1929,* 23–24.
33. Preston, *Braddock's Defeat: The Battle of the Monongahela and the Road to Revolution*, 210, 345.
34. Journal of Bougainville, *Rapport de L'Archivist de la Province de Quebec, 1923–1924*, 234.
35. "The Narrative of Marie Le Roy and Barbara Leininger," *Pennsylvania Archives* 7, 410–411.
36. Ibid.
37. John Armstrong to William Denny, September 14, 1756, *Colonial Records* 7, 257–263.
38. Robert Robison's Account, as printed in Loudon, *Interesting Tales*, 162–163.
39. Ibid.
40. Betts, *Rank and Gravity*, 96.
41. Robert Robison's Account, as printed in Loudon, *Interesting Tales*, 162–163.
42. Ibid.
43. *Pennsylvania Gazette,* September 30, 1756, as quoted in Betts, *Rank and Gravity*, 97–98.
44. Betts, *Rank and Gravity*, 100–101.
45. John Armstrong to William Denny, September 14, 1756, *Colonial Records* 7, 257–263.
46. Ibid.

EPILOGUE: VICTORY

1. "Ode to the Inhabitants of Pennsylvania," as published in the *Pennsylvania Gazette*, September 30, 1756.
2. Minutes of the Philadelphia Council, October 5, 1756, as quoted in Betts, *Rank and Gravity*, 106.
3. John Armstrong to Philadelphia Council, January 24, 1756, as quoted in Betts, *Rank and Gravity*, 107–108.
4. Ibid.
5. Barr, "Victory at Kittanning?," 25.
6. Thomas Barton to Thomas Penn, February 28, 1757, as quoted in Hunter, "Victory at Kittanning," 407.
7. Ibid.
8. Zimmerman, "*Benjamin Franklin and the Quaker Party*, 311.
9. Benjamin Franklin to Peter Collinson, November 5, 1756, FranklinPapers.org.
10. Journal of Christian Frederick Post, as published in Craig, *The Olden Time*, 119.
11. Betts, 109.

BIBLIOGRAPHY

PRIMARY SOURCES

A Journal of the Captivity of Jean Lowry and Her Children Giving an Account of Her Being Taken by the Indians, the First of April 1756, from William McCord's, in Rocky Spring Settlement in Pennsylvania. Mercersburg: The Conococheague Institute, 2008.

Colonial Records of Pennsylvania: *Minutes of the Provincial Council of Pennsylvania from the Organization to the Termination of the Proprietary Government.* 10 vols. Harrisburg, PA, 1852.

The Papers of Sir William Johnson, Volume II. Albany: University of the State of New York, 1922.

"The Treaty of Logg's Town, 1752." *Virginia Magazine of History and Biography* 13 (1906).

Brunner, D. B. *The Indians of Berks County, Pennsylvania.* Reading: Spirit of Berks, 1881.

Cope, Thomas Pym. *Passages from the Life and Writings of William Penn.* Philadelphia, 1882.

Fitzpatrick, John C. *The Writings of George Washington.* Charlottesville: University of Virginia, 1931.

Franklin, Benjamin. *The Papers of Benjamin Franklin.* FranklinPapers.org.

Kopper, Kevin P. *The Journals of George Washington and Christopher Gist: Mission to Fort Le Boeuf.* Slippery Rock: Slippery Rock University and Historic Harmony, 2009.

Le Roy, Marie, and Barbara Leininger. "The Narrative of Marie Le Roy and Barbara Leininger." *Pennsylvania Magazine of History and Biography* 29, no. 4 (1905).

Loudon, Archibald. *A Collection of Some of the Narratives of Outrages Committed by the Indians in the Wars with the White People.* Vols. 1–2. London: Loudon, 1808.

Pennsylvania Archives 2–7. Harrisburg, PA (1900).

Rapport de L'Archivist de la Province de Quebec, 1922–1924 and 1928–1929. Quebec: Bibliotheque et Archives Nationales du Quebec, 1929.

Sparks, Jared. *The Works of Benjamin Franklin.* Vol. 1. Chicago: Townsend Mac, 1882.

Thwaites, Reuben Gold. *Early Western Travels, 1748–1846.* Vol. 16. Cleveland: Arthur H. Clark, 1905.

Toner, J. M. *The Journal of Colonel George Washington.* Albany: Joel Munsell's Sons, 1893.

Transactions of the Moravian History Society. Vol. 1. Nazareth: Whitefield House, 1876. Yale, and the American Philosophical Society.

SECONDARY SOURCES

Anderson, Fred. *Crucible of War: The Seven Years' War and the Fate of Empire in British North America, 1754–1766.* New York: Vintage Books, 2000.

———. *The War That Made America: A Short History of the French and Indian War.* New York: Penguin, 2006.

Barr, Daniel P. "Victory at Kittanning? Reevaluating the Impact of Armstrong's Raid on the Seven Years' War in Pennsylvania." *Pennsylvania Magazine of History and Biography* 131 (2007).

Betts, William W. *Rank and Gravity: The Life of General John Armstrong of Carlisle.* Westminster: Heritage Books, 2011.

Bond, Beverly. "The Captivity of Charles Stuart, 1755–57." *Mississippi Historical Review* 13 (1926).

Brands, H. W. *The First American: The Life and Times of Benjamin Franklin.* New York: Random House, 2000.

Busch, Clarence M. *Report on the Commission to Locate the Frontier Forts of Western Pennsylvania.* Vol. 2. Harrisburg: State Commission of Pennsylvania, 1896.

Calloway, Colin G. *New Worlds for All: Indians, Europeans, and the Remaking of Early America.* Baltimore: Johns Hopkins University Press, 1997.

———. *The Scratch of a Penn: 1763 and the Transformation of North America.* New York: Oxford, 2006.

———. *The Shawnees and the War for America.* New York: Penguin, 2007.

Craig, Neville B. *The Olden Time.* Pittsburgh: Dumars and Company, 1846.

Crytzer, Brady J. *Fort Pitt: A Frontier History.* Charleston: History Press, 2012.

———. *Guyasuta and the Fall of Indian America.* Yardley, PA: Westholme Publishing, 2013.

———. *Major Washington's Pittsburgh and the Mission to Fort LeBoeuf.* Charleston: History Press, 2011.

Dixon, David. "A High Wind Rising: George Washington, Fort Necessity, and the Ohio Country Indians." *Pennsylvania History* 74 (2007).

———. *Never Come to Peace Again: Pontiac's Uprising and the Fate of the British Empire in North America.* Norman: University of Oklahoma Press, 2005.

Dowd, Gregory A. *A Spirited Resistance: The North American Indian Struggle for Unity, 1745– 1815.* Baltimore: Johns Hopkins University Press, 1993.

Downes, Randolph C. *Council Fires on the Upper Ohio.* Pittsburgh: University of Pittsburgh Press, 1940.

Fischer, Laura S. *Pennsylvania's Forbes Trail.* New York: Taylor Trade Publishing, 2008.

Flexner, James Thomas. *George Washington: The Forge of Experience, 1732–1775.* Boston: Little, Brown and Company, 1965.

Ford, Worthington Chauncey. *The Writings of George Washington.* New York: Knickerbocker Press, 1891.

Halpenny, Francess G., and Jean Hamelin. *Dictionary of Canadian Biography,1771–1800.* Vol. 4. Toronto: University of Toronto Press, 1979.

Hanna, Charles A. *The Wilderness Trail, or Ventures and Adventures of the Pennsylvania Traders on the Allegheny Path.* London: G. P. Putnam's Sons, 1911.

Harper, Stephen Craig. *Promised Land: Penn's Holy Experiment, the Walking Purchase, and the Dispossession of the Delawares, 1600–1763.* Bethlehem: Lehigh University Press, 2008.

Hoffman, Phillip W. *Simon Girty, Turncoat Hero: The Most Hated Man on the Early American Frontier.* Franklin: Flying Camp Press, 2009.

Hunter, William A. "Victory at Kittanning." *Pennsylvania History* 23 (1956).

James, Alfred Proctor, and Charles Morse Stotz. *Drums in the Forest: Decision at the Forks, Defense in the Wilderness.* Pittsburgh: University of Pittsburgh Press, 2005.

Kelsay, Isabel Thompson. *Joseph Brant, 1743–1807: Man of Two Worlds.* Syracuse: Syracuse University Press, 1984.

Kenny, Kevin. *Peaceable Kingdom Lost: The Paxton Boys and the Destruction of William Penn's Holy Experiment.* New York: Oxford University Press, 2009.

Kopperman, Kevin. *Braddock at the Monongahela.* Pittsburgh: University of Pittsburgh Press, 1977.

Mayer, Brantz. *Tah-gah-jute, or Logan and Captain Michael Cresap.* Baltimore: Maryland Historical Society, 1851.

Moretta, John A. *William Penn and the Quaker Legacy.* New York: Pearson, 2006.

Morgan, Boone. *Boone: A Biography.* Chapel Hill: Algonquin Paperbacks, 2007.

Myers, Albert Cook. *Narratives of Early Pennsylvania, West New Jersey, and Delaware, 1630–1707.* New York: Charles Scribner's Sons, 1912.

Myers, James P. "Pennsylvania's Awakening: The Kittanning Raid of 1756." *Pennsylvania History* 66 (1999).

O'Meara, Walter. *Guns at the Forks*. Pittsburgh: University of Pittsburgh Press, 1965.

Peckham, Howard Henry. *Pontiac and the Indian Uprising*. Detroit: Wayne State University Press, 1994.

Pencak, William A., and Daniel K. Richter. *Friends and Enemies in Penn's Woods: Indians, Colonists, and the Racial Construction of Pennsylvania*. University Park: Pennsylvania State University Press, 2004.

Preston, David L. *Braddock's Defeat: The Battle of the Monongahela and the Road to Revolution.* New York: Oxford University Press, 2015.

Rupp, I. Daniel. *The History and Topography of Dauphin, Cumberland, Franklin, Bedford, Adams, and Perry Counties.* Lancaster: Gilbert Hills, 1846.

Shannon, Timothy. *Iroquois Diplomacy on the Early American Frontier.* New York: Penguin, 2008.

Silver, Peter. *Our Savage Neighbors: How Indian War Transformed Early America.* New York: W. W. Norton & Company, 2009.

Sipe, C. Hale. *The Indian Chiefs of Pennsylvania.* Lewisburg: Wennawoods Publishing, 1998.

Soderlund, Jean R. *Lenape Country: Delaware Valley Society Before William Penn.* Philadelphia: University of Pennsylvania Press, 2015.

———. *William Penn and the Founding of Pennsylvania: A Documentary History.* Philadelphia: University of Pennsylvania Press, 1983.

Spencer, Richard Henry. "The Carlyle House and Its Associations." *William and Mary Quarterly* 18, no. 1 (1909).

Steele, Ian K. *Setting All the Captives Free: Capture, Adjusmtment, and Recollection in Allegheny Country.* Canada: McGill-Queen's University Press, 2013.

Sullivan, James. *The Papers of Sir William Johnson.* Albany: University of the State of New York, 1921.

Thomson, Charles. *Causes of the Alienation of the Delaware and Shawanese Indians from the British Interest.* London: John Campbell, 1867.

Tuckerman, Bayyard. *Peter Stuvyesant: Director-General for the West India Company in New Netherland.* New York: Dodd, Mead, and Co., 1893.

Wainwright, Nicholas B. "Governor William Denny in Pennsylvania." *Pennsylvania Magazine of History and Biography* 81 (1957).

Wallace, Paul A. W. "Conrad Weiser and the Delawares." *Pennsylvania History* 4 (1937).

———. *Historic Indian Paths of Pennsylvania.* Harrisburg: Pennsylvania Historical and Museum Commission, 1952.

———. *Indians in Pennsylvania.* Harrisburg: Pennsylvania Historical and Museum Commission, 1981.

Watt, Gavin K. *Rebellion in the Mohawk Valley: The St. Leger Expedition of 1777.* Toronto: Dundurn Press, 2002.

Weslager, C. A. *The Delaware Indians: A History.* New Brunswick: Rutgers University Press, 2003.

Zimmerman, John J. "Benjamin Franklin and the Quaker Party, 1755–1756." *William and Mary Quarterly* 17, no. 3 (July 1960): 291–313.

ACKNOWLEDGMENTS

This book was an ambitious project that required a great deal of support from many people. I would like to thank my family and friends for their patience as I completed this project, with special consideration to my wife, Jennifer, for her helpful critiques, and Carter for reminding me to take breaks from time to time. I would like to thank my numerous colleagues for providing the opportunity to join the ongoing conversation of Frontier studies. I would like to acknowledge my publisher, Bruce H. Franklin, for taking on the project, as well as the staff at Westholme Publishing for their tireless efforts to prepare it for publication.

INDEX